Photo by Samantha Brown

2013

STARTING
LINES

AN ANTHOLOGY
OF STUDENT WRITING

UCSB Writing Program

Twelfth Edition—2013

HAYDEN
McNEIL

Hayden-McNeil Sustainability

Hayden-McNeil's standard paper stock uses a minimum of 30% post-consumer waste. We offer higher % options by request, including a 100% recycled stock. Additionally, Hayden-McNeil Custom Digital provides authors with the opportunity to convert print products to a digital format. Hayden-McNeil is part of a larger sustainability initiative through Macmillan Higher Ed. Visit http://sustainability.macmillan.com to learn more.

Printed in the United States of America

10 9 8 7 6 5 4 3 2 1

ISBN 978-0-7380-5642-5

Hayden-McNeil Publishing
14903 Pilot Drive
Plymouth, MI 48170
www.hmpublishing.com

Miele 5642-5 F13 (*Starting Lines*)

CONTENTS

WRITING 2

TEXTUAL CARNIVALS

SERIOUS INQUIRY

EXPLORING GENRES

BOUNDARY CROSSINGS

PHOTOGRAPHER PROFILES

ACKNOWLEDGMENTS

Christopher Dean and Ilene Miele

Santa Barbara, California
June 2013

Thanks to all those who played a part in the publication of *Starting Lines*.

To all of the students who worked through multiple drafts to revise and edit their writing and then took the time to submit their work, we appreciate your energy and interest.

Congratulations to the students whose words fill these pages. We celebrate your success and look forward to hearing more from you. Your enthusiasm will encourage other students to share their ideas and tell their stories.

Our sincere gratitude to Dean David Marshall for his steady support and generosity in providing the funding that made this issue possible.

Thanks to Writing Program Director Linda Adler-Kassner for her support and encouragement in getting our first expanded issue off the ground.

Great appreciation must go to the Editorial Board for the generous contribution of their time to read and evaluate submissions.

A special thanks to Randi Browning, Robert Krut, and Randy Rightmire for devoting their expertise this year to select the Writing 1/Linguistics 12 prizewinners for this issue. We also wish to express our gratitude to Brian Ernst, Caren Converse, and Cissy Ross for their willingness to read every Writing 2 piece in this collection and do the very hard work of selecting prizewinning essays in each category.

Of course, none of this would be possible without our dedicated instructors who inspire students to realize their potential. Thanks to the Writing Program and Linguistics faculty for motivating students to learn and for encouraging submissions. A particular thanks goes to those who have promoted the ongoing publication by using *Starting Lines* as a supplemental text for their classes.

Writing minor interns Dominique Koudsi, Alyssa Vergun, Diane Mooshoolzadeh, Carley Ryckman, and Christine Van Beek have been especially helpful, and their fine editorial work is much appreciated.

Thanks to Arianna Meza, Shannon Dalton, and Meghan Ummel for their helpful assistance throughout the year.

Starting Lines has had the good fortune again this year to receive the sponsorship of the UCSB Bookstore, which provided several of the prizes. Thanks to Bookstore Director Mark Beisecker for the donation of prizes and to Cynthia Ellestad for her assistance in coordinating publication and sales.

To all the students in Writing 1, Linguistics 12 and Writing 2, we hope that you enjoy these pieces and that they will inspire you to submit your work to the next issue. We look forward to hearing your voices.

PREFACE

Linda Adler-Kassner
Director, Writing Program

University of California, Santa Barbara
June 2013

"What new thing can you bring to the table?" Luis Carlos García Verduzco, whose Writing 1 essay "An Invitation to Dine" is included in this volume, opens his piece with this query from his instructor, Dr. Mashey Bernstein.

This question seems especially important right now. Politicians, policy makers, parents, and our students are asking the same question of college education: what new things does university learning bring to the table? Here at UC Santa Barbara, what new things do we bring?

To continue with Luis's metaphor, this year's *Starting Lines* provides forty-six compelling responses to this question. The pieces included in this volume are illustrations of what engaged, committed students and caring, dedicated instructors bring together to the feast that is college learning.

Reading through *Starting Lines*, you'll see that these essays illustrate a bounty. New insights into seemingly familiar ideas, like "home" or what it means to write. New questions about issues seemingly "answered" that open up avenues for inquiry and additional thinking. New ways of exploring and representing research through work in multiple genres.

Especially exciting is the expansion of this year's *Starting Lines*. Since its inception in 2002, *Starting Lines* has always included the brilliant work of students in Writing 1 (Approaches to University Writing) and Linguistics 12 (Approaches to University Writing for Multilingual Students). This year, for the first time, we're excited to add several new place settings to the table with the inclusion of work from Writing 2 (Academic Writing) students. This course focuses on helping students develop strategies for analyzing expectations for writing in specific contexts, especially academic disciplines. In the pieces from this course, you'll find explorations of how different disciplines engage in and represent inquiry, multigenre work that puts into practice the idea of writing for different audiences, and podcast transcripts that use writing to represent research in creative and lively ways.

With these pieces, *Starting Lines* answers the question about "new things at the table" in compelling ways. New insights, new ideas, new senses of self as writers and as contributors to the community of inquiry that exists at UC Santa Barbara—tasty, indeed.

NOTES

EDITING

These selections are presented as outstanding examples of student writing, not as flawless models. For this reason, we have maintained, for the most part, the students' choices in wording and punctuation. However, some editing has been done for the sake of clarity.

SUBMISSIONS

Students are encouraged to submit their best work from Writing 1, Linguistics 12, and Writing 2 by the deadline immediately after the quarter in which they complete the course. Sources should be cited properly using MLA, APA, or CMS format. The selection committee looks for pieces that represent the range of formal and informal writing done in these courses. Campus photos and graphics for cover art and for use throughout the book are also accepted. For more information about how to submit your work, see the submission form available on the Writing Program website: http://www.writing.ucsb.edu/publications.

AWARDS

WRITING 1/LINGUISTICS 12

INTERPRETING EXPERIENCE

1ST PLACE
Ruiqi Ye,
Shipai

2ND PLACE
David Diaz,
Elaborate

HONORABLE MENTION
Louis Lin,
More than Just Words

RESPONDING TO TEXTS

1ST PLACE
Luis Carlos García Verduzco,
Invitation to Dine

2ND PLACE
Eli Wolf,
Don't Think, Just Play

HONORABLE MENTION
Anabel Hernandez Torres,
Pedagogy of the Oppressed

POSING PROBLEMS/ TAKING POSITIONS

1ST PLACE
Wenxi Xiao,
Gap Year: High School Graduates' Best Choice

2ND PLACE
Anyssa N. Luna-Oropeza,
Tattoos, Women, and the Judgment

HONORABLE MENTION
Amber Garcia,
Grades and Progress

MULTIMODAL TEXTS

1ST PLACE
Joyce Liu,
A Moment in Time

2ND PLACE
Kay (Sue Jeong) Lee,
Me Speaking Out (Spoken Word)

2ND PLACE
Marilou Razo,
Accidentally Pursuing Self-Identity

WRITING 2

TEXTUAL CARNIVALS

PRIZEWINNING ESSAY
Meagan Reece,
The Sex Pistols

PRIZEWINNING ESSAY
Blanca Lopez,
Are Media and Learning Compatible?

HONORABLE MENTION
Bradley Afroilan,
Why Not? The Unknown Potential of the Proper Use of Cognitive Enhancement

SERIOUS INQUIRY

PRIZEWINNING ESSAY
Zoe Kam,
What Effects Do Sexually Degrading Lyrics Have on Young People's Image of Modern Gender Roles and Sexual Politics?

PRIZEWINNING ESSAY
Jaime So,
Not the Average Outing

HONORABLE MENTION
Melissa Carlos,
Why do the Terms in Senate Bill 1070 Lead to Racial Profiling?

EXPLORING GENRES

PRIZEWINNING ESSAY

Kelley Coe,
The Dimensions of Genre: Twitter and Political Speeches

PRIZEWINNING ESSAY

Michael Sprague,
The Importance of Literacy Practices in Computer Science

HONORABLE MENTION

Mackenzie Keil-Long,
Eating Disorders in Ballet for the Medical and Psychology Disciplines

BOUNDARY CROSSINGS

PRIZEWINNING ESSAY

Jared Payzant
Inside the World of Sam-I-Am

PRIZEWINNING ESSAY

Linda Phan,
Ports of Writing

HONORABLE MENTION

Danielle Butler,
"Dear Danielle"

PHOTOGRAPHY

COVER PHOTOGRAPH

Samantha Brown

CAMPUS PHOTOGRAPHS

Leo Vargas

OTHER CONTRIBUTORS

EDITORIAL BOARD FOR WRITING 1

Mashey Bernstein
Ryan Boyd
Randi Browning
Judy Gough
Roberta Gilman
Leslie Hammer
Deborah Harris-Moore
Jennifer Johnson
Kathy Patterson
Randy Rightmire

EDITORIAL BOARD FOR WRITING 2

Linda Adler-Kassner
Can Aksoy
Sasha Metcalf
Peter Romaskiewicz
Vincent Rone
Roy Vallis

PHOTOGRAPHERS

Samantha Brown
Loriel Davila
Marisol Jimenez
Shannon Mirshokri
Leo Vargas
Yuqing (Augustina) Wang

Starting Lines Photo Editor
Kathy Patterson

Photo by Yuqing (Augustina) Wang

Photo by Leo Vargas

WRITING 1 / LINGUISITICS 12

Photo by Yuqing (Augustina) Wang

WRITING 1/
LINGUISTICS 12

INTERPRETING
EXPERIENCE

SHIPAI

Ruiqi Ye

Instructor: Roberta Gilman

> **"At the time, opportunities for success were like blooms floating on the air. A little bit of courage was all that you needed to catch one."**

"Where are you from?" Annoyed by the waves of heat in mid August, I questioned the candidates impatiently, keeping my eyes on the notes.

"Guangxi. We are from Guangxi," a young couple answered together in Mandarin, with an unfamiliar accent.

While skimming through their application forms, I continued, "What are your educational levels, any graduation certificate?"

"Uh…I just graduated from high school," the man stopped, avoiding my gaze, "and…her too. This is my certificate."

Before I could start, the man eagerly added, "She…um…left her certificate at home. Would you please give us the interview opportunity and she'll send it here later? I promise!" The woman nodded and smiled embarrassingly.

"Sorry, I can't give you anything without seeing your certificate, since you want a position in QA[1]." I shrugged at the girl with a there's-nothing-I-could-do face.

"Please, please!" they pleaded.

The last picture of their frustrated looks in my mind is as vivid as the hot weather today. It was three years ago that I worked informally in my dad's factory as a human resources intern in Shipai, a small town in Dongguan city, Guangdong province.

Shipai, also my birthplace, had been a quiet agriculture-oriented town up to the time when Deng Xiaoping forwarded his reform and opening up policy[2] in the 1980s. All of a sudden, numerous Hong Kong and Taiwan investors came, worked with the local government, and built their factories in the town, turning it into a world factory. At the time, opportunities for success were like blooms floating on the air. A little bit of courage was all that you needed to catch one. These blooms attracted not only locals like my father, but also uncountable others (like the couple I spoke with) who left their homes all over China for Shipai, to seek a better job and life. Most of the newcomers were farmers, their children, and high school graduates. They came to Shipai with a dream to explore, succeed, or merely survive.

Of those who came, some left while some stayed, like my mom. She was born in 1966 into a middle-class family with both of her

---

1   QA stands for quality assurance, a typical position in a factory to assure the quality of products.

2   This policy allowed private ownerships of property and opened Guangdong for foreign enterprise, including Hong Kongese and Taiwanese investments.

parents working as government officials in Hunan Province. In her early 20s, she left her home with a bunch of friends for Dongguan city. Later, she was lucky enough to get a job as an English translator in a Taiwanese-owned electronics factory in Tangxia town. She met my father in the factory and they started their romantic relationship. However, there was always one thing I did not understand well enough: why my mom left her home. All I knew was that she could have had a comfortable, leisurely life there because she was the daughter of government officials. She could have gotten herself a job in an office through my grandparents' connections. But she left.

"I moved just because I wanted to," she told me. "You know, I got a job in the library from my mom's friend before I left, and I was getting bored with it." My mom seldom told me about her past, but when she did, there were always interesting stories. "Life there was so dull. My work was so easy that I just sat on my butt and waited for 5 p.m. everyday!" she laughed. "So, I decided to do something on my own, something fresh and worthy of my time and passion. And I heard Dongguan was a nice place with tons of new companies. So, on this one morning, I left without telling my mom, leaving just a note on the table at home."

Was it a dream for a different life that drove my mom to Dongguan?

It must have been, to some extent.

What is more, why did she marry a local from a farmer's family? How did she cope with their differences in values, and even more difficult, with the local hostility and misunderstanding that struck newcomers in general and non-local brides in particular?

I remember my mom told me how angrily my grandma from my father's side reacted to the marriage. She fought with my father and refused to talk to him for weeks, just because my mom was an *ai po*, a local derogatory word describing women from other provinces. To me, Grandma's rejection made sense because locals did not trust those newcomers, who invaded their territories and nearly outnumbered them. Even now, my grandma is still suspicious of non-locals in the markets. She always accuses *ai lo*[3] and *ai po* of selling spurious goods,

like selling roast duck for the price of roast goose. Whenever I try to take the side of non-locals, she either insists on her claim or ignores me.

I wonder how my mom and other newcomers have survived and continued their dreams in such a hostile place. But then I notice that they have had their communities, too. Most of the newcomers, despite whatever dreams they carry to Shipai, usually end up working in factories as general workers, since the positions require limited education and have a relatively high salary because the Chinese government is continuously pushing up the minimum wage. It is easy and perfectly desirable for them to make friends when they are stuck in the assembly lines and behind the gates of factory complexes all day. The newcomers, however, are less visible during the day than at night, when they, along with their friends, crowd into shopping malls, night markets, and parks.

This past summer, newcomers, or non-locals, really amazed me when I saw them dancing in groups in Shipai Park. Though the music seemed to come from some cheap speakers, they had a lot of fun. Actually, I was on my way to meet my friends in the barbeque square, which was in the deepest end of the park. Walking all the way down with my little brother, I found it ironic that I met more newcomers than locals. Oh no, wait! My friends were the only locals I saw that night[4]. Those newcomers were dancing in the center, riding mini roller coasters in the adventure square, resting on the grass, wandering around the artificial lake. They were everywhere!

"Where are the locals?" I exclaimed.

No sooner had my brother made a sound to answer that than I realized it was just a rhetorical question—because we both knew that Shipai Park was a lost place for the average locals. We ourselves had seldom been to this place. It being far away from our homes was one reason, but more deeply, feeling out of place in that park was the other.

Interestingly, the city government coined a name for all these newcomers—*Xin Guanren*, meaning "New Dongguanese." Banners and advertisements about building a harmonious society and helping New Dongguanese secure their lives were

---

3 Same as *ai po* but is used for males

4 Locals and non-locals can be distinguished by the languages they speak. Locals speak a dialect of Cantonese, while most of the non-locals speak some versions of Mandarin.

ubiquitous, and they especially focused on the low-rent housing project. Despite all its efforts, the local government still cannot provide enough for these *Xin Guanren*. As a result, some of them leave, while some give up.

The word "suicide" had been so distant from me until two years ago, when my aunt told me about a male general worker from my dad's main factory who jumped to his death from his dorm in the middle of a night. I physically shook.

"Why?" I could not help asking.

"Who knows? The police are still working on that." With a finger pointing to her temple, my aunt said, "Probably some sort of problem here."

Lost with the young life were his hopes and dreams. Yet, the stories I am telling here are not so much about individual success or tragedy as they are about a "sense of place." In the face of economic globalization, more and more people from different social and economic backgrounds are drawn to Shipai to seek a better job and life. However, these newcomers may not expect the complexity and problems in their interaction with local people. *Xin Guanren* and locals are like numerous lines that were once parallel but now intersect—they meet, interact, and then move on. Within their interactions are confrontation, cooperation, silence, and often, any combination of the three.

People in this town have their own ways of living, regardless of marrying a local or selling roast duck or goose or sitting beside the assembly lines or dancing in the Shipai Park or giving up dreams. These ways of living transform Shipai and simultaneously affect deeply each individual in the place. Some people are able to survive on the hostility, mistrust, and helplessness created by this increasingly congested modernized town. Some are not.

This place holds a pool of dreams but fulfills only a small portion. The lucky ones, like my mom, are able to secure their "sense of place" in Shipai and eventually climb up the social ladder. However, the unlucky ones, like the male general worker, may be stuck in the lower class and gradually lose their hopes. But what makes one lucky or unlucky?

Surely good luck is not a sufficient explanation for the difference in fortune of people like my mom and other newcomers. As Tim Cresswell argues in "Imagining a Telescopic view," different social groups

have distinct relationships to mobility because some people are in more control of resources and power than others are (14). Here, "mobility" refers to the ability to move to any geographic or social location. Considering the case of my mom, surely her greater control of resources can explain her higher social mobility—that is, her ability to move towards a more fulfilling life. But control of resources can be expressed in many ways, and one of them is through educational level because it largely determines the kinds of jobs people do in a factory. Working as an English translator in a Taiwanese-owned electronics factory marked my mom as middle-class and college educated because in the 1980s, not many Chinese people could afford to learn English, since it was only offered at colleges and a few high schools. Also, at that time, getting into a college was almost as difficult as finding a job now because of the limited spots offered and the fierce competition among so many people. Therefore, my mom distinguished herself from other newcomers through her mastery of English. Such benefit offered her more control of financial resources and helped her rise in the social hierarchy in Shipai.

Unlike my mom, many newcomers in Shipai did not have a college education, so they ended up working as general workers in factories. Many of them graduated from junior high schools and some, especially newcomers in their mid-40s or older, only finished elementary school. Furthermore, educational level is an effective indicator of one's human capital, or in other words, talents and capabilities, and these are valuable resources that improve one's social status, too. Being a local, however, promised an even better job than high human capital at the time. Although my dad did not finish his college education, he worked as a factory manager when he met my mom simply because he was a local with a good reputation. But such "insider's advantage" was exclusive to locals—people who were supposed to be in control of the place. Therefore, for general workers who lacked both local connections and high human capital, moving up the social ladder seemed almost impossible.

Luckily for my mom, her marriage to my dad helped her cross the boundary between newcomers and locals, and provided her with advantages and opportunities not available for most newcomers.

Through this marriage, my mom was able to claim her identity as a local not only because she was associated with a husband and a mother-in-law from Shipai, but also because she learned the local language and resocialized herself based on longstanding ways of living in the town. All of the three were essential in making my mom "a local" because differences between family, culture, and especially language are the very small yet significant stones that draw a line between locals and newcomers.

In fact, the most convenient way for locals to distinguish themselves from others is through language. Although my mom still made pronunciation mistakes and spoke with a Hunan accent, she learned the local language, Cantonese, eventually. In contrast, most of the general workers with whom I spoke did not know how to speak any language other than Mandarin, though they understood some Cantonese. Since language skills are closely related to people's social skills, speaking Cantonese allowed my mom to communicate well with locals despite her accent and to embrace a new culture. Her higher human capital in both linguistics and social awareness eventually won locals' acceptance for her and aided her integration into the local community—the privileged group that enjoyed more power and resources than newcomers.

As Cresswell argues in "A Global Sense of Place," "It is not the economy alone which determines our experience of space and place" (3). What contributed to my mom's higher social mobility was a mixture of multiple factors and definitely not limited to financial means. With her high educational level, marriage, language skills, and social skills my mom distinguished herself from other general workers. But let us not forget good luck, which gave her middle-class parents who could afford her higher education. These five elements all provided her with more control over resources like a good job and local connections, and these resources eased her transition from a newcomer to a local, supporting her higher social mobility. With so many advantages, she was able to develop a positive "sense of place" in Shipai and therefore live a fulfilling life.

WORKS CITED

Cresswell, Tim. "A Global Sense of Place." *Place: A Short Introduction.* Malden: MA: Blackwell, (2004) 63–70. Rpt. in *Linguistics 12 Course Reader* Santa Barbara, University of California, Santa Barbara, 2012. 4–5. Print.

Cresswell, Tim. "Imagining a Telescopic view: The Power-Geometry of Time-Space Compression." *Place: A Short Introduction.* Malden: MA: Blackwell, (2004) 63–70. Rpt. in *Linguistics 12 Course Reader* Santa Barbara, University of California, Santa Barbara, 2012. 14. Print.

AUTHOR PROFILE

I'm the girl from Shipai! I'm currently a sociology major and a feminist studies minor. I really love the sunshine and beaches here in Santa Barbara. Life is full of uncertainties, so enjoy it.

—*Ruiqi Ye*

ELABORATE

David Diaz

Instructor: Jennifer Johnson

> **"I was so exhilarated and impressed with his essay that I knew there was more to writing than I had previously thought."**

"Elaborate." I'll never forget that word for the rest of my life. After walking up the flimsy platform leading to the gloomy building known as Bungalow 21, I first encountered her. The classroom was silent. I was late and unsure of what to do as I stood in the doorway looking into the classroom. I slowly made my way through the room to the only empty seat left, feeling her piercing gaze all the while as I quickly averted my eyes from classmate to classmate. The looks on their faces were unmistakably telling one thing: this class was going to suck. My tardiness had apparently halted her analysis of a Givenchy perfume ad, so she thought it appropriate for me to continue the analysis since I had so rudely interrupted her. She asked me to explain the rhetorical purpose of the royal purple staircase leading up to darkness that the model was standing on in the ad. I simply said what I thought—that it was to make the perfume seem "mysterious" and therefore desired by the audience. It was then that I first heard the word slither out of her cold, calculating mouth and into my ears for the very first time: "elaborate." I didn't know what to say; I thought I had justified my answer with a satisfactory reason, yet she wanted me to elaborate? I sat there, my eyes darting from face to face, not knowing what to say. My cheeks burned red-hot as I looked at my teacher for mercy, yet her mind was set to the task, so I bowed my head in defeat and uttered those three shameful words: "I don't know." Never had I felt this stupid and embarrassed before in my life. A feeling of shame and worthlessness loomed over me, and it was only the first day of junior year in high school.

Mrs. Ciotti certainly proved her point that day, so I remained in the background of the class in fear of reliving that one horrifying memory. It was not until a couple of months after that episode that I started regaining my confidence, becoming bolder in class discussions—although still avoiding difficult questions. By this time in the year, we were fully engaged in the ways of argument and rhetoric, studying Aristotle's three means of appeal: ethos, pathos, and logos—and putting them to the test in persuasive writing. I never had considered myself a great writer, so I always tried to work with exceptional writers during peer review. It was especially helpful to get feedback from them because they would write a lot of comments on my essay explaining what I needed to change in order to improve my essay. But I wasn't using their comments in the way I should have; I was solely focused on getting that "A," so I could feign being a good writer to my friends and parents. The truth was that I hated writing because I was a bad writer. To me, writing was one of the hardest and most frustrating things to do because there are so many possibilities and avenues of reason you can explore, yet it's very difficult to tie key points together to make a cohesive idea. Little did I know, though, it was all about to change.

The day after a timed writing assignment in class, Mrs. Ciotti slowly walked up to the overhead and displayed one of our classmate's essays. As I turned my head to look at the board, I noticed something that's never happened before in Mrs. Ciotti's AP English class: an essay received a score of nine out of nine points. I was in complete awe, my jaw visibly dropping as she read the essay aloud to the class while analyzing certain parts of it and commending its brilliance. It was a masterpiece. This essay had exceptional flow, making it easy to follow the writer's thought process, and it had a never-ending source of diverse references and analogies to imprint those ideas onto the reader's minds for days to come. The writer, Binh, who was easily recognized due to his unique handwriting, referenced the Battle of Thermopylae and a quote from Abraham Lincoln all in the same sentence—and he made it work! How could someone write such an amazing essay in the brief time span of 58 minutes? I was so exhilarated and impressed with his essay that I knew there was more to writing than I had previously thought. Binh opened my eyes to a world of the seemingly impossible and instilled in me a great appreciation for excellent and masterful work.

Toward the end of the school year, we received increasingly more difficult assignments that had to do with analyzing every single aspect of an ad to understand its underlying rhetorical purpose and the argument it's trying to make. These aspects included the focal point, position of the model, color, background, facial features, meaning of texts, and subtle sexual hints. Mrs. Ciotti surprised us one day when she brought in a Tiffany's ad that she had enlarged and planned to analyze for us during the entire class period. "Sweet," I thought, "I don't have to pay attention in class today," because it seemed like she was going to be doing all the work. Little did I know that I was about to have an epiphany. The teacher I'd hated for the better part of a year was about to unlock some hidden area inside of me that actually made me respect her deeply.

I can still remember the ad vividly; it was a picture of young girl, no older than eight, holding onto a metal sled with presents wrapped in teal paper and tied with white ribbons, over a snowy forest with a white light in the background. The little girl, dressed in all white with white nylons, white slippers, and a teal ribbon in her hair, was looking back at the camera over her shoulder. Mrs. Ciotti began to break down the ad piece by piece, starting off with the focal point; she claimed that the focal point was not the presents themselves, but the little girl tempting the audience with a teal ribbon in her hair and saying "Come and get me" in a very sexual manner even though the girl was but a child. The advertisers displayed the girl in all white to show that she is a "good girl," or innocent, although her body language and incentive of gifts suggest otherwise. Mrs. Ciotti pointed out that the little girl also seemed to be going toward the bright, snow-white forest, indicating that there's a little mystery and danger about her, that if you buy one of Tiffany's products, you'll be mysterious, somewhat dangerous, and sexy.

Once again, that feeling of exhilaration and astonishment had returned, yet this time it was due to something I came across in spoken form. I was on the edge of my seat the whole time during class, shaking from excitement, ready for more. That's when it hit me. I realized there was no way I could hate someone as professional and inspirational as Mrs. Ciotti was to me that day. It's truly amazing that I could go from hating Mrs. Ciotti all throughout junior year to developing a deep respect and appreciation for her unmatched knowledge in the field of rhetoric and argument. Binh and Mrs. Ciotti both seemed to have a certain skill that I didn't: elaboration. Binh utilized this skill by expressing his views and opinions through a wide variety of examples and appeals in his writing, whereas Mrs. Ciotti relied on decades of experience and knowledge to guide her through the process of uncovering the rhetorical purpose and argument of a piece. I find it fascinating that a few enlightening experiences can outweigh numerous unpleasant ones, and that I could grow to love what I used to hate.

Binh and Mrs. Ciotti have both helped me discover that I have an inner appreciation for excellence and mastery. I've taken the skills acquired from having Mrs. Ciotti as a teacher and used them to further my understanding of a topic or subject matter. Whether it be detecting the rhetorical purpose of an ad in a magazine or underlining the subtle themes and messages the director is trying to portray in a movie, I use my knowledge of elaboration, developed through one painful year in high school, to try and find the deeper meaning behind it all. Because of Binh's essays and Mrs. Ciotti's demonstration on elaboration in the field of rhetoric and argument, I have finally established a positive relationship with my literacy and have developed a deep reservoir of appreciation and passion for those willing to commit to excellence and mastery.

AUTHOR PROFILE

I am a math/science person, and I hope to land a career in the medical field as an emergency room doctor. Although writing is not my strong suit, it is something that I enjoy doing especially when it turns out to be a good piece of work.

—*David Diaz*

MORE THAN JUST WORDS

Louis Lin

Instructor: Jennifer Johnson

> **"I have never read a Nicholas Sparks novel, but I imagine that what I said to her could qualify."**

My mom moved to Vancouver in British Columbia, Canada from Guangzhou, China over eighteen years ago, unable to speak even a single word of English. Even today, she has trouble with the language. Despite this language handicap, she constantly challenges herself to improve. When I was growing up, she would often tell me how important communication, especially written communication, is, but I never believed her until a particular experience happened in my life.

Because she is a realtor and an insurance salesperson, my mom is constantly in communication with her clients, whether it's by talking on the phone or by writing e-mails. When she wrote an e-mail, she would often have me revise and sometimes even rewrite the message. I can still hear her calling my name from her home office, her demanding tone indicating that there is another e-mail to be reviewed. I would trudge over to her as part of my reluctant obligation as her son. While I would be looming over her shoulder, tapping on the keyboard, eyes studying the screen, she would be lecturing me on the importance of written communication. She would tell me that learning how to write is important because writing has more impact than speech. She would say letters hold more meaning than your voice. "Yeah, yeah. Whatever, Mom," was always my apathetic response. I would walk back to my room, disregarding her advice, so I could continue being unproductive, spending countless hours cruising through useless internet pages and social networking posts merely for moderate amusement.

It took several years and a painful breakup for me to realize how true her message is. My first love and I were in an argument and after a few days of "giving her space," as she requested, her best friend called to tell me that she was done with the relationship. At this point, a psychologist would have diagnosed me as being in the first of five stages of grief: denial. *No way had that just happened. We love each other... right? She's just upset; I'll give her a while to cool off.* But after a while, nothing changed. My dumb stubborn self was convinced that we were still together and that this was just a fight. *Just a fight? Louie, get over it. There is nothing you can do now. No, that's just how she is when she fights, trust me. We'll be fine.* It was not until I logged onto Facebook that I realized the weight of the situation.

I checked her profile and read her new relationship status: single. The breakup was "Facebook official," the 21st century way of establishing anything. Then I found I had a new message from her. I opened it as slowly as I could, knowing I would not like whatever she had to say to me. As I read the first few lines, all the words just seemed to fuse together. Something about it not being the same. Something about moving on. Something about this. Something about that. I had been told it was over and I did not believe it, but to read that it was finally over convinced me.

Second stage of grief: anger. I had always thought that writing angry letters was childish, but somehow I found myself writing one. I was upset. I felt I was being treated unfairly and that she had overlooked the mistakes she had made and the chances I had given her. In my letter, I wrote about what I had done wrong and compared it to everything she had done wrong. I poured all my rash and erratic post-breakup complaints into that letter, which was so hot with my rage that I am surprised it did not explode. However, I found that as I was finishing the letter, my frenzy was subsiding. I was no longer a fuming teenage boy playing with fire. I was a child holding a pen and paper. I was totally confused and ended up tearing the paper up, ashamed of myself for even having that mentality towards someone I loved.

I am glad she did not have a chance to see my second-stage, immature self. Instead, she saw me in my third stage: bargaining. I wrote back to her explaining myself and telling her how I could change. I have never read a Nicholas Sparks novel, but I imagine that what I said to her could qualify. After an hour of writing about how much she meant to me and another hour of reading my lines repeatedly, I sent the message. Immediately after, I handwrote a list of all of the things I loved about her, something I had wanted to do for her for a long time but regrettably never did while we were together. I wrote the list with hope that she would read it, cry, and take me back. But a few days later with no reply made me realize it was definitely and finally over.

Fourth stage of grief: depression. I became just a mopey mess. I refused to go out with my friends, and I refused to even make an effort to make myself happy. I found solace in depressing songs and bent the meaning of the lyrics to fit my situation. As I dragged along through life, I decided to do something. I needed a habit, so I asked my mom what I should do. She reminded me that writing is a powerful tool and suggested that I practice my abilities. I knew she was only trying to cunningly bring me to revise another e-mail, but what she said rang true. So I began to write about how I felt about everything. I filled pages with thoughts about how stupid I was and how I could have changed everything if I were smart enough to see it happening. Over the next few days, those pages began to serve two purposes: they helped me cope with the situation, and they gave me something to laugh about when I finally got over the breakup. As I became more lighthearted, I found myself writing about other things. I found myself thinking of other things. I found myself finally getting over it.

Fifth stage of grief: acceptance. Rather than stay inside and keep writing, I began to contact my friends and go out again. My playlist changed to a more upbeat one. My journal entries became significantly less frequent and significantly less dejected. When the thought of her did cross my mind, it became easier for me to brush it off and move on. I was fine again.

My mom was absolutely right about the importance of writing. Writing is more than just words. When I was told about the breakup, it did not have as much of an impact as reading the words my ex-girlfriend had written; there was something about those written words that gave them so much more meaning. And later, writing about my experiences helped me speed up the five stages of grief in my breakup and bring me closer to acceptance and happiness; it allowed me to connect with myself and find my true feelings. Writing may seem like the simple act of stringing words together, but I know now that writing is a powerful therapeutic tool that can help us find meaning and understanding, even in our most painful moments.

A few days ago, I went home to visit my mom. After unpacking and settling back into my room, I heard her calling my name from her office, asking for help with another e-mail. I just smiled and gladly agreed.

AUTHOR PROFILE

The story I wrote is only half true. I wrote about how writing about my break up helped me get over it, when I was actually writing about an actual break up I was going through at the time. It helped; writing about writing about my break up helped me get over it. Thank you for reading. Enjoy!

—*Louis Lin*

MEN OF HONOR

Juan Afanador

Instructor: Kathy Patterson

> **"**As we slide in the mud and score goals, the refreshing mist that falls from the clouds washes away our sweat. The adrenaline is unstoppable, and our excitement uncontainable.**"**

Nestled in the heart of the northernmost South American nation of Colombia lies a majestic city named Bogotá. As the booming capital of a third world nation, the city's problems of violence, poverty, and corruption are inevitable. Yet despite these adversities, and those that have given the country a dark connotation, usually involving drugs and war, *Bogotanos* are amiable people who have learned to live past these challenges and who are guaranteed to always show you a smile. *Gimnasio Campestre*, a male pre-kindergarten to eleventh grade private school is a perfect example of this, as regardless of its academic rigor and prestige, happiness is abundant. Here, both the teachers and the students follow a philosophy focusing on chivalry, philanthropy, fraternity, honesty, and Catholicism. This philosophy teaches "*Gimnasianos*" to be role models for their school, developing a clear sense of justice and fairness while working towards the ultimate goal of becoming "men of honor" ("Misión & Visión").

The sun is peaking through the unpredictable tropical grey clouds. The distinctive smell of the wet grass lures my friends and me to come and play *fútbol* on the immense soccer complex. As we slide in the mud and score goals, the refreshing mist that falls from the clouds washes away our sweat. The adrenaline is unstoppable, and our excitement uncontainable. It is through these perfect conditions that we are able to cherish everything: from the second the ball leaves the laces of our cleats to the whipping sound it makes when it hits the back of the net after a goal. Most of this excitement originates from the turf's inexplicable charm that causes our imaginations to expand every time we set foot on it and pretend that we are wearing the school's jersey while playing against *Gimnasio Moderno* in our yearly derby. This moment of creativity is soon cut short as the bell rings and the teachers herd us back to our respective classrooms.

Although the setting changes, the enthusiasm doesn't disappear. Our excitement continues to flow, evident in the post-game reactions that echo through the redbrick halls while we snake our way into the classrooms. Once we're settled in, our teacher takes this opportunity to get us into "learning mode" by conversing with us about our lunchtime game. Nimbly, she transitions into the day's lesson and keeps us engaged throughout, using her amiable personality regardless of the academic subject. She makes sure to conclude class with a final thought about moral wisdom, aiming to reinforce the theme of making a difference in the world and setting goals to accomplish that.

The teacher reinforced the founder's belief that the role of a teacher is to provide students with unique tools and abilities that will help them make a difference in their lives ("Historia"). Alfonso Casas also believed these tools then had to be humbly spread throughout the neighboring community so others could uptake these abilities and use them for their benefit. From school fundraisers to sports rivalries, *Gimnasianos* always displayed good sportsmanship, charisma, and devotion, growing into content and satisfied students. The most prominent activity was the weekly competition between grades to see which class could bring in more non-perishable food items. All of these were then donated to the deprived neighborhood just a couple of streets away, where people shivered and starved daily. Such actions broke down social barriers and helped kids like me begin to understand that despite the monetary discrepancies, everyone should be treated as equals and the less fortunate should be helped in any way possible.

Three years after my first day of school at *Gimnasio Campestre*, my family decided to move to the United States. Of course I missed my extended family, the food, and the Colombian lifestyle after the move, but one of the most important things I lacked in my new home was the community I had helped build at school. The shift to a public school was a momentous one, as I was exposed to completely different teaching styles and an environment lacking enthusiasm from my peers. My new teachers tended to focus only on academics and not the moral aspects of learning as I was accustomed to—which had almost as big an impact on me as learning a new language. This overall transition was similar to starting life over from scratch, yet I had to be ready to continue and hope that the values I had grasped in Colombia would be reinforced here.

When I concluded elementary school and started middle school, the environment changed once again as I was exposed to a much more diverse group of students that varied from jocks and nerds, to slackers and "in-betweeners." There, I was again placed in an unfamiliar medium in relation to my values. In addition, I had a few inconsistent teachers who tried implanting their personal philosophies into our brains as if they held the only truths about political ideology or social etiquette. However, this was rare since most of the time teachers focused on their main priority—preparing us for standardized tests so that the school's scores would be higher than those of competing schools. Although these exams were important, I realized that successful people weren't just those who proved to be "book-smart," but also those who showed personality and values, a correlative situation to the ideals of personal development instilled by *Gimnasio Campestre*. By limiting themselves to teaching only "the standards," some of the teachers lost the connection with their students, as they did not teach but rather bombarded them with information. Consequently, the competitive environment between students was catalyzed as they each tried to be the best of the best at whatever cost, making some students simply give up and fail. This was when it truly hit me that everyone had not learned the same values I had learned at *Gimnasio Campestre* and that people were unhappy. The principles of spreading ideas of brotherhood, philanthropy, and social justice to students seemed to have been lost, and I felt as if I were on an island where the guiding motto was "Every man for himself." Regardless, I did not let myself fall victim to that way of thinking and continued to live by my childhood philosophies, through which I was able to find a couple of good friends with similar mentalities. Oddly enough, they continue to be great friends while maintaining an academically and socially successful life that's bound to prosper.

Despite having these ideals taught to me as a boy for only three years, I continue to live by them and they continue to remind me of *Gimnasio Campestre*. Now every time I pick up that distinctive smell of wet grass, or drive past a red brick building, my mind flashes back to those instances of muddy games at the field, memories that remind me of all the things I learned from that influential institution. Occasionally, I wonder if the move was as beneficial as my parents had hoped. I especially wonder if I gained more than I lost through my transition to different educational systems. However as I study here at the world-prestigious UCSB, I realize that although it was knowledge that got me here and not morals, it's the wisdom and astuteness that I learned here in American schools that guarantee a successful future for me (at least financially speaking). Yet in terms of developing my personality, I realize my values weren't reinforced or increased here. Regardless, I know that for my social future to thrive, I need to be the one to strengthen these ideas and follow *Gimnasio Campestre's* motto of "being men of honor."

WORKS CITED

"Historia." Conocer El Campestre. Gimnasio Campestre, n.d. Web. 04 Dec. 2012. <http://campestre.edu.co/conocer_el_campestre/historia>.

"Misión & Visión." Conocer El Campestre. Gimnasio Campestre, n.d. Web. 09 Dec. 2012. <http://campestre.edu.co/conocer_el_campestre>.

AUTHOR PROFILE

I was born in Bogotá, Colombia and moved to the San Francisco Bay Area (Foster City) when I was eight years old. I am currently a first year pre-bio student and aspire in making the best out of the rest of my time here at UCSB. Writing is not my forte, yet a combination of hard work, passion on the topic, and having a good time allowed for my piece to be selected. Enjoy.

—*Juan Afanador*

A FEW GOOD MOTHERS

Jessie Jazlyn Wall

Instructor: Christopher Dean

> **"I am blessed to have had so many women to help me grow and teach me about life."**

My mother was killed in a car accident involving a drunk driver when I was a toddler. This does not mean I am lacking mother figures; in fact, I grew up with a handful of mothers. My non-biological mothers held the flashlight that guided me when I was in the dark, left a trail I could follow, and encouraged me to climb every mountain in my way. I am blessed to have had so many women to help me grow and teach me about life. These women have shaped a nurturing, strong, light-hearted, and independent me. My great-grandmother, grandmothers, aunts, and father made sure my upbringing had no holes in the mother department.

First and foremost is my grandma on my dad's side, Mama. She has kissed the boo-boos, helped with Spanish homework, and showed me what a kind soul is. She always has time for family, even now when we are two time zones apart. Mama teaches me patience through example; she rarely yells and always has time for me if I want to ask a question, share an idea, or just have an urge to talk. Mama is extraordinarily intelligent and always believed education was a must for me; she encouraged me to take higher-level courses and to try classes I did not think I would ever succeed in. An excellent example is that in eighth grade Mama encouraged me to take Spanish. None of my friends were taking the class, but Mama knew that it would help me out later. In high school, I was able to take second level Spanish as a freshman and therefore was ahead of the majority of my class. Mama helped me to understand concepts in ways my teachers could not convey. She has taught me how to cook some of her best recipes, including her zucchini bread (which is usually three quarters gone about an hour after it comes out of the oven). Mama always pushed me to be the very best of myself. When I was a young child, she encouraged me to join sports teams, even though I could not dribble a basketball or catch a softball to save the polar bears. Despite my lack of athletic ability, she was always in the front row, cheering me on. She has shown me that it is best to be calm and strong in the face of outrageousness or tragedy. Mama was silent and collected as she comforted the rest of my family, when my mother's unforeseeable death had them all in a state of sheer insanity. She has been my coach, my teacher, my nurse, and my biggest cheerleader.

My grandma on my mother's side would make sure to do things alone with me, without my plethora of cousins. She always made me feel special during our one-on-one time together by eating pretend food

I had made and playing with dolls with me. These are the kinds of things I will always remember. We had a very unique connection. She loved country music and now, whenever I am feeling down or stressed out, I listen to some George Strait or Tim McGraw and feel instantly comforted. Grandma had multiple heart attacks in her lifetime. Every time she dusted off her boots and went for a ride on her filly, "Leon," just to prove that she was still a tough little cowgirl. When she had to bury two of her children, as well as her parents, she showed me that no matter how terrible things seem, you can always move forward. After we lost loved ones, she kept them alive in our hearts by telling us stories we had forgotten or had not been told because they were embarrassing to the deceased. One that comes to mind is the story about the night before a planned family vacation to Disneyland when my mom's older siblings snuck the family car out at night to cruise around with their friends and in their ignorance broke the transmission. As a result, there was no family vacation for seven in the morning! Even in her sixties, my grandma had a young, vibrant, full-of-life personality. She never let herself get worn down and outdated. Grandma showed me that life is short, but what matters is what you make of it. It does not matter if social norms say that people in their sixties should not wear Disney characters on their shirts. Do what makes you happy in life, even if others do not accept it. Wear that Tinker Bell top if it makes you smile and do not worry about the people who roll their eyes. I want to age like she did—full of fun and young at heart.

My great-grandmother has instilled a sense of fun in me. Granny loves to introduce herself to new people as a current Dallas Cowboys cheerleader; she keeps everyone guessing for her own amusement. At almost ninety years old, she continues to attend Pilates classes and is a member of several clubs, one of her favorites being the Santa Ynez Valley Hookers, a group of women who knit and crochet Afghans for any elderly people who spend time in the local hospital. Granny loves to throw people off their game. One Thanksgiving dinner, she included her own addition to grace, "Up yours bin Laden!" Her reasoning was that he was hiding in a hole somewhere while we were all enjoying a delicious dinner, but the statement definitely had a

powerful shock value on all of us. She has taught me that no matter who you are, whether you are a retired senior citizen just looking for something to do, a teenager looking to be a part of something worthwhile, or anyone else who just feels the need to offer their abilities and services for a more meaningful purpose, you can contribute to help better your community. In high school, I took on this value and joined a group that organized several community service projects throughout the year. Some projects helped raise money for the less fortunate, such as ringing the bell near the winter holidays for The Salvation Army donations; other projects were just genuine good deeds such as placing flags, medallions, and crosses or Stars of David on veterans' graves. From these community service projects, I learned that a simple gesture like decorating a veteran's grave can have meaningful effects on others. When I helped with The Salvation Army donations, many people stopped to talk to me and thanked me for volunteering to help those who were less fortunate. I was standing under an umbrella on a windy, cold, rainy day, but I felt genuinely warm inside. Granny has shown me that contributing to your community and being silly and slightly odd will bring more to life.

My dad's two sisters have become sister-like to me as well. They guided me through my teenage years with support and advice regarding problems with boys and cliques, but could not help but tease me about my first pimple. Molly has always had a clear plan for her life: finish college, have a worthwhile career, get married, and have children. I admire her determination and drive. She has worked extremely hard to receive all that she has now—a degree in radiography, options for a new career, a caring husband, and a baby due in May of 2013. She is extremely generous to others and I find myself wanting to give more, as she does. Whenever someone in the family needs financial help, Molly is the first to offer. For birthdays and holidays, Molly always pays attention to detail to ensure the event is absolutely perfect. Never adhering to clichés or stereotypes, Erica has taught me that it is good to be unique, and that individuality is the key to discovering yourself. Erica is a woman who has always been confident and independent. She is a large woman and has never been ashamed of her size. Instead, she embraces it by having a full personality. She is fun and silly, and does not change when she is with different people. When I was a young child Erica took me to Knott's Berry Farm, Disneyland, and the movie theater. She was in her thirties and thoroughly enjoying Winnie the Pooh alongside me. She was never embarrassed to act younger than her age and or to make a goof of herself in public by talking to the Disney characters to make me giggle. She has taught me to stay true to my quirks and funny mannerisms, because people will learn to love me for them.

My mom's many sisters have shared stories and memories with me. They all have a few shared personality traits that I feel my mom would have had as well. All of my aunts are compassionate and regard family high in their hearts. No alcohol is necessary to get my mom's sisters silly. My aunt Kelly works in a Hallmark card shop and brings along silly singing stuffed-animals, figurines, and cards for the holidays. She and my other two aunts will sing along to the characters' songs loudly, obnoxiously, and proudly, just to get giggles from the rest of us. I am similar to them in personality, which I feel connects me to my mom as well as to my aunts. All of the sisters are strong like their mother; they have had to deal with burying their siblings, parents, and grandparents and remain full of life when that life has obviously taken a toll on them. In addition to the deaths in the family, all of my aunts have had to deal with financial troubles along the way. Lisa is very well-read; she often has book suggestions for me. My mom's younger and closest sister is very artistic; she and I connect when we discuss art projects. The elder sisters offer a glimpse of what my mother would be like now. I feel that if I were to combine all of my aunts' characteristics, I would have a very close representation of whom my mom would be today.

My dad has kept my mother a part of my life by showing me pictures of her, her artwork, her poetry, and telling me stories about her from when they were teenagers. He likes to tell me about the music they would listen to, mostly rock and alternative rock such as Green Jellö (later renamed "Green Jellÿ" due to a legal conflict with the owners of the Jell-O trademark), Nine Inch Nails, Anthrax, Faith No More, Pantera, and Guns N' Roses. He also enjoys telling me stories about the mischief they often

found themselves in. He recently gave me a VHS that is a home video displaying the inside of a tunnel that my mom covered with her street art; it took her just a few days to complete. I think he does these things to help me get a feel for what kind of woman she was. I know it hurts him to talk about her, but he continues to do so for my benefit. My dad and other family members help to keep my mom's image alive by sharing their own thoughts and memories of her with me. I have no personal memories of my mom, but thanks to the retelling of stories and the memories of others, I feel like I know who she was. My mom had a shy artist side, a loud and crazy Jane's Addiction–loving side, and a nurturing side with which she took care of me. My dad wants me to know the amazing human being she was.

Instead of one mother, I have had multiple mothers, and as I grow up I realize that I am a better person due to the variety in my upbringing. The women who mothered me have provided me with a better sense of who I am and who I can become. I have had multiple life experiences and perspectives to learn through. Each woman, and even my dad, has helped in mothering me; each in their own unique way. This variety has made me a more dimensional person with multiple layers, and for this I am thankful. To me, a mother is not defined by the sharing of half of my DNA. Instead, a mother is a life teacher, a confidant, a friend, a helping hand, and a push when one is needed. I miss my mom and wonder what she would be like; I wonder if what I dream her to be is an accurate representation. I try not to dwell on the "what ifs" because I know I have many women helping to shape me into a lady my mom would be proud of. Maybe it does not always require a village to raise a child but just a few good mothers.

AUTHOR PROFILE

I am a freshman and hope that my essay touches a few people.

—*Jessie Jazlyn Wall*

SEEING AHEAD

Benjamin Kambiz Ghiam

Instructor: Christopher Dean

> **"After explaining the surgical procedures that he could perform to help get my vision back, he looked into my eyes again and saw that my profound burden was beginning to diminish."**

It's always difficult to explain, but I can only describe it with fuzzy blotches and stains of dull colors. Listening makes it easier to discern what these hazy motions actually are. It's almost impossible to tell that those are my own hands out in front of me. This is the ill-fated truth of individuals suffering from severe keratoconus, a degenerative eye disorder. I was one of those individuals, and what I describe above was what my vision was like for months until Dr. Wachler performed a procedure on my eyes. I am forever grateful for Dr. Wachler and I can never thank him enough. However, the ability to see clearly was not the only gift I received when I walked out of that chilly surgery room. Once I realized what an impact one man can have, I too wanted to have that same effect on others. Because of the pressures and expectations from my family, I usually denounced the notion, but after the surgery, I knew I wanted to become a surgeon.

Growing up in a traditional and stern Middle Eastern family, I was never given many options. Whether it was clothes, food, or even girls, I was constantly expected to abide by a strict set of guidelines. From day one I always thought of myself as the "outcast," the rebel. My mother insisted I play the piano, but I chose the electric guitar. My father pushed me to play soccer, but I preferred Greco-Roman wrestling. I even refused to accept the BMW that everyone in my entire extended family is automatically issued the instant they turn sixteen. I preferred the rusty orange 1999 Jeep Wrangler that can hardly manage to merge onto the 101. I had always been the unconventional character who did not quite fit into my family's mold. Even my career choice seems to be a product of my family's authority and expectations; the only choice I was given was to pick either law school or medical school. I refused to accept this powerless reality. In middle school, I was convinced I could be the next Jimmy Paige, not Doctor Benjamin Kambiz Ghiam, and it wasn't until I was unexpectedly diagnosed with an unfortunate disorder that my views, both literally and figuratively, took a sharp turn.

I had never suffered any traumatic accidents. I never experienced any life-threatening instances, nor had I broken a limb. That's why it was an unprecedented shock to my family and me when I had nearly lost, arguably, my most fundamental sense. In my freshmen year of high school, the school optometrist recommended that I get a pair of glasses to help focus in class. By that spring, I had found myself "four-eyed" most of the day. By the time sophomore year started, I had gone to the optometrist every other week for a new prescription. The doctors explained to me that I had a form of astigmatism, and that this corneal disorder commonly starts to develop around my age. They said it was "normal." However, my progression was in no way, shape, or form "normal." Every week or so, it became more and more of a challenge to see. After months of agonizing optometry appointments and new prescriptions, my vision had gone from 20-20 to clinically blind in one year. I suffered from very severe keratoconus, and according to the state of California, I was "too blind to function without correction." The only form of correction at this time was rigid gas permeable contact lenses that are as painful as they sound. Because keratoconus is a very rare disorder, treatment was particularly limited, and the surgical procedures were not promising.

One optometrist recommended this hotshot ophthalmologist in Beverly Hills who had apparently developed his own surgical procedure to help with my disorder. Upon walking into his waiting room, it was easy to tell that this man was both well qualified and indeed a "hotshot." The room was large and lavish with modern white furniture, dark mahogany wood finish on the floors, and an everlasting buffet of warm pastries and coffee in the corner that filled the office with an incredible aroma. There was a massive window with a view of what looked like the entirety of southern California, and to top it all off, a colossal wall covered with medical diplomas, certificates, newspaper and magazine articles, and celebrity photos signed "Thanks Doc!" I remember feeling an overwhelming sense of relief upon meeting him. Dr. Wachler looked exactly like his waiting room—tall, elegant, and attractive. As he looked into my eyes, he began to diagnose my disorder in its entirety. The doctor explained the details of keratoconus and how his collagen reviving procedure could both stop the disorder's progression and help restore vision lost. After explaining the surgical procedures that he could perform to help get my vision back, he looked into my eyes again and saw that my profound burden was beginning to diminish.

Shortly after meeting with Dr. Wachler, I found myself flat on my back in an all-white surgery room. I was kept awake and shivering in light blue scrubs as three trained doctors operated on my clamped-open and restless eyes. The surgery took only thirty minutes, followed by a moment of darkness to sedate my eyes. Dr. Wachler slowly helped me out of my chair and gave me eye drops to help ease the tension. As my pupils started adjusting to the light, I was able to walk out of the room on my own. It was an incredible sensation and everything seemed so new to me. I could discern shapes and colors, and I was able to see the emotions on people's faces. It was as if I had raised my head out of the water to breathe for the first time in fifteen months. It was an incredible feeling of liberation that I owed entirely to the hands of Dr. Wachler. And then I realized that this man gives dozens of helpless individuals this same feeling of liberation every week. My prior rebellious disposition towards my parents' tyranny did not matter anymore—I wanted to become a surgeon. I wanted to be a doctor who has the ability to change the lives of those who desperately need it. I understood the challenges that face me in medical school, but the fulfillment I will receive from changing someone's life is worth the struggle to get there.

It has been a few years since the surgery and I have transformed into a changed man—I can now see. I can see my aspirations, my goals, and my future. Today, one footstep at a time, I am finishing up my pre-med undergraduate degree in hopes that one day I will be able to rid a boy of a similar misfortune. With any luck, I will leave an overwhelming impact on him through an impactful moment that makes him see clearly—provide not merely his eyesight and the ability to clearly see around him, but the clarity that allows him to glimpse into his future and envision his goals. That's what did it for me. I will never be able to fully express my gratitude to Dr. Wachler, nor will I ever forget the vision he has given me. Perfectly told by ancient Roman philosopher Lucius Seneca, "People pay the doctor for his trouble; for his kindness they still remain in his debt."

AUTHOR PROFILE

Born and raised in LA Valley, I'm a third year here at UCSB. I'm a biopsychology major hoping to go to medical school.
— *Benjamin Kambiz Ghiam*

HOMELESS

Gabrielle Castleberry-Gordon

Instructor: Daniel Pecchenino

> **"The burden of home haunts me every day."**

Monday, April 23rd. The day that I was dreading was here. Why did I take this Writing 1 class, and why did I feel so indignant about these elementary essays? Why was I agonizing over this huge paper? Four to six pages. Six pages? I can barely conjure up a one-page reading response. Six pages on "the burden of home," some abstract term that meant nothing to me. I was already not a strong writer, yet somehow I had to formulate six pages about a concept completely foreign to me. What does Joan Didion even know about me? In "On Going Home," she plainly states how she has a home and she wants her daughter to know what it is like to be her. If I had a daughter, how could I expect her to understand where I have been and what I have been through, where my home is, or how to feel at home anywhere? In Didion's essays, she describes in detail the experiences she had in Sacramento during a time when I was too young to enjoy life; I was bouncing around between the bickering of my parents, the door slams, the seclusion of my room, and the denial of my feelings.

"The burden of home." What does that even mean? Analyzing Didion's text "Notes of a Native Daughter" gave me no concrete images, only vague memories. She talks about how everything around her changed, much like my hometown Detroit changed from a booming metropolitan center to a ghost town with the economic crash. It got me thinking that I would have taken Advanced Placement Language and Composition if my high school had not been so crappy, and then I would not have been in this remedial writing class in the first place. That was a burden I lived with every day, struggling to get a good education in a town where most teenagers become farmers or mothers. I grew up in Dublin, Georgia, a place so small that the only thing it is known for is being halfway between Atlanta and Savannah. A town so rural, our biggest festival was for St. Patrick's Day. Even in that tight knit community, I didn't feel like it was a home.

What is a home? Home is not a house where you live. Home is a refuge, acceptance, the place in your life where you belong. By this definition, I know I do not have one. When I moved to California, I was so excited to escape that suffocating speck called Dublin, but I had a hard time adjusting to the new atmosphere. The food was bad, the people were fake, and the parties were not as good as everyone thought they were. For many weeks, I had no friends. I was sick for more than half of fall quarter. I never thought I would fit in. I secluded myself from everyone else. "Where are you from?" new smiling faces would ask. I struggled to reply, "Georgia?" because even I did not really know. Before I moved to the country, I was a big city girl. My life had been completely different there. I had a father. I had money. I attended a great private school. I had no friends, but I had no need for them then. In California, I learned to open up more and more to the girls on my floor, made close friendships and started to grasp a basic understanding of what home should be like. But I still carried the burden of not truly having one. It was like moving to Georgia all over again. At first, living in Georgia was great: fresh air, wide open spaces, cows and horses grazing on the side of the road. The country was so peaceful, just the break I needed from the cold, hectic life of the city. Later, I began to feel withdrawn and depressed. My "friends" did not understand me. "Where do you come from again? Why do you talk so funny? You seem so stuck up." Those inquisitive little girls were capable of irreparable damage, questioning my northern accent and starched uniform from my old private school. Quickly, I began to put on weight. First 100 pounds, then 200. Everyone had their curious eyes on me. I just wanted to go back "home." But home was replaced by something else. The burden.

Moving from the Detroit of my childhood to the Dublin of my adolescence was torture. I was ripped away from those cool nights lying in my bed listening to the cars drive by chased by police sirens in the urgency of the night. I remember coming home from school one day and hearing those words for the first time: "Papa had a stroke." The turning point of my life. My mom decided to move us to Georgia. My dad decided to stay. In that instant, I knew I would never have a home again. Not really remembering home, the burden strongly imprinted in my fragile mind. The burden is the weight held on your heart by nostalgia, sharp feelings, lingering words, broken dishes and picture frames, and the smell of your room from your childhood. The burden is everything that fades as you age and is replaced by painful loss. The burden is moving.

Recently, my grandpa became very ill again. It was the weekend of my 18th birthday. I had just left from smoking my first hookah in downtown Santa Barbara, something that my mother strictly forbade,

when I received a panicked message from her. My grandpa had a blood clot and a brain hemorrhage simultaneously and was in need of a surgery that they could not perform. He had suffered from another stroke, the problem that caused us to move to Georgia in the first place. I dropped all my classes and flew back immediately; it felt just like the time before when my life in Detroit stopped. The doctors did not expect my grandpa to live long. But his brain stopped bleeding and the clot dissolved. I stayed in Georgia a month and watched as he moved from palliative care to a nursing home, started therapy, and returned to decent health. Being at home all that time while thinking about the final I was missing at UCSB stressed me out, but I wouldn't change my decision. I had to be there with my grandpa. It was because of me that he got better.

What does all this have to do with the burden of home? Didion says she feels trapped when she is at home. When you go home, it consumes you and forces you to redirect your life to focus on family issues. The day before I was to fly back after spring break, my great aunt mysteriously died. She had just called the day before. She said she was going to the doctor because she felt sick. Then we got a call that she was dead. Diabetes. Last time I talked to that woman, she cursed me for going to California, leaving the family in debt for my own personal gain. I was furious and stormed out. I had no idea that the next time I heard from her would be a call from the mortician. It was a shock to the whole family. Should I stay? Should I go? "Go back," my mom said. *Don't worry about us* is what she meant.

Now I am sitting here, 2000 miles away, writing this paper about the burden of home and it is because of the burden of home that I am writing this paper. It is so hard for the words to flow when I am thinking about when I can make up my finals, when I can meet with my professors, whether or not I can earn any extra credit. Will my professors listen to me? Even though I am back, will the burden of home stop following me and influencing everything? No, life cannot stop when home gets in the way. It will not stop when I eat the food at the dining commons and think about the smells that come from my mother's kitchen. The beautiful palm trees will never replace the millions of pines in the Georgia countryside. The Santa Barbara traffic doesn't amount to the Detroit or Atlanta rush hour. Sitting here struggling to fill these pages with repressed memories has made me realize many things. My weak education. My single-parent household. My change in socioeconomic status. All the events that changed my life culminate inside me and make up who I am. Everything I am determines if I finish this essay, pass calculus from last quarter, have enough financial aid to even go to this school next year. This summer I am supposed to be taking study abroad classes. My layover is in Detroit. I have not been there in almost ten years. Everything will be different. Will I feel "the burden of home" then? When I'm walking through the airport and the memories of vacations to my grandparents' country home overwhelm me, will I understand where my true home is? Or will I continue to sit on the fence until I am dead, homeless forever?

I realize that the burden of home is not some abstract concept that existed only when I was confined to the inevitable pain and emotional heartbreak I experienced when I visited my family. The burden of home haunts me every day. It determines if I succeed or fail, win or lose, graduate or drop out, live or die. The burden of home never stops following me no matter where I go. It holds my hand tight, comforting me in my depression and suffocating me in my happiness. The burden of home is a straitjacket, meant to help but managing only to hinder growth and independence. The burden of home is a crutch when weak. The burden of home is my flaws. The burden of home is breathing air that has been polluted; I need it so badly even though it kills me. The burden of home is me.

AUTHOR PROFILE

I am Gabrielle. I was born in Detroit and moved to California from Georgia in pursuit of a better education. I recently turned eighteen and have been coping with issues of culture differences this year. They provide an interesting college experience.
— *Gabrielle Castleberry-Gordon*

DESIRE FOR EXCELLENCE

Jose Hernandez

Instructor: Jennifer Johnson

> **"**This quest to improve my literacy skills would prove to be a difficult one, yet for the sake of progressing in life, I was up for the challenge.**"**

Coming from an all Spanish-speaking family that had a history of minimal education, I was never encouraged to speak English as a child, much less to read or write it. And because I would never practice my English skills or apply them in my household, it was way too easy for me to fall behind in my literacy skills. While the native English speakers would be getting ahead by hearing English everywhere they went in school and at home, I would come back home from school and listen to uneducated Spanish slang; this definitely held me back. It was not until high school that I started to challenge myself and develop my own desire and motivation to become a better reader and writer. This quest to improve my literacy skills would prove to be a difficult one, yet for the sake of progressing in life, I was up for the challenge.

In high school, I was placed in the lowest level English class in order for me to catch up with my peers. Although I did not like it and was embarrassed by the fact that I thought I was stupid, this motivated me to work harder than the average student. We first started with basic writing and basic reading. Our teacher would read short stories and we would write half-page summaries on them. This continued on the whole year, mainly, I think, because our teacher was just plain lazy. She would do the least amount of work possible; she would hand out our assignments and expect us to complete them without any prior knowledge of what to do or without teaching us what we needed to know. I realized that I was not learning much and was frustrated by her lack of energy to teach. I started to think that my whole life had been like this because I never moved out of my comfort zone or challenged myself. I realized that if I ever wanted to truly challenge myself, I would have to do things on my own. This desire to challenge myself was fueled by the fact that I wanted to go to college and succeed. Yet, at that time, I was nowhere close to "college material."

I knew that I was at a disadvantage because never before had I picked up a book and read or written essays on my own, unless it was assigned in school. Other students would tell me how their parents always encouraged them to read and write when they were younger. Those same students would tell me, "I read for fun." How was this possible, I wondered? How could reading be so much fun? It was not until I was motivated to read that I got an idea of what they meant by "fun." My desire would eventually lead me to head to the school's library to check out my first book, *The Sound and the Fury* by William Faulkner.

I must admit, at first I was intimidated by the reading because all I saw was page after page filled with words I did not understand. Nevertheless, my desire to read more complex material was greater than my intimidation. I would read the book whenever I got the chance. The book fascinated me as it told the story of a dysfunctional family. This family had a tradition of having bad luck; first one of the family members, Benjy, is born with a severe mental disorder that makes him act like a young child even though he is thirty-two years old. Then another family member, Quentin, goes to Harvard and commits suicide. As I read, I made up scenes in my head, picturing how the family's bad luck in the book played out. This was when I realized what the other students meant when they said that they "read for fun."

As I finished that book, I was eager to start on another one, then another, and another. My desire to read more introduced me to different worlds I never knew could exist. These books gave me a whole new perspective on how to look at reading and to not be afraid of it. This new perspective confirmed that reading was actually fun. Now I try to have a book with me at all times because of the stories they hold and the power of imagination they can produce. Reading different books certainly did challenge me and soon I was reading college-level books like *Angels and Demons* by Dan Brown and Richard Dawkins's *The God Delusion*. I knew I was progressing in my quest to improve my literary skills. I would then start to challenge myself even further and analyze different books by writing book reports. Performing this arduous task required lots of time, and therefore, it interfered with my personal life. However, I never let this stop me, and I knew I had to continue practicing because it would only help me become a better writer.

Reading paved the way to writing—as I read and read, I understood more complex writing styles and how they were used. It fascinated me to see the many different forms of writing. Learning all these new things only benefited me. It helped me do better in my English classes as I kept getting only As and helped me formulate a pretty darn good UC personal statement, which is the reason, I think, that I got accepted into UC Santa Barbara. Writing let me figure out that I can be on the same level with all the other students as long as I would continue to challenge myself to my full potential. This was the only way to improve on my literacy skills, and as it turned out, I enjoyed sitting down and letting the hours pass as I would write anything from book reports to more personal reflections on my life, which allowed me to see the world from a different perspective.

Because of my commitment to challenging myself, I was able to become more comfortable with the English language. Reading and writing gave me a whole new perspective on my relationship with literacy. I think I have gotten to that point in my life where I would not know what do with myself if I ever lost the ability to read and write because of the excitement they bring me. Because of these skills I have obtained, I don't feel as though I am at a disadvantage from the native English speaker anymore. On the contrary, it makes me feel ahead of them because I am now mastering two languages, which I know will help me be successful as I continue my academic career.

AUTHOR PROFILE

I grew up in the most violent places East LA has to offer. It was always my dream to get out of there. My only way out was by pursuing my education here at UCSB. I am currently a political science major. I hope to give back to my community some day, to make it a better place.

—*Jose Hernandez*

LIVING THROUGH THE TRANSITIONS

Cheng Zhang

Instructor: Judy Gough

> **"**For me, living between two worlds was challenging at first because I was away from the country where I spent my first fourteen years of life.**"**

Sometimes, people do not realize the difficulties of being an immigrant. I know that I had no idea how hard it would be to start a new life in a new country. However, my opinion changed when I experienced it personally. In fact, living between two different cultural worlds is a unique experience and not all people have the opportunity to experience it. It is unique because people who live between two cultures have to adapt to a new environment while keeping their own native traditions and customs. For me, living between two worlds was challenging at first because I was away from the country where I spent my first fourteen years. However, through this experience, I have learned that although living through transitions is difficult, striving for goals with perseverance will help overcome hardship and lead to success.

Four years ago, my parents and I emigrated from China to Rowland Heights, California. Because of the drastic changes in our new surroundings, this experience was one of the turning points in my life. In China, I lived in the city with a large and dense population and here I live in the suburbs where the neighborhood is quieter. At first, I was not used to the change, but later on, I began to enjoy the tranquility in the neighborhood. Another difference was the change in education. In China, the teachers give lectures and make students take notes through the whole class period. But here in the United States, students tend to participate and become involved more in group activities such as discussions, projects, and presentations with other classmates. When I first went to class here, I was shy and was not used to the brand new learning method. But after collaborating with other students as groups in and out of class, I became more interactive and outgoing. And by having more interactions and activities while learning in class and participating in the classroom assignments, I gained the ability to become a thinker, communicator, and contributor.

As newly arrived immigrants from China, my parents and I had to restart our lives in every way imaginable. Personally, as I began attending high school, another big challenge I faced was communicating through a new language. I had to rely heavily on the dictionary for almost every school assignment and lecture. At the same time, I realized that it was hard for me to communicate with teachers and classmates because the speed of their speech was too fast for me to comprehend, and I had no knowledge of their slang or idioms. But when I thought about how my parents sacrificed themselves in order to give me a better education in the United States, I felt that I could not let their efforts be wasted. I realized that they had limitations in selecting careers because of their limited English. One way for me to address the situation was to practice my listening and speaking skills in English. Often, the children of immigrants speak the language better than their parents, and they serve as interpreters, who translate their native tongues into English for their parents. I did this, too. By translating for my parents, I saw my efforts to improve my English rewarded. Therefore, my motivation to learn was not only to better myself, but also to help my parents to communicate.

Determined to improve, I repeatedly listened to English recordings and CDs in order to get accustomed to the speed of normal conversational English. In the Chinese communities in Southern California, new arrivals to the United States will sometimes limit their contact with people to fellow Mandarin speakers, preventing them from learning to speak English fluently. However, I would force myself out of my comfort zone of friends and family and seek situations where I would have no choice but to speak English. By putting all my time and energy into practicing daily, I skipped an entire level of an English Language Development course and got out of the program within half a year. After another year, I was reclassified by the school from a limited-English-proficient student to a fluent-English-proficient student. Like Carlos Aldape, the author of "Challenging and Changing for Success," I struggled with the language and with communication when I first came to the United States. Also like Carlos, I took extra English classes at the community college after the school year ended and in summer because I needed those classes to fulfill the University of California requirement. Because of my efforts, I was in the top 7 percent of my graduating class and got into the college of my choice, the University of California, Santa Barbara. This experience taught me the life lesson that you have to work hard to achieve goals.

Besides the transition between two cultures, the transition from high school to college is challenging as well. First of all, the grades are calculated in different way: in high school, homework and classwork are worth a considerable percentage of the final grade, which means I could keep my grades up by doing well on homework and classwork. At the same time, the teachers check the progress of the students closely. On the other hand, homework is only worth a small percentage of the grade in college, and the professors do not check on progress. This requires more self-control, because if I do not do homework, I will do poorly on the quizzes and tests that count for a majority of the percentage of my grade. In terms of daily life, I have to take care of myself instead of living under my parents' shelter, and therefore must assume responsibilities and make daily life decisions.

By living through the transition between two cultures and the transition from high school to college, I have learned that working and striving with perseverance will lead to success and that the hardships in the transitions will be overcome eventually. Moreover, in light of all the sacrifices that my parents have made, I hope to make them proud and show them my gratitude through my actions.

WORK CITED

Aldape, Carlos. "Challenging and Changing for Success." *Starting Lines 2012*. Ed. Ilene Miele. Santa Barbara: UCSB Writing Program, 2012. 20–22. Print.

AUTHOR PROFILE

I am a freshman pre-biology major. I was born in Tianjin, China and came to the United States with my family during my freshman year of high school.

—*Cheng Zhang*

Photo by Loriel Davila

Photo by Yuqing (Augustina) Wang

Photo by Loriel Davila

Photo by Yuqing (Augustina) Wang

Photo by Loriel Davila

WRITING 1/
LINGUISTICS 12

RESPONDING
TO TEXTS

AN INVITATION TO DINE

Luis Carlos García Verduzco

Instructor: Mashey Bernstein

"Students should be 'inventors,' drawing the connections between sources while keeping in mind that they should not leave themselves behind, even when writing academic essays."

I sit at my desk and ponder about my professor's question, tapping my pen against the surface. "What new thing can you bring to the table?" he asked. As I think about it, I imagine myself holding a lidded china dish and walking into a formal dinner party. There is a large refectory table covered in all kinds of appetizing foods and stunning silverware at the event. Looking for a place among the dishes to set mine down, I see Orwell's apple dumplings, King's corn bread, Freud's Roman-style artichoke, and many more I recognize. All of these edibles, all of these ideas, are fascinating. In fact, they are so fascinating that I am embarrassed of and sometimes even forget my own. "What am I doing here?" I think, "My dish, my idea, is not worthy enough to bring to the table." I turn to leave. Remembering something, however, I immediately stop. To the table I return and I sort through the multitude of dishes. After a while, I find what I look for. It is Sommers' fragrant chicken, and it is as fascinating as the other dishes. Despite my worries, I place my lidded plate next to hers on the table of ideas. My professor's question still floats unanswered in my mind, though. Seeing the need to do so, I remove the lid from my dish. Nancy Sommers helped me understand that I need to bring my judgment and interpretation to bear on what I read and write in order to bring something new to the table.

In her essay "I Stand Here Writing," Sommers analyzes and interprets scenes from her life, connecting them through the theme of being an innovative thinker. While cooking in her kitchen, Sommers brings to mind her family: an encouraging mother, a father who wishes his daughter were his parent, and two little girls—one of them speaks Urdu while the other writes lists of things to do. Sommers tries to understand what each of them brings into her life, looking for the answer to her questions in library sources that, more often than not, fail to clarify uncertainties. To explain her use of sources, she delves into a pair of memories set apart by several years. In one, during a high school debate, she quoted an authority she did not understand. Her opponent, Bobby Rosenfeld, questioned her reference, disarming her and leaving her without words of her own. In the other memory, she picked Emerson's essay "Eloquence" for her college senior thesis. Through Emerson, she learned that even if she knew all the sources that existed, she must be an "inventor" in order to draw the connections between them. She reveals that her desire is to teach her students "to see themselves as sources." She wants them to be "personal," in the sense that they are the interpreters of what they read and write. Students should be "inventors," drawing the connections between sources while keeping in mind that they should not leave themselves behind, even when writing academic essays.

There are times when the judgment and interpretation I bear on my writing is inappropriate. Essay writing is a skill used in almost every academic field. From biology to philosophy, from engineering to the creative arts, practitioners are required to express information and concepts through the written word, thus informing the reader on the subject. However, there are essays in some fields that are not supposed to be interpretive. Beginning with the most obvious of this kind, in the fields of biology, chemistry, and physics, scientists write papers that explain the processes taken during an experiment to reach a desired goal. As I did in my chemistry laboratory classes, I wrote the steps and the chemical equations associated with each step to demonstrate how a certain chemical formed, decomposed, or changed color. There is no personal interpretation of the data. Certainly, bearing my judgment on this type of essay would cause it to lose track of its purpose, which is only to describe something. Another example is the subject of history. During the fall 2011 quarter, I had a class about the history of human civilization from prehistory to before the Middle Ages. At the end, the students had to write an essay on several possible subjects. One of my classmates wrote an astounding essay that compared the civilizations of Mesopotamia, Egypt, and India and how they were influenced by nomadic tribes. In her essay, she did not bring her personal interpretation and judgment. She used historical data to reach her conclusion. Even if personal interpretation is sometimes inadequate it should be used whenever possible.

To be a creative writer, I need to bring my understanding and meaning to what I read and write. In my first essay for this class, I wrote about Malcolm X with a thesis on why he is still important in the contemporary United States. My thesis says, "[He] is not an obsolete figure because he was able to achieve self-mastery." Truly this claim lacks originality and inventiveness. I certainly could write something better about Malcolm that delved deeper into modern times, connecting the issues to my life

and experiences. However, I did not. Reading the work, I find the same lack of originality and inventiveness scattered throughout. I attribute this mistake to two reasons. The first one is that my thesis, being the most important part of the discourse, guides how the paper is going to be. Since it is devoid of my creativity, the rest of the paper also lacks imagination. The second yet most important reason is that I did not engage myself in the reading and writing enough. I sought to use Malcolm's words in my favor as a passive listener without entering into "reflecting conversations with sources," which is what Sommers says an essay should do. When Sommers debated in high school against Bobby Rosenfeld, she was left speechless because she did not use her own ideas. She used the ideas of someone else, also acting as a passive listener that did not engage in the words she read. I, like her, learned a lesson. Even though there are great people who said great things, I can still use my own words to express my ideas. The ideas of great people form part of my thoughts as I converse with them, but their ideas are not mine.

Putting forth my interpretation and judgment into what I read and write will result in clever concepts for me to propose. The second essay I wrote for this class concerned George Orwell and his proposition that the decadence of the English language is due to bad politics and economics. In the essay, I applied his concept of a decaying language to the Spanish tongue and how Mexican politicians use it to manipulate the masses. As I read the work, I remember how I managed to understand Orwell's text well enough in order to apply it to my ideas. By connecting his ideas on the British Empire and, therefore, all other empires during his time to a government of present days, I established my idea. Of course, my writing has its follies. In some parts, I am not explicit enough as to precisely demonstrate what I mean, like forgetting to indicate that the use of a euphemistic and vague language is bad. In other parts, I do not concentrate enough on a single subject. I go from talking about the war on organized crime to how a politician uses a condemnable language. However, I understood Orwell's idea and entered into a conversation with it, exploring it by adding my judgment and interpretation. Sommers unexpectedly found the answer to her questions when she stumbled upon Emerson for her senior thesis. When she read "One must be an inventor to read well," she understood that she must be the one to create the connections between what she reads and her experiences. She continues her conversation with Emerson through her essay, implementing her judgment and interpretation on what she reads and writes. I, then, continue the conversation in the hope that I shed a new light on this idea and whatever other ideas I come into contact with.

The formal dinner party continues in my mind. This time, however, my dish's scent flows freely in the air, mingling with the rest to form a delightful aroma. I am not embarrassed by my dish, my idea. It may or may not be as good as the rest placed upon the table, but I at least hope it will cause a good thought when served to one person and start a dialogue when served to two or more. With my judgment and interpretation placed upon the recipe that Sommers gave me, I brought something new to the table. As I see it, there is enough room on the refectory table for new edibles. Even though what one will bring to the table is a mystery, I have to live with this uncertainty. My wish for now is to be creative enough so, when those new dishes arrive, I can go into a good conversation with their makers.

WORK CITED

Sommers, Nancy. "I Stand Here Writing." *Writing 1 Course Reader.* Santa Barbara: University of California, Santa Barbara. 2012. Print.

AUTHOR PROFILE

Born in Coronado, California, I have had a life on the border between Mexico and the United States, shaped by strong familial and religious ties. When I entered UC Santa Barbara, I was a biology major. However, after deliberating for more than a year, I changed majors and am now double majoring in economics and Spanish along with a minor in Japanese.

—*Luis Carlos García Verduzco*

DON'T THINK, JUST PLAY

Eli Wolf

Instructor: Jennifer Johnson

> **"If second order thinking can be associated with practice, then it follows that first order thinking is associated with game time."**

It was the top of the fifth inning and I had just finished warming up in the bullpen. Coach had me slated to close out the last three innings of the game. As I approached the pitcher's mound, or "the bump" as I like to call it, I was trying to "clear the mechanism" as Kevin Costner would in *For the Love of the Game*. I was focused only on pitching, thinking about all the little details that I had been working on during practice: stay balanced, follow through, bend over, watch the glove, and grip the ball before starting the wind-up. Every step of a pitch was going through my head like a little movie replaying itself over and over, just to make sure I didn't forget anything, and then I heard something that pulled me back to reality. "ELI!!!!!" I stopped thinking and immediately recognized my father's voice. "Don't think son, just pitch and play ball."

There are two types of thinking: first order and second order, which Peter Elbow, a professor of English, describes in "Teaching Thinking by Teaching Writing." On the one hand, first order thinking is "intuitive and creative and does not strive for conscious direction or control" (Elbow 37). Basically, you don't think; you just do, and let happen what happens. I think of it as a leaf being blown in the wind. The leaf does not think about what is happening or where it is going; it simply lets itself get taken by the wind to wherever the wind takes it. The leaf does not try to take control of any aspect of the situation. On the other hand, Elbow argues that second order thinking can be considered the opposite. He describes it as "conscious, directed, controlled thinking" (Elbow 37). Elbow suggests that you can improve your writing skills by using a balance between both first order and second order thinking. He recommends that you find a balance between the amounts of each type of thinking you should use and then find a rhythm for when to switch between the two. This method can be described as a back and forth style that requires the extended use of each type of thinking without interruption (Elbow 39). Whether I knew it or not, before reading Elbow's "Teaching Thinking by Teaching Writing," I have always used first and second order thinking to improve my skills as a baseball player. The two most obvious situations in which first and second order thinking can be applied in the game of baseball are in practice versus in a game.

Second order thinking is crucial when critiquing your performance during baseball practice. Starting with something as simple as throwing a baseball—which is in fact a piece of cork, wrapped in string, covered in leather—requires a series of precise actions just to move it from point A to point B. Most people don't use the proper technique the first time they throw a baseball. They either do the steps in the wrong order, neglect to do all the steps, do at least one or more of the steps wrong, or most commonly, they do a combination of all three. Practice exists so that you can analyze what you are actually doing and how it is different from what you need to be doing. Repetition is essential for breaking bad habits or instincts and forming good mechanics. All methods require some form of analysis or another. In fact, many players rely on someone who is knowledgeable about the game and who will watch them in real-time and analyze their execution of the steps. This sort of analysis is a direct application of second order thinking, as reflected by another definition Elbow provides: "Second order thinking is a way to check, to be more aware" (38). Probably the most effective way to check for flaws in your form would be to film yourself so that you can watch your form over and over, in slow motion, to see exactly what you are doing. This method works for any aspect of baseball, whether hitting, pitching, catching, fielding, throwing, relays, pick-offs, stealing, base running, lead-offs, you name it; second order thinking works, and it makes the process of discovering flaws much easier than any other method. While practicing, you are trying to control what happens by consciously thinking about it and making an effort to go in the desired direction of improvement.

If second order thinking can be associated with practice, then it follows that first order thinking is associated with game time. Ever since I can remember, my dad and all of my coaches have told me to stop thinking when I'm on the ball-field and just play. Yet I was not able to do this until about a year or two ago, the summer between my junior and senior year of high school. I was always under the impression that if I stopped thinking on the field, I would cause all sorts of problems. Elbow points out that it's a common misconception that if we stop using second order thinking then everything will fall apart. It turns out that my mind was so cluttered trying to focus on performing all the steps of a play that I was unable to do them correctly and quickly.

If I did all of them quickly, then they wouldn't get done correctly, and if I did them all correctly, then I would not do them fast enough. I would either field the grounder and make a poor throw, or not have the baseball reach the base in time. But last year, I played without thinking, and to my surprise, I played the best baseball I have played in my entire life. I was able to let instinct from years of practice take over, and I played like I actually knew what I was doing—because I did. I let baseball happen, and without making any conscious effort, I succeeded on the field. I know now that I play better baseball when I just play rather than try to execute all the parts of baseball individually. As Elbow would say, "I wasn't steering, I was being taken for a ride" (39).

Yet, as with everything in life, playing baseball well is not as simple as first order thinking during a game and second order thinking during practice. During games, it is in fact necessary to instead switch back and forth between the two in order to maintain optimal performance as a player and a team member. While in the dugout, during the offensive half of the game, analysis of the pitcher and locating the opponent's weaknesses in the field are crucial for success. This second order thinking determines what strategies to use while on offense. First order thinking is needed while at bat or during the pitch. Between plays, second order thinking is required to make sure that the right actions are being applied in the right situation. The need for switching between the two applies when on defense as well. Fielders need to know exactly what to do with themselves, no matter where the ball is put into play. At times the player could even be switching back and forth between the two types of thinking in quick succession. For example, when at bat, before each pitch the batter should be using second order thinking by analyzing where to hit the ball to best help the team, predicting what pitch will likely be thrown and where, as well as paying attention to what signs the third base coach is giving. Then, once the pitcher begins the pitching sequence, the batter should immediately switch to first order thinking and let the subconscious mind take over. Everything worked on during practice is ingrained in the mind and all that is left to be done is let it come to the surface via first order thinking. The act of balancing first and second order thinking is just as important as being able to separate the types of thinking from each other. In baseball, this balancing act enables a player to play better baseball, as well as to be a better team member.

I have always seen myself as an analytical baseball player, focusing carefully on the technical side of the game, or what Elbow would refer to as second order thinking. I have only recently learned to use first order thinking in baseball, and it has served me well. As a result, I can't help but agree with Peter Elbow that first and second order thinking can be applied to improve one's performance in baseball, or for that matter, almost anything. As usual, my dad was right. I should have listened to him all those times he told me to stop thinking and just play. Now that I have, I am a better baseball player and I love the game so much more, for now I am both thinking about the game and enjoying the fun of playing it.

WORKS CITED

Elbow, Peter. "Teaching Thinking by Teaching Writing." *Change* 15.6 (1983): 37–40. JSTOR. Web. 5 Apr. 2010.

AUTHOR PROFILE

I am a first-year physics major in the College of Creative Studies. I love to conduct my own rocket experiments in my backyard at home in Elk Grove, CA.

—*Eli Wolf*

PEDAGOGY OF THE OPPRESSED

Anabel Hernandez Torres

Instructor: Leslie Hammer

"Four times four is sixteen; the capital of Para is Belem. The student records, memorizes, and repeats the phrases without perceiving what four times four really means or realizing the true significance"; this situation occurs because of the style in which students are taught in society (31). In *Pedagogy of the Oppressed* Paulo Freire calls this style of teaching the banking concept of education. Freire believes that teachers are treating students as containers that need to be filled with knowledge without any interaction. With this process, "education thus becomes an act of depositing, in which students are depositories and the teacher is the depositor," much like a bank account (31). Freire believes this is a problem because instead of analyzing the material being taught and applying it to real life, students are memorizing the information being "deposited" into their brain. I agree with Freire's outlook on the banking concept of education. Without interaction, emotion, or explanation, students do not retain knowledge, nor do teachers gain anything back.

> **"Many argue that teaching is a two-way street. Students learn from teachers, but teachers also learn from students."**

Freire believes that the banking concept is mirrored by society. Society has let the banking concept continue for so many generations that it has become one of the "norms" of teaching. Most lectures in college are taught by the banking concept, in which "the teacher teaches and the students are taught; the teacher knows everything and the students know nothing; the teacher is the subject of the learning process, while the pupils are mere objects" (32). The problem with this, as Freire states, is that students are not interacted with. They are not asked to repeat what they learned in class, which in my personal experience has helped me retain knowledge. When I came to UC Santa Barbara about a month and a half ago, I did not know what to expect from my professors' teaching methods. The first lecture I attended was for Biological Anthropology. I remember walking into Campbell Hall, along with five hundred other students. I sat down, ready to participate in lecture, when I realized I was but merely just another face in the crowd; another dollar to the professor's pocket. The professor stood in front of the hall and read off the screen for an hour and fifteen minutes. Fact after fact—I was barely able to retain so much information. Needless to say, he did not feel the need to interact with us or explain what in the world he was talking about. My professor was depositing information into my brain as if I were a bank, expecting that I would understand it all. Because of his teaching method, every day after lecture I would sit with my friend and go over the PowerPoint slides to discuss key points so that I could understand what he was saying.

From experience, I know that I cannot simply have information "deposited" into my head and be expected to maintain it. During my senior year in high school, my history teacher seemed to teach by the banking concept. The most boring man anyone will ever meet, Mr. Conacka had no sense of humor, fun, or ability to start a conversation. His daily appearance consisted of the same outfit—a button-up single-colored flannel shirt and dark-washed jeans. He stood daily in front of the classroom and spoke as if he were a robot. He did not even have PowerPoint slides to help students follow along. He spoke aloud with no emotion or passion about history. Mr. Conacka did not engage with us, and we did not engage with him. It was miraculous if I could remember what he spoke about in class. Everything he said went through my head like a Frisbee through the cold wind. His methods were anything but helpful. I did not feel that I was able to think critically or be self-expressive when it came to this subject. To retain the knowledge, I had to learn the material on my own because his teaching ways were impossible to withstand for more than twenty minutes. Students are not barrels that will retain anything that is "deposited" into them. This is the problem with the banking concept. Information is more difficult to retain. The more effective way to teach is when the teacher "presents the material to the students for their consideration, and re-consideration, and re-considers her earlier considerations as the students express their own" (36). Because of such methods, Freire created a resolution called the "problem-posing" method in which educators must "abandon the educational goal of deposit-making and replace it with the posing of the problems of human beings in their relations with the world" (35). Educators must learn not to think of students as objects and should teach through interaction.

When someone asks the question, "What do you want to be when you grow up?" and hears the reply "A teacher," the questioner can usually assume that this person enjoys being in the company of younger people and discussing a subject they are truly passionate about. The banking education style shows anything but this. All it expresses is a person who enjoys treating others as objects who are putting money into their bank accounts. Freire describes education as "the practice of freedom," while the banking concept would have education described as "the practice of domination—that man is abstract, isolated, independent and unattached to the world; The world exists as a reality apart from people" (36). In high school, I found that the best teachers were the ones that spoke with the students instead of at the students. My favorite teacher was Ms. Mishra, who would have each student express his or her outlook on the subject. She always had a way of being able to relate to students, which all educators should have the ability to do because they too were students once before. This would be the "problem-posing" method of teaching that Freire suggests society should do.

Many argue that teaching is a two-way street. Students learn from teachers, but teachers also learn from students. With the banking education concept, teachers are not necessarily teaching to their students, but merely standing in front of a group of students and depositing information into their "banks." Teachers receive feedback when interacting with students. By teaching to students, teachers learn and gain the confidence to have the ability to interact in such a way that allows knowledge to be given. In my opinion, teachers that are the most experienced are the teachers that are the most talked about and most recommended for a subject due to their passion for teaching and willingness to interact with others to gain a common goal—knowledge of the subject.

Freire blames professors, teachers, staff, and all educational figures whose role is to teach. His solution is to have educators change their way of teaching, and to directly associate students to the learning and education process as a whole—the "problem-posing" method. An educator's job is to "regulate the way the world 'enters into' the students. The teacher's task is to organize a process which already occurs spontaneously, to 'fill' the students by making deposits of information which he or she considers to constitute true knowledge" (33). Freire gives interesting points, in my opinion, when he says that education has to be a two way street in which both the teacher and student are involved in the teaching. The depositing of education must come to an end—anyone can memorize facts and information for a test, but learning what they actually mean allows students to apply the concepts to real life and be able to express themselves in the subject.

WORK CITED

Freire, Paulo. "Chapter 2" *Pedagogy of the Oppressed. Writing 1ACE: Approaches to University Writing.* Ed. Leslie Hammer. Isla Vista: Graphikart, 2012. 31–39. Print.

AUTHOR PROFILE

My name is Anabel Hernandez Torres. I am from a small town in Northern California. I am the first in my family not only to graduate high school, but also to pursue a higher education at a university. I am currently undeclared but have discovered my great interest for writing after taking my first writing class here at UCSB.

—*Anabel Hernandez Torres*

STRUGGLES IN SOUTH AFRICA

Cayla Bergman

Instructor: Mashey Bernstein

> **"If people aren't given an option to think for themselves in society, then they are likely to conform and believe that what they are doing is right, just like my parents did."**

I've never really asked my parents about their time in South Africa during apartheid. When they immigrated to the United States in 1988, they came to a better, more equal, and just society. As a result, I grew up in America and never experienced the segregation of blacks and whites the way my parents did. Not only did I think that this separation of people based on skin color was wrong, but so did everyone else, including my parents. So why do people tell me that my parents are bad people? Why do they blame my parents for the injustices in South Africa during their childhood? With apartheid's end in 1994, there were many influential people who spoke up against this injustice who petitioned for many years for it to subside, such as Nelson Mandela. He was a South African anti-apartheid activist who followed the nonviolent approach famously started by Mahatma Gandhi. This nonviolent approach carried on throughout America, where both Ralph Waldo Emerson and Martin Luther King, two influential and famous activists, advocated for others to have a sense of individuality and confidence in order to speak up in society. If people aren't given an option to think for themselves in society, then they are likely to conform and believe that what they are doing is right, just like my parents did.

Emerson exclusively studied and taught individuality and nonconformity. In the essay "Self-Reliance," he proposes that people must be true to themselves and tend to think that they are better than society. He explains the reforms and changes needed in society to show that society is a barrier against the individuality of its members and that people need to embrace themselves. Emerson believes that individuals need to strive to be defined and only then can they bring peace to themselves. It is also important to disallow society from suppressing one's individuality and responsibility. Martin Luther King preached for equality and justice for African Americans living in America in the 1960s. In "Letter from Birmingham Jail," King responded to the clergymen who believed that the battle of racial segregation should take place in the courts rather than on the streets. King wrote in a respectful manner and calm tone, demonstrating his patience to deal with the injustice against blacks that at the time needed immediate attention. Although he wrote his letter in the Birmingham jail after his unsuccessful non-violent protest on the streets, he never ceased to preach what he believed in and how he felt about segregation within society.

King believed that a society must be just and that people's God-given rights are legitimate to have no matter who they are or where they live. In America, he was given an opportunity to preach his beliefs because he lived somewhere that allowed unalienable rights of speech. This isn't always the case, especially where my parents were brought up. Although my parents grew up half way around the world from America, they were taught that segregation between blacks and whites was normal. My parents conformed to society because it was expected and they didn't know any better. Their nannies, servants, and gardeners had to ride at the top of the bus that allowed only whites to sit on the bottom of the double-decker. There were all-white schools that my parents attended, and all-black schools located in the predominantly black areas. Blacks also weren't allowed on certain beaches; they were only allowed to go to these beaches and into the cities if they had a permit with a white family. Despite what blacks had to go through, many still seemed happy, as if they also didn't know any better. Although apartheid was happening half-way across the world, it was also occurring in many southern states of America. King was a strong advocate for justice and peace in South Africa during apartheid. He believed he could eliminate apartheid by using an economic approach. He proposed that if America and the United Kingdom stopped purchasing South African goods, such as gold, South Africa would stop earning revenue and apartheid would end. King protested nonviolently against South Africa saying, "Injustice anywhere is a threat to justice everywhere," which brought attention to many people around the world (88). If people don't question society, they will believe that injustice is the normal and right thing and not believe in any other alternative.

My parents grew up assuming that what they thought was right. My dad told me that he was never really exposed to the lives of the oppressed during middle school and believed that this situation was normal and existed everywhere else in the world. Even though apartheid laws oppressed the blacks, to my parents, they seemed to be happy in their environment. A lot of white families, including my parents', looked after black workers by providing jobs, housing, food, and basically treated them as part of the family. My parents were brought up in a very sheltered environment. My dad said

he learned about apartheid when he went to high school, but since he was at an all-white high school, it still seemed to be a normal way of life. Once he got to college, he was then exposed to the way the country was run. In 1988 after college, he and my mom left the country at a time that was very unstable for South Africa politically. At the time, people were very unsure of what was going to happen with society. Now that apartheid was ending, there was a lot of doubt about how the country was going to be run. Many educated people emigrated from the country, such as doctors and lawyers, who didn't believe that the country could sustain a democratic society. Despite all that happened with my parents, they never really knew how it felt to be on the oppressed side. King was a strong advocate for anti-apartheid and believed that South Africa was home to the world's worst racism. He realized that even the mildest form of non-violent resistance resulted in years of imprisonment or worse. King's nonviolent solution to rid South Africa of apartheid through an economic approach was approved by the United States and the United Kingdom, and four decades later, apartheid finally came to an end.

When Nelson Mandela was released from prison in 1990 and became prime minister of South Africa, he was the symbol of freedom from apartheid. Mandela was a militant anti-apartheid activist and after a non-violent protest in 1962, he was convicted of sabotage and sentenced to life in prison. Following his release from prison, he set off a political campaign where he established democracy and became president in 1994. Mandela promised all blacks jobs, shelter, food, education, and electricity; however, this task was too monumental to be effective. To this day, there is still a lingering problem of unemployment in South Africa (approximately 25% unemployment), which leads to crimes such as robbery, carjacking, and other forms of violence just in order for people to survive. Mandela exhibited many of the qualities famously demonstrated by Emerson, such as strength, determination, and belief in himself. He used self-reliance to stand up for what was right against apartheid, and although it landed him in prison, he still never gave up. Emerson's quote, "envy is ignorance; imitation is suicide" depicts what kind of a person Mandela is and how he built his own power to create a democratic society in a distressed country (95).

Most people do not agree with the way oppression was handled in South Africa. For four decades, segregation between blacks, whites, and other people of color was a normal way of life. Although my parents do not agree with what happened during apartheid, they still didn't know any better when they were younger. The main contributors to the anti-apartheid movement in South Africa used ideals from both Emerson as well as King to act non-violently against the regime. Through years of protest, violence, sentencing to prison, and non-violent acts of protest, apartheid came to an end. It is evident that in order to really make something happen, it is important to not stand idly by and conform to society, but rather to make a difference and speak up for what is right. No matter where someone lives, the same ideals can flourish and become stronger. Knowing what was right and acting on it changed a country for the greater good and allowed people to realize that the oppressed will not stay oppressed forever, as they just need to take a stand and be confident that it is possible to change.

WORKS CITED

Emerson, Ralph Waldo. "Self-Reliance." *Writing 1 Course Reader.* Santa Barbara: University of California, Santa Barbara. 2012. Print.

King. Martin Luther. "Letter from Birmingham Jail." *Writing 1 Course Reader.* Santa Barbara: University of California, Santa Barbara. 2012. Print.

AUTHOR PROFILE

I am eighteen years old and a freshman at UCSB. I am from Los Angeles, CA. I love music, soccer, and traveling the world.

—*Cayla Bergman*

KNOWLEDGE SHOULD FLOW AND BE GIVEN

Judith Martinez

Instructor: Leslie Hammer

> **"Questioning one of our teachers was never an option because as students we were taught to assume that the teacher knew everything."**

Sitting in class from 1st through 12th grade, did you feel like a little flash drive just being filled up with information? Having to follow certain guidelines in every single assignment you had to complete? Scoring a bad grade simply because you hadn't imitated what the teacher had shown you before? During my last year in middle school, my teacher continuously gave my essay assignments low grades. She argued that because I did not follow her guidelines, my essays were not well developed and therefore not worthy of a good grade. However, I believed that I was not acquiring knowledge by solely following her guidelines, by simply using only the information she had filled me up with. I wanted to experiment with my writing skills and the outcomes of structuring my essays differently than what she had taught. Paulo Freire describes this teacher's approach as the "banking concept of education" and says that it limits the amount of knowledge a student can acquire (31). While I agree that the banking method limits the amount of knowledge a student can acquire, I disagree with Freire's idea of imposing "problem-posing" education because not every classroom setting can adapt to this method (31). Students need a foundation to work up from that is set forth in Freire's idea of the banking method of education.

According to Freire, banking education functions by letting a teacher simply deposit ideas into the student, making them memorize everything, and consequently only serving to oppress the student. He claims that this type of education is useless because the student can only act to a limited extent—merely receiving and storing these deposits. He argues that knowledge emerges only through continuous and relentless questioning of the world with others. During that last year in middle school, I never understood why the teacher insisted that my essays come out a certain way. Now, I realize that she only worried about our essays being in a particular format so that when we took the state assessment test, she would be recognized as an "excelling teacher" due to our test scores. The knowledge we acquired did not matter to her. Every single day it was the same thing: I had no passion for writing at all as she simply filled us up with information, which is what teaching meant for her. I felt like my education consisted of being a robot that did only what the programmer had programmed it to do. According to Freire, the solution to this problem is to implement "problem-posing" education, which works by "adopting the concept of women and men being conscious beings" (38). They can reflect upon situations, pose problems, reflect upon them, and therefore become critical thinkers.

Freire argues that banking education oppresses students and limits their actions. He describes this as "[Turning students] into 'containers,' into 'receptacles' to be 'filled' by the teachers," and claims that, "The more completely she fills the receptacles, the better teacher she is. The more meekly the receptacles permit themselves to be filled, the better students they are" (31). In other words, Freire believes that teachers get acknowledged as excelling if they can successfully get students to imitate what they have taught, and it is the ones who do so that are noted as the top students. According to him, the teacher controls what the student learns and is possessor of consciousness; the student is just a spectator and is only open to learning what the teacher deposits. In response to this, he claims that the best way to obtain knowledge is by letting the knowledge flow through the classroom setting, so that everyone learns from each other. He argues that knowledge is gained through critical thinking, which is what problem-posing education encourages. Freire states that critical thinking skills are obtained by constantly being exposed to and presented with problems and by reflecting upon them continuously. Furthermore, this knowledge is needed in order for humans to coexist and revolutionize, so they need to be continually questioning the world around them.

As I said earlier, my middle school teacher would simply fill us up with information. She never liked the idea of us questioning her or challenging her by not following her strict guidelines for writing essays. Questioning one of our teachers was never an option because as students we were taught to assume that the teacher knew everything. I am not implying that the teachers either do or don't know everything, but as Freire stated, we can all learn something new from each other when knowledge flows, just as it does in my writing class here at UCSB. Our professor questions us about the readings and asks for our opinions, and then she puts our opinions together to create one main central idea. She is helping us to develop as critical thinkers. We always work in groups and although she determines what we will talk about, the ideas we bring

forth during this discussion are completely ours, unique to every student. We learn from each other. But this is at a higher level of education. In lower levels, such as elementary or middle school, this method of education would be difficult since those students are not yet trained to think critically and question ideas.

Just like a house must be built upon a sturdy foundation, every student needs a strong foundation from which to begin in order to become a critical thinker. Freire is surely right in stating that banking education limits the knowledge a student can obtain, but I disagree with the idea that problem-posing education should be used throughout all classroom settings. In college lecture hall settings, this method is impossible since there would be so many ideas set forth that discussion would be endless. This would result in a negative impact upon the learning process because such a large number of subjects could not be covered during the lecture period. This is similar to elementary school. In kindergarten, students don't know how to read or write. These are basic skills that can only be taught by having the student repeat what the teacher is doing. Something like writing or knowing the difference between a verb, an adjective, and a noun cannot be taught with a problem-posing type of education. The method of banking education should be introduced in late elementary school, when the students are being geared to become critical thinkers during their middle and high school years.

Therefore, problem-posing education should be used in middle school. Before that, banking education is the only way to equip students with the knowledge necessary in preparation to critical thinking and exposure to problem posing. In order to develop into critical thinkers, we need to know what a question is in the first place. We must all acquire basic knowledge first, level off the soil of the ground, and build a foundation—a steady one, so that as we continue to travel through our many years of education, we can be active critical thinkers, thus making the world a much more intellectual place. I am astonished by the ideas about education, put forth by Paulo Freire. I had never thought of education in this way. I wish our high schools would introduce students to these perspectives on learning so that many more of them can find an incentive towards obtaining higher education.

WORKS CITED

Freire, Paulo. "Chapter 2." *Pedagogy of the Oppressed. Writing 1 ACE: Approaches to University Writing.* Ed. Leslie Hammer. Isla Vista: Graphikart, 2012. 31–39. Print.

AUTHOR PROFILE

I am a first-year student, currently declared as a mathematics major. Originally from Venice Beach, I reside in Santa Catalina. I am a first-generation Mexican-American and the first in my family to go to university.

—Judith Martinez

ANALYSIS OF "MY PLACE"

Yanfei (Emphy) Wang

Instructor: Roberta Gilman

> **"In other words, it is possible that people who haven't found their place yet could be on the way to achieving that some day."**

In today's globalized world, many people have trouble attempting to establish a sense of place in another country. In the article "My Place," Emphy Wang relates her experiences of facing difficulties living as a foreigner in Japanese society. As far as I am concerned, situations vary a lot during the process of achieving one's own place. Many people continue trying to establish their own sense of place in spite of suffering while they are spending their lives overseas. Others find that maintaining a place is more difficult than creating one, while some think achieving a place for themselves is not necessary if they have other choices.

First, Wang wonders whether people could have a sense of place at all in another country, and all her examples reveal difficulties people had when they lived overseas. For example, as a foreigner, she found it hard to get a part-time job in Tokyo. Is it really impossible to achieve a sense of place? Perhaps while it seems hard or even impossible for people to find their place, some people may successfully do that. As for the question of whether or not they are able to maintain that place, we know that Korean immigrants who lived in Los Angeles's Koreatown did create a "place" overseas. They gathered together and worked hard as a big group. Consequently, many Korean restaurants, karaoke lounges, and miscellaneous shops were built, and most Koreans were able to make a living in the US. As a result, it seemed that they had already found their place in another country. However, according to the *Los Angeles Times* article "Two Worlds Blend Uneasily in Koreatown," things appeared to change in time. Koreatown was supposed to have its peculiar characteristics, but Western shops and restaurants slowly invaded it. "The old shops have given way to Coffee Bean & Tea Leaf, Nine West, Cold Stone Creamery, and other familiar names," says Gerrick Kennedy, the article's author (4). Additionally, people living in Koreatown had to compete with other local people to get a job. When it became a place that was cross-assimilated into American culture, it was no longer the place only for Koreans. In other words, people in Koreatown started losing their own place, which they had created. In this way, it was possible that some people were able to find their place; however, it was hard for them to keep it.

Secondly, many people have struggled to create their own place in another country when in reality it was not necessary to do so. Wang gives an example of Japanese people in China. As the Chinese economy became strong, many Japanese people went to China to find a good job. Recently, due to the territorial dispute, some Chinese people held protests and became very hostile towards Japanese people, which caused some degree of violence. Therefore, many Japanese people in China returned to Japan. Wang argues that in this case, going back was almost the only way out for Japanese people. It seemed that they were forced to "physically move" because they didn't have their own place in China, and if they did, Japanese people in her hometown would never have to go back to Japan after the protest. In other words, if there had been a solid Japanese community and those émigrés had owned property, they would have been able to survive the crisis and stay. However, it could also be argued from another perspective. Tim Cresswell, who did a lot of work researching the relationship between time and space, points out some examples of people who did not have the freedom to move or communicate: "The refugees from El Salvador and Guatemala and the undocumented migrant workers from Michoacan in Mexico" (14). If Japanese people were these people who did not have the power of mobility, they would have had to stay in China and continue suffering from local resistance. However, they were a group that possessed control over their mobility because they did not necessarily have to find their place in China. In other words, Japanese people in the story did have the power: they could go back anytime they wanted and they could still earn a living after they returned to Japan. Therefore, finding their place in China was not necessary for them because they had other options to be better off even if they failed to make it.

Lastly, while Wang concludes in her paper that it was still very tough for people to find their own place and that many people failed to fit into local societies, I think the most important thing for those who succeeded was that they never gave up. While she argues that limits and boundaries exist, what she neglects to mention is the fact that people still kept trying and never slowed their pace in spite of difficulties. In her story, there was a Chinese girl who had tried her best to act like Japanese people: "The Chinese girl had a Japanese name, put on a Japanese style make-up and dressed up like a Japanese girl." In my opinion, this was her own way of finding her place in Japan—at least she put a lot of effort into changing herself and fitting in with local Japanese society. Moreover, the author of "Fugitive Visions," Jane Jeong Trenka (who is a Korean adoptee with an American background), said that she would "never" go back to America (9). In a way, although Trenka was treated as an "outsider" and had difficulty communicating with local people, it can be said that she still wanted to get used to Korean life. Furthermore, both the Chinese girl and Trenka have a very tightly focused desire of place, although due to their identities, they seem to be out of place to the locals. Therefore, even though most people find it hard to live in another country, some, including Wang herself, try very hard to keep on going. In other words, it is possible that people who haven't found their place yet could be on the way to achieving that some day. More importantly, having a sense of place requires the seeking of it first—that is, the desire for a sense of place.

It is tough for people to find their place in another country. However, situations vary a lot among people. Some people may have already found their place but they have difficulties keeping it. Some don't have to struggle since they have more options, like going back to their own place. Others are still on the path to achieving their place because they have great desire for that. Furthermore, I believe that this corresponds to what Cresswell argues about in his article, "a highly complex social differentiation" (14). Different people are placed and locate themselves in different ways under different circumstances. Therefore, I believe that the question of whether people can find their own place overseas does not have a clear answer, nor does the meaning of "overseas," sometimes. Instead, a better way to understand "place" may be to think about how people act distinctly when they feel "out of space" in another country.

WORKS CITED

Cresswell, Tim. "A Global Sense of Place." *Place: A Short Introduction*. Malden: MA: Blackwell, (2004) 63–70. Rpt. in *Linguistics 12 Course Reader* Santa Barbara, University of California, Santa Barbara, 2012. F 2012. 4–5, 14, 19–20, 29–30. Print.

Trenka, Jane Jeong. *Fugitive Visions: An Adoptee's Return to Korea*. St. Paul, MN: Graywolf Press (2009). Print.

Kennedy, Garrick D. "Koreatown's Two Worlds Blend Uneasily," *Los Angeles Times*. 23 Aug. 2009: A-3. Print.

AUTHOR PROFILE

I study in the UCSB Economics Department as an exchange student and this is my third year. My hometown is Suzhou, which is a beautiful city on the east coast of China. After graduating from high school, I started learning Japanese and entered Waseda University in 2010. I am very interested in different countries and cultures around the world and want to work in international organizations in the future.

—*Yanfei (Emphy) Wang*

Photo by Loriel Davila

Photo by Loriel Davila

Photo by Loriel Davila

Photo by Loriel Davila

Photo by Loriel Davila

Photo by Loriel Davila

Photo by Yuqing (Augustina) Wang

Photo by Loriel Davila

POSING PROBLEMS/ TAKING POSITIONS

GAP YEAR: HIGH SCHOOL GRADUATES' BEST CHOICE

Wenxi Xiao

Instructor: Deborah Harris-Moore

> **"**The gap year allows students to be in the real world, to do service, and to approach college more deliberately.**"**

On April 1, 2012, Liu Wa, a Chinese high school graduate from Beijing No. 4 High, got an offer from Yale University to attend the school with a major in education. While she was excited to embrace one of the most important stepping-stones of her life, she started thinking about her next step. Normally people think that a college acceptance letter is a pass to success, but this may not always be the truth. Motivation surveys show that college students' "learning motivation is going along a downward trend worldwide" (Martin 561). There is no doubt that those who idle away their university studies are further away from success. Most high school students may lack the life experience to choose what they want to pursue in college. For this reason, prospective college students might be better off considering taking a year off before starting school. Scholars refer to this as a "gap year." According to Tom Stehlik, a senior lecturer at the University of South Australia as well as an expert of education, "The 'gap year' is a time between the end of school and the beginning of further studies in which young people engage in a variety of activities, including paid or voluntary work" (363). Based on the research done on gap years, taking a gap year after high school is very beneficial to one's overall college success as well as one's happiness.

The historical origin of the gap year dates from the Victorian era when well-educated upper-middle-class young men undertook a "Grand Tour" before going to a university. At that time, however, only certain groups of young people were able to gain advantages over others during a period of educational expansion. "The gap year has a historical association with privileges," concludes Sue Heath, a sociology professor at the University of Southampton (103). "[The] Grand Tour provided a moratorium between the completion of education and the commencement of a professional career, and invariably involved 'improving' experiences such as visits to sites of classical European culture as well as to the sites of outstanding natural beauty" (Heath 100). Accordingly, the gap year has been seen for a long time as a beneficial experience that people of privilege should take to explore the world.

Unlike its early history, the gap year has lost its social class features and is open to all students who have just graduated from high school. Students with rich parents can spend a lot of money to travel around the world while students in lower classes can find jobs or internships to not only earn experience but also to earn the money to pay their college tuition. There are more opportunities waiting for students to grab them. It is Britain's custom that after accomplishing high school, graduates will take a year off before going to college. Normally they take this chance to travel around the world or to find jobs in the fields that they are interested in. In Austria, there are a variety of gap year programs offered to students, such as traveling, volunteering, or working abroad. In some countries like Yemen, taking a year off before going to college is mandatory. Even in countries where the gap year is not obligatory, all of the students generally take a year off, like in Ghana. Evidently, the gap year is a lot more popular among students across the world than before. Also, due to the great demands of high school graduate students, a gap-year industry has emerged all over the western world, such as gap year agencies, volunteering programs and guidebooks, as well as social networking websites. For instance, "Travel, Experience, Share" is the slogan of a social networking website called gapyear.com, which is a travel advice website committed to providing students with everything they need to know about taking a gap year.

Going to college immediately after graduating from high school has potential dangers to students in terms of college completion. Many students do not realize their future plan so clearly, which leads them to lack the motivation to study and waste their time in college. "There is some evidence to suggest that students who had taken a gap year are less likely to drop out of university than those who had not" (Stehlik 375). Having a sabbatical time between high school and college is not a waste of time; going to college directly then dropping out of college is. There is a Chinese saying that goes, "Preparation may quicken the work." During my more than ten years of study at primary schools and high schools, I have seen that nearly all the students are struggling to cope with all kinds of tests and papers; their physical fatigue is obvious. Besides, most of them have little time to think about their future life or choices. Before they formally enter the university, they can not only take this opportunity to relax themselves physically and mentally, but also to slow down their life pace to think about their future direction. "Not every seventeen-year-old is ready to enter college," argues Karen Giannino, senior

associate Dean of Admissions at Colgate College (qtd. in Gutner). Most seventeen-year-olds do not have perspective of the world. They may spend their whole seventeen years in the same city and same town, and never have a chance to see what the world is about. So once they enter college with a very narrow perspective and lack of discipline, they may end up failing. Some students drop out of college due to the fact that they are not able to meet the academic standards or develop interpersonal communication with their professors and friends. One study found that, "three reasons were identified for freshman attrition: inability to handle stress, mismatch between personal expectations and college reality, and lack of personal commitment to a college education" (Zhang and Stephen). Without a full understanding of the reality of college life and the motivation to study, students just waste their time and end up dropping out of college. Thus, a gap year would help to prevent some of these problems and serve as a smooth transition between high school and college for students who are not able to.

It is the gap year that offers a time for students to see their future clearly as well as to reflect on their career orientation, especially when choosing a major in college. For instance, as a normal seventeen-year-old high school senior in London, Tom Hart had to make a tough decision with potentially lifelong ramifications: which degree program (major) to study in college. "I found it quite difficult, to be honest," admits Hart (qtd. in Grose). Tom is not alone with his difficulties. Suzanne, an acquaintance of mine, who is an incoming freshman majoring in pre-biology at the University of California, Santa Barbara, says "I just took the biology AP test and got a very good score, so I chose to major in Biology in college." However picking a major does not depend on just a test score, but depends on how dedicated a student is in that area. Jessie Qi, another friend of mine and also an incoming freshman at Vanderbilt University, says, "Although I chose psychology as my major, I have no idea what it is. At the beginning I just thought a psychologist can read people's minds, like a magician." This answer is not uncommon among college students. Although they are assigned a certain major, they do not know how the major applies in the real world. Li Li, a high school graduate from China and a freshman at Bucknell

University, says, "My mom said that being a doctor can earn a lot of money, so I have always wanted to be a doctor. But when I entered my university I suddenly realized that there was no med school!" Some students just listen to their parents to choose their major. They may decide later to take their own path, and will have to make up their course requirements as well as grades all over again. The evidence is consistent: choosing a major is an onerous task. Even though students have decided a major, most of them do not know what the major is really about.

This is not a surprise for me. When I faced the same situation, I not only struggled a lot but my parents were also worried about which major was suited for me. After talking to my counselor, I took a month off from my high school study during my senior year winter holiday and sought an opportunity to do psychology research with a professor at the North China University of Technology. It is this practice that exposed me more broadly to the science of psychology, but I just wished I could have had more time to further understand it. So taking a year gap could have definitely provided me with the experience to help me decide a major. Through this year or just several months, I could have looked for jobs or internships in psychology. Or by taking a year off to volunteer, do an internship, or travel, I could have thought beyond simply taking tests and getting good grades for the first time. Some may argue that I could have time to do those things during summer or winter vacations; notwithstanding, the jobs, the internships and the traveling are long-term activities and according to my own experience, my vacations were rifted with either homework or extra curricular activities. Moreover, I should have been able to consume the time at my own pace, which would have led me to better moods and would have been more helpful for me to reflect on those inspirational ideas and opportunities. Therefore, a gap year would have helped me to develop a post-school plan.

There are other advantages to take a gap year. For instance, many students feel that the long time they spend in school is excessive, so after graduating from high school they get tired. "We're in school for 14 years, followed by at least three more at university," expresses Matthew Holehouse who has just finished the 12th grade at Harrogate grammar school in the UK (1). Students spend such a long time studying all the way to high school; they deserve a transition, which can spare some of their strength before going to college. "After a couple of months of long hours stacking shelves, [it would be nice to] see the world, of course," Matthew admits (1). Hence, the gap year is a time for students to take a respite. Andrew Martin, a professor at the University of Sydney specializing in motivation, engagement, achievement, and quantitative research methods, conducts two studies to explain this phenomenon from a psycho-educational perspective. He examines the academic factors that predict gap year intentions among 2,502 high school students as well as gap-year participants of 338 students in college or university. Martin states: "Findings in Study One show that post school uncertainty and lower levels of academic motivation predict gap year intentions, that lower motivation and lower performance predict post school uncertainty. Findings in Study Two show that gap year participation positively predicts academic motivation and this effect is significant" (576).

This research among students intending to take a gap year and students who have taken a gap year indicates that the gap year can serve as a smooth transition between high school and college. Therefore, a gap year is a time for students to refresh.

What if a student has already overcome the tough decision and has determined which major he or she wants to concentrate on in college? Is considering taking a year off useless for them? The answer is no. Getting into college is still a challenge without well-rounded applications. Planning a well-structured gap year can always provide students with a good résumé on the road toward college entrance. In this generation, attending a college is easy because there are oceans of universities as well as liberal arts colleges in United States. However getting accepted into a decent university is more and more competitive for current high school graduates. Nowadays, only having a good SAT or ACT score as well as a high GPA is not enough to reach the dream of most high school graduates to get an offer from more than one decent university. The trend leads more high school counselors and college admissions officers to suggest that students participate in extracurricular activities and gain leadership experience. A gap year is a good choice for these students.

Even when students master the college application with outstanding grades and extracurricular experience, they can still use the gap year to develop their social values as well as shape their soft skills, such as communication, organization, working with a team, and many other skills. Equipped with these soft skills, not only can students better acclimate to challenging college life, but they will also become more attractive to employers out of school. Nowadays, more and more college graduates are leaving school with good grades, which means it is hard for employers to choose which students to hire. One study found that "more that half of the employers (54%) said they found graduates who had taken a gap year more rounded interviewees than those going to college straight from high school. While seven in ten said they would be impressed by a candidate who had undertaken volunteer work" (Marshall). Even on the Harvard College Admissions website there is a page called "Taking Time Off" which states: "Harvard College encourages admitted students to defer enrollment for one year to travel, pursue a special project or activity, work, or spend time in another meaningful way." As the most prestigious university in the world, Harvard University recommends that their students take a year gap before college to do something interesting or important. Then it suggests that students can truly benefit from a gap year.

If there are so many advantages to taking a year off and students all across the world are taking the gap year seriously, why has this trend not become popular in the United States? Some may argue that taking a year off between high school and college will create a crack in students' academic career; in other words, the gap year interrupts student's study mood. They believe that students cannot adjust to learning in college soon after having a one-year break. Others may argue that it is hard for gappers to receive scholarships when they enroll in college. Nevertheless, many psycho-educational studies suggest that a gap year does not adversely affect students' academic motivation once they enroll in a university; in fact, "students who defer university are found to have higher marks than students who

commence university directly after completing high school" (Birch and Miller 329). Moreover, because of the gap year, many students come to college with new visions of their academic plans and new extracurricular pursuits, the intangibles they hope to gain in college, and the career possibilities they observed in their year away. Their goal is narrower and more specific, which will let students concentrate better on it. On the other hand, it is true that most of the universities are likely to offer scholarships to the students who go directly to university from high school. However, students need to maintain a high academic performance level to keep their scholarship. If a high school graduate got a scholarship at first but lacks academic motivation and fails in courses, they will no longer obtain the scholarship. Furthermore, at most universities, students can always apply for scholarships when they are qualified. Worst-case scenario, the gapper does not receive scholarships at all, but what they gain during the gap year is much more than the money is worth. Therefore, gappers should not worry about not getting scholarships.

Currently, many college students are not maximizing their potential to advance in education because they do not have a specific goal as a result of lacking real life experience. Therefore, taking a year off before going to college is a wise idea for most high school graduates as they can take advantage of this opportunity to broaden their horizons and get in contact with society. The gap year allows students to be in the real world, to do service, and to approach college more deliberately. As a life-altering experience, a well-structured gap year can even lead the students to a lifelong lesson. Through a gap year, students are evidently able to set proper goals for their future development and manage themselves objectively and pragmatically, and its full value can never be measured and will pay dividends the rest of the young people's lives. Is it better to defer your education a year and learn more or to continue the education and risk dropping out? Liu Wa has already decided to take a year gap and she is on her way to volunteer teaching English in rural China. What is your choice?

WORKS CITED

Birch, Elisa R and Paul W Miller. "The Characteristics of 'Gap-Year' Students and Their Tertiary Academic Outcomes." *Economic Record*. 83.262, (2007): 329–344. *Wiley Online Library*. Web. 09 Sept. 2012.

Grose, Thomas K. "Taking A Page From Britain." *U.S. News & World Report* 146.8 (2009): 46. *Academic Search Complete*. Web. 10 Sept. 2012.

Gutner, Toddi. "New High-School Elective: Put Off College." *Wall Street Journal–Eastern Edition* 30 Dec. 2008: D5. *Academic Search Complete*. Web. 12 Sept. 2012.

Harvard College Admissions § Applying: Taking Time Off, Harvard University, 2012. Web. Sept. 12. 2012.

Heath, Sue. "Widening the Gap: Pre-University Gap Years and 'Economy of Experience.'" *British Journal of Sociology of Education*. 28. 1 (2007): 89–103. *Academic Search Complete*. Web. 02 Sept. 2012.

Holehouse, Matthew. "Feed the world and get a tan." *Times Educational Supplement*. 4647 (2005): 21. *LexisNexis Academic*. Web. 03 Sept. 2012.

Marshall, Michael. "Document Round-Up." *Education* (14637073) 197 (2005): 6. *Academic Search Complete*. Web. 10 Sept. 2012.

Martin, Andrew J. "Should Students Have A Gap Year? Motivation And Performance Factors Relevant To Time Out After Completing School." *Journal of Educational Psychology*. 102.3 (2010): 561–576. *Academic Search Complete*. Web. 03 Sept. 2012.

Stehlik, Tom "Mind the gap: school leaver aspirations and delayed pathways to further and higher education" *Journal of Education and Work*. 23:4, 363–376. *Academic Search Complete*. Web. 02 Sept. 2012.

Zhang, Zhicheng, and Stephen R. RiCharde. "Prediction and Analysis of Freshman Retention." *AIR 1998 Annual Forum Paper*, 1998. *ERIC*. Web. 12 Sept. 2012.

AUTHOR PROFILE

My name is Wenxi Xiao, which means the tide of knowledge, and I am a freshman at UCSB. I came from China and have studied English for five years. I love singing and meeting new people. I am also a traveler and have been to Canada and the UK.

—*Wenxi Xiao*

TATTOOS, WOMEN, AND THE JUDGMENT

Anyssa N. Luna-Oropeza

Instructor: Christopher Dean

> **"**Society should not standardize females; they should accept tattoos as a form of self-expression and individuality as they have been in past centuries.**"**

In past centuries, tattoos were accepted as a form of beauty and expression. This form of art remained consistently popular through time, but within the past century a stigma has arisen. Even as tattoos are becoming more popular in society, women with tattoos are being scrutinized within the eyes of many. Women's self-expression can result in stereotyping and discrimination. Society should not standardize females; they should accept tattoos as a form of self-expression and individuality as they have been in past centuries.

Tattoos are created by artists using a needle to inject carbon-based ink into the dermis layer of the skin to produce permanent images. However, this has not always been the practice. It is believed that tattoos were discovered by accident; colored material such as ash or dirt would enter an open wound and then stay under the dermis layer of skin, creating a permanent mark now known as tattoo (Burnell). Since this discovery, tattoos have been popular throughout centuries. According to Burnell, author of "Where Did Tattoos Come From?" "Tattooing became a mark of courage, as the process was often long and painful." Although tattoos were once viewed as a rite of passage and mark of courage, this has not always been the case. In the 1990s, the popularity of tattoos declined because they became associated with criminals ("A History of the Tattoo"). They displayed toughness, strength, and their loyalty to a group. For example, the members of the outlawed motorcycle club "Hell's Angels" acquire tattoos to represent their commitment to the club and their willingness to protect their own and defeat outsiders. The perception of tattoos therefore became very masculine. This is where the stigma against tattoos began. Thereafter, the respect for the art continued to decline. In 1961, a hepatitis outbreak occurred in New York and was blamed on tattoo parlors ("A History of the Tattoo"). Therefore, parlors were shut down, making it nearly impossible to get a tattoo done. Thus people with tattoos during this time were seen as dirty, unclean, and a threat to public health because they had a disease due to shared needles.

Although time has passed and we are now in the 21st century, people have continued to have a negative bias on tattoos. According to Burleson Consulting, a website that talks about the dos and don'ts in corporate America, tattoos are more popular among the poor and uneducated. Supporting this is the statement that tattoos are for hookers, not lawyers by "Poll Results: Professional Women and Tattoos," which reflects the potential judgment from not only the corporate world, but society in general, towards the personal form of self-expression. However, this is pure ignorance. Marisa Kakoulas is not only a New York lawyer but also a journalist, writer, and author of a blog that focuses on tattoos. She attended New York University, Brooklyn Law School, and Columbia University. Ms. Kakoulas is a perfect example of a woman with tattoos who does not fit the stereotype of uneducated.

Though some find tattoos trashy, others see the beauty in them. People believe that there is no longer a "type" to get this body art and believe it is a freedom of expression. According to Erika Icon, "Thirty years ago, 1 in 100 people in this country had tattoos. Now 1 in 10 have them." With these statistics, one can assume that a wide range of people take part in this art; doctors, lawyers, CEO's, actors, managers, etc. Nicole M. Stata is a former graduate of the University of Vermont. She is the founder and managing director of Boston Seed Capital and has a Japanese-inspired tattoo located on her back (Stata). She proves society wrong as she does not fit the stereotype of a woman with tattoos. Therefore, society shouldn't base their thoughts of a woman off her body art.

Just like the corporate world, the medical field is not accepting of tattoos. This field's main focus is to assist people in their physical needs; thus they must provide a safe professional environment that comforts the patient. Therefore, tattoos should not be visible because they could cause a patient to feel insecure about the person who is helping with their health. However, Leah is currently completing her residency at a children's hospital in St. Louis. She has tattoos on her chest, arm, and foot. The tattoo on her foot is a symbol of medicine, a tribute to herself and her father (Lucille). This woman is making something of herself and pursuing a life goal. Therefore, neither does she fit the stereotype of an uneducated woman.

Sandra O. Luna has worked in the medical field for fourteen years and has been able to withhold from tattoos and hide them from visibility. After a lot of thought on design and location, at the age of twenty-three she got her first tattoo. She took

into consideration that sentimental meaning may change within time, but went forth with her first tattoo. Since then, she has acquired three more tattoos, to make a total of four tattoos. She has been employed with the same company for twelve years. However, she understands that if she were to seek employment elsewhere, depending on the city and community, she would choose to be discreet with her tattoos for fear of them focusing on her tattoos rather than noticing her and what she can offer. She stated that she did not want to be stereotyped; she wanted to avoid the categorizing that people would place upon her. For this reason, she chooses the location of her tattoos carefully as she makes sure that the exposure would be varied upon her clothing. She lives in a community where tattoos are popular. They are seen on people of various statuses ranging from lawyers, to gang members, to students, etc. Living in a place where there is a lot of gang activity really did affect the decision of which tattoos she wished to acquire, as she did not want any to resemble these factors in any way.

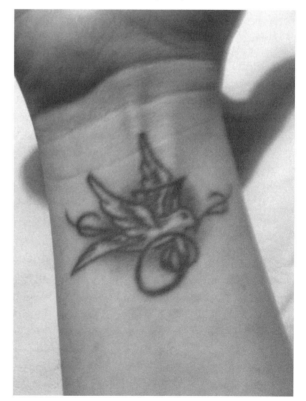

When asked for her views on women with tattoos, she stated:

> My view upon tattoos on women especially women who are seeking a professional career is that tattoos are in itself a form of self-expression, so why not go on and get what makes you…you. There is however a line between expressing yourself and going overboard. Yet, that shouldn't stop you from persuing your dreams, goals, and aspirations. Nonetheless, it is a shame that society's opinions and views on personal art determine what is acceptable or not. Society has been trained to place a persons' value and worth based on their appearance. They focus on the outward appearance rather than giving a person to reveal who they are and what they can offer in their career of choice. I would see it as acceptable since for me the character of the person is far more important than what they choose to put on themselves; ranging from clothing to tattoos.

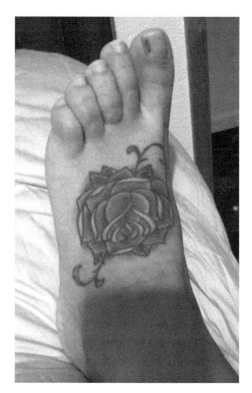

However, she does believe that with time, things have become "easier" to a point with people and their tattoos. Although stereotyping continues, she believes that people have become a bit more understanding to how many generations have taken this art into personal matters to express themselves.

When asked about their views on women with tattoos, a group of teenagers seemed to be stunned; some just gave the look of "why does it matter?" Because they are exposed to tattoos so often, they are indifferent about this idea. However, this didn't mean that they didn't see the negative effects of women having tattoos. Growing up, they have often been told that "tattoos will affect how people judge you." A majority of the group plan on getting tattoos—family members' names or symbols that represent them individually. A common tattoo that teenage women aspire to get is the dove, resembling freedom and purity. However, when asked for location in which they wanted to place the tattoo, they hesitated. They stated that they had not decided because they did not know what career they wanted to pursue yet. This clearly reveals how society affects how people choose to express themselves. However, young generations are already slowly changing how society works and will continue to do so as they grow.

Women should not stay away from tattoos because of the stigma in society. People will judge a woman with tattoos—that is inevitable—however, their status should not be dropped for wanting to decorate their body. The women that were demonstrated here have all been able to hide their tattoos in one form or another, and have been successful in their work environment. They prove that women don't fall under the stereotype that people have built from tattoos. Therefore, society has to come to an understanding that tattoos are now popular throughout a large spectrum of people and soon will have to accommodate the new generation.

WORKS CITED

"A History of the Tattoo." *Socializing Bodies.* 26 July 2008. RandomHistory.com. 21 Nov. 2012. <http://www.randomhistory.com/2008/07/26_tattoo.html>.

Burnell, William. "Ezine Mom articles." *Tattoo History—Where Did Tattoos Come From?*. Web. 21 Nov. 2012. < http://ezinearticles.com/?Tattoo-History---Where-Did-Tattoos-Come-From?&id=4634064>.

Icon, Erika. "Tattoos and Piercings in the Workplace." *Working World.* Web. 21 Nov. 2012. <http://www.workingworld.com/articles/tattoos-and-piercings-in-the-workplace>.

Lucille, Diego. "Ink Meets Inc.: Twenty Tattooed Professionals." *Rank My Tattoos Magazine.* N.p., n.d. Web. 04 Dec. 2012. <http://mag.rankmytattoos.com/ink-meets-inc-20-tattooed-executive-and-white-collar-professionals.html>.

"Marisa Kakoula." Linkedin. N.p., n.d. Web. 4 Dec. 2012. <http://www.linkedin.com/in/kakoulas>.

"Nicole Stata." *Walker's Research.* N.p., n.d. Web. 04 Dec. 2012. <http://www.walkersresearch.com/profilePages/Show_Executive_Title/Executiveprofile/N/Nicole_M_Stata_100031594.html>.

"Poll Results: Professional Women and Tattoos." *Tattoos and Professional Women.* Web. 21 Nov. 2012. <http://corporette.com/2008/10/23/poll-results-professional-women-and-tattoos/>.

"Professional Dress Code and Tattoos." *BC Oracle Consulting.* Web. 21 Nov. 2012. <http://www.dba-oracle.com/dress_code_tattoos.htm>.

PROJECT REFLECTION

The first draft of this project really did cause me to stress out a bit. Because I was indecisive on what to do my presentation on, I kind of just went with my first instinct—transgender and how it is not a mental disorder. I quickly came to realize that this was not a topic for me; therefore, I decided that during Thanksgiving break I'd decide on my topic. I researched two topics that really did interest me: football and tattoos. Soon after I made my decision—women with tattoos and how they are perceived by society. I found this topic interesting and important because tattoos are common in my generation but they are frowned upon. I quickly thought about my mother as a resource and how my English teacher in high school had a sleeve of tattoos and how these two amazing women used tattoos to express themselves. As my topic changed, so did my idea on how to present my argument. I decided to work with a blog because it is an easy way to guide a reader. I would be able to state all the arguments and then come against them neatly.

Overall, I think just choosing topics is the hard part with this project (well for me, I'm very indecisive), and also knowing how specific to be. I know I wrote a lot more than what was expected and part of it is that I wasn't sure how much to expand on. However, I really liked this piece of writing because it really drew my attention.

AUTHOR PROFILE

I'm a first-year student from Watsonville, CA. I am the first generation in my family to attend college.

—*Anyssa N. Luna-Oropeza*

GRADES AND PROGRESS

Amber Garcia

Instructor: Jennifer Johnson

> **"**Grades and tests should be used in higher education as a way to demonstrate where we stand and to serve as a guide for realizing what subjects we do well in, in order to lead us to a career that best fits our talents.**"**

When we think of grades, we think of where our progress stands in comparison to others. A high grade means success while a low grade means failure. The system in which we average together an accumulation of grades throughout a course to make a final grade is a beneficial way to show how we progress throughout a course. In our early years, we should not focus so much on the importance of a letter grade but rather focus more on learning the material and grasping the idea that effort and perseverance will help guide us to the knowledge we hope to acquire. Even though effort is an essential part of learning in our early years, it is not the only important factor. The more we learn, the more we must test ourselves and our progress to ensure that we retain the knowledge. Therefore, the higher we go in education, the more necessary letter grades are to our progression. Grades and tests should be used in higher education as a way to demonstrate where we stand and to serve as a guide for realizing what subjects we do well in, in order to lead us to a career that best fits our talents.

In early schooling years, children are not accustomed to the grading system or how school functions and therefore they should focus more on effort and progress. As five-year-old children start out on their first day of school, they know nothing of letter grades and therefore do not understand the importance of them. In my elementary school, we were graded on effort until the fourth grade. I never saw my grades since they were mailed to my parents. I did not know what my report card would say but I was motivated by this need to prove to my parents that I was trying at school. When we are young, we see our parents as this deciding factor that determines whether we are good at things or not. No child wants to face the anger of disappointed parents; at least that was the way I saw things. However, the more I learned and succeeded in mastering the material, the more I realized that my curiosity led me to the desire for more knowledge. Putting forth effort was no longer an issue because it was instilled in my mind that I would do better in life with perseverance and knowledge. As Jerry Farber states in his article "A Young Person's Guide to the Grading System," "Learning happens when you *want* to know" (385). Oftentimes, we hear that our minds are at their most curious peak when we are young. This desire for knowledge encourages children to work hard and therefore put effort forward when working towards learning. Letter grades, which have no value to students when they are quite young, should gradually evolve into a combination of points based on effort and results.

Although it is easy to grade based on effort, sometimes effort alone may not be the best measurement of progress, and therefore points and letter grades become helpful in not only motivating students, but also in evaluating how much a person knows and how willing they are to put forth the effort to learn. In some instances, effort may be undervalued or overestimated. For example, a teacher may not know how much a student studies when they go home. Simply showing up to be tutored is not enough. Or perhaps, the teacher is biased to give more or less points based on how well they like the person. It is in moments like these when tests using a point system are beneficial. One would think that a lot of persistence would lead to some improvement. Although it is no guarantee that a student may fully understand a concept, some progress is bound to show if there is effort put forth. Combining effort points with test points should give a balanced demonstration of how well a student is doing. In putting these two methods hand in hand, one would hope to do well in one or both areas and do well in the class. As stated in the article "Zen and the Art of Grade Motivation" by Liz Mandrell, "Learning must somehow be linked to a product" (383). In her experiment, when she guaranteed every student an A in the hopes that students would feel less stressed and more willing to focus on putting in effort, the students took advantage of her system. The results of this experiment bring us to the realization that grades are a motivating factor to try harder and to do better, rather than giving people the benefit of the doubt and hoping for the best. It may be considered unfair when a student who is better at one subject may not need to put in as much effort as others, but even the smartest kid needs to learn the material just like everyone else. It is simply a matter of finding a study habit that works for each student. With that being said, a balance should be made between grades and effort by giving points in both areas and averaging out the two. That way, we can bring some fairness to the playing field while instilling the habit of working hard towards a good outcome.

Once a student reaches levels of higher education such as college or beyond, effort is more of an obvious necessity and expectation. Therefore it should no longer be relevant in the grading system. After more than twelve years of continuous effort to learn, the focus should tend more towards knowledge of the material and constant evaluations. Some may say that college is not for everyone and that some people's calling may be to do something that may not need schooling. Either way, numerous years in school with the grading system helps with similar evaluations in life. If you do well in a job, you keep your job or possibly get a higher position; if you do badly, you may get fired. In college, the concept is similar. Effort is expected, therefore, focusing on evaluation with grades is a beneficial system to maintain in our society. As stated in the article "Grades and Money" by Steven Vogel, "In my college, like most others, grades are money. They're the currency around which everything revolves" (390). Grades in higher education demonstrate what subjects we excel in and in which ones we do not. That is the positive side of choosing a major; you can pick a subject you know you excel in and will most likely enjoy. If you enjoy something you are good at, the motivation will not be difficult to come by and the fear of struggling endlessly for something you may never fully understand is not a determining factor.

Each school may have its own ways of evaluating students, but the main focus of the grading system should be to instill curiosity and the need to work hard at an early age. If it is a constant reminder, it will become a habit, and old habits die hard. Once this habit is maintained alongside curiosity, it will not be too difficult to strive to learn material in order to receive good grades on constant evaluations. Although many people see letter grades as having a negative impact in schooling, it should not have to be such a threat. It is simply another motivator to do well in school, and therefore, life.

WORKS CITED

Farber, Jerry "A Young Person's Guide to the Grading System." *Reading and Writing in the Academic Community*. Eds. Mary Lynch Kennedy and Hadley M. Smith. Upper Saddle River, NJ: Prentice Hall, 2012. 385–388. Print.

Mandrell, Liz. "Zen and the Art of Grade Motivation." *Reading and Writing in the Academic Community*. Eds. Mary Lynch Kennedy and Hadley M. Smith. Upper Saddle River, NJ: Prentice Hall, 2012. 379–383. Print.

Vogel, Steven. "Grades and Money." *Reading and Writing in the Academic Community*. Eds. Mary Lynch Kennedy and Hadley M. Smith. Upper Saddle River, NJ: Prentice Hall, 2012. 389–392. Print.

AUTHOR PROFILE

Born and raised in Pasadena, I come from a Mexican family and have no idea what my future holds. I may hope to be a writer or a psychologist. I truly see myself impacting lives some day.

—*Amber Garcia*

POSING PROBLEMS/TAKING POSITIONS Grades and Progress

FLAWS IN THE GRADING SYSTEM

Pamela Tint

Instructor: Jennifer Johnson

> **"**We learn from our failures, and we should not be penalized for them. If we fear failure, we will not grow and learn from our experiences.**"**

"Mommy and Daddy look, I got an A and a smiley face sticker on my test!" Ever since I can remember, getting good grades came with rewards and getting bad grades came with penalties. As a child, whenever I got good grades my parents would reward me with simple gestures such as taking me to McDonald's for a Happy Meal, buying me something that I really wanted, or praising me with kind words that made me feel good about myself. And whenever I got a bad grade, it was always expected that my parents would lecture me about how important it is to get good grades. My dream is to become a physical therapist because I find that the most rewarding thing is to help other people. Sometimes I find myself over obsessing over grades, and I have to stop for a moment and take a deep breath to remind myself of my goals. Grades and the grading system should be an extrinsic factor that encourages students' goals to educate themselves and further their knowledge. Unfortunately, the way our society runs has made getting good grades and a high GPA the most important goal for success and rewards rather than education and learning itself.

The grading system is supposed to advocate learning and broadening your own knowledge, but it can actually inhibit learning in some circumstances. Through my personal experiences in school, I have to admit that I am guilty of letting the grading system inhibit my learning interests. Steven Vogel, who wrote the article "Grades and Money," states, "By tying grades to money, we give incentives not to take risks" (392). When I pick my classes during my pass time I have to admit that I check the online site Rate My Professors to see how difficult or easy a class is in order to determine which classes I should take. Last quarter of college I was picking between a few GE classes. I really wanted to take a religious studies class. Rate My Professors ranked it as a difficult class to receive an A in, so I ended up picking psychology because I took it in high school and thought it would be easier to get a better grade. I was concerned about the religious studies class because I had not been exposed to it in high school. Because of this concern, I decided to play it safe with a class that I have already taken. Why take classes that will threaten your GPA when you can take easier classes that will lead to good grades and success? Through my past decisions, I find that I have developed habits that are in favor of boosting my grades or GPA rather than in favor of taking risks to broaden my knowledge and going out of my comfort zone. My past experiences show how the grading system may prevent students from learning to the best of their abilities because of their fear of failure. We learn from our failures, and we should not be penalized for them. If we fear failure, we will not grow and learn from our experiences.

Some may argue that the grading system and grades are needed because it is a way to evaluate and assess students for various kinds of works. As Liz Mandrell, who wrote the article "Zen and the Art of Grade Motivation," states, "Product must be measured or graded to gauge the worth of the product according to the merit it deserves" (383). However, if students are more concerned about high grades and GPAs than learning itself, I would imagine that it is not a completely accurate way to determine a person's qualification for fields in the work force. Jerry Farber, who wrote the article "A Young Person's Guide to the Grading System," states that "grades don't make us want to enrich our minds; they make us want to please out teachers" (385). Through high school I saw multiple instances where people cheated to get a higher grade in class because they needed the GPA to get into a school of their choice. If it wasn't cheating, then it was finding strategies and other possible ways that will produce the best results with minimal effort. In high school, my friends and I had a symbiotic system in which one of us took notes for one section of a chapter while the other did the other section, and we would exchange notes without ever having to read it ourselves. Memorizing the notes from my friends compensated for actually reading the whole chapter myself. Vogel points out that "if grades are money and, if the product for which they pay is learning, then it's perfectly rational for students to try to minimize that learning while maximizing their return" (391). Why take the time to read the whole chapter when you can "learn" it in a faster way and use the extra time to study for another class? The grading system has taught students how to find loopholes in the system and has convinced students that the main goal is to fulfill the teacher's expectations rather than their own expectations, because meeting the teacher's expectation is what brings good grades and success.

I believe that extrinsic rewards and punishments have great influences over a person's intrinsic goals and motives. Flora and Poponak, who wrote the article "Childhood Pay for Grades Is Related to College GPAs," point out how "reinforcement for academic work conditions reward value of academic work and helps to create intrinsic interest in academic behaviors" (394). If rewarding students for academic work helps create intrinsic interests in learning then wouldn't penalizing students produce an opposite effect of making students disinterested in knowledge and learning? I find this to be true through my experiences with writing. As a child, I loved to read and write, and it was something that I was good at. However, through my school years I gradually started to dislike it because of the critical feedback I kept getting from some of my English teachers. This led me to believe I was bad at it and that I hated it when, in actuality, I enjoy it and find that I am actually good at it. Because society believes that grades are what determine our abilities, when we get a bad grade in a subject it leads us to believe that we are incapable of doing well in that subject and may influence us to avoid it entirely. This explains why people categorize themselves as a math person or a writing person. Why can't we be both? It's because past bad grades have made people believe they don't like that subject; therefore, they are not a "math" or a "writing" person. The way grades serve as an extrinsic punishment for students can influence them intrinsically to believe that the only way to succeed is through loopholes for good grades. Because students start to learn to find loopholes in the grading system, education proves to be the opposite of what it's supposed to be, something to encourage and motivate students to broaden their knowledge and educate themselves. As a student, it is hard to freely set learning and expanding your knowledge as your main priority. Unfortunately for some students, their main priority often turns to getting good grades no matter the cost because they feel it is what actually defines their abilities.

I believe that there are other systems that can be more effective in the education system, ones that will allow students to set learning as their main priorities rather than the main goal of getting as much points for the highest grade. Vogel suggests that "what grades ought to be is a report, nothing more: how did the student do, how much did he or she learn, how much were his or her skills and critical self-consciousness and knowledge of the world expanded?" (390). As I am writing this paper, I find flaws in our grading system, but I didn't really have a replacement system to suggest up until now—when I think back and reflect on how I have been graded in this writing class. In Writing 1 class, I find it very helpful and beneficial that we are graded on the process that leads up to the outcome of our final product and work. The points that we earn for the brainstorming process, revising process, and even the reflection process with our composing paper serve as a form of extrinsic rewards that motivate us to learn, which is exactly what grades are supposed to do.

If we can develop an education system that considers grading on both the process that leads up to a final product and the final product itself, like in Writing 1 class, it will shift students' goals and motives to learning and education itself without losing a way to evaluate students' abilities through grades. By grading students on their work process and their reflection process, this system will allow students to learn through learning. This will eliminate the negative extrinsic effects of grades, such as finding loopholes in the grading system, and emphasize the positive extrinsic effects of grades.

WORKS CITED

Farber, Jerry. "A Young Person's Guide to the Grading System." *Reading and Writing in the Academic Community.* Eds. Mary Lynch Kennedy & Hadley N. Smith. Upper Saddle River, NJ: Pearson, 2010. 385–388. Print.

Flora, Stephen and Stacey Poponak. "Childhood Pay for Grades is Related to College Grade Point Averages." *Reading and Writing in the Academic Community.* Eds. Mary Lynch Kennedy & Hadley N. Smith. Upper Saddle River, NJ: Pearson, 2010. 393–394. Print.

Mandrell, Liz. "Zen and The Art of Grade Motivation." *Reading and Writing in the Academic Community.* Eds. Mary Lynch Kennedy & Hadley N. Smith. Upper Saddle River, NJ: Pearson, 2010. 379–383. Print.

Vogel, Steven. "Grades and Money." *Reading and Writing in the Academic Community.* Eds. Mary Lynch Kennedy & Hadley N. Smith. Upper Saddle River, NJ: Pearson, 2010. 389–392. Print.

AUTHOR PROFILE

I am a nineteen-year-old from Northern California. I am a pre-biology major but planning on majoring in biopsychology. I hope to pursue a career as a physical therapist. I enjoy playing basketball, rock climbing, cooking, and watching movies.
—*Pamela Tint*

LOVE IS LOVE

Debbie Lum

Instructor: Christopher Dean

Barack Obama announced in an interview on May 9, 2012: "I've just concluded that for me personally it is important for me to go ahead and affirm that I think same-sex couples should be able to get married" (Weigner). I grew up in San Francisco, and growing up in this community has led me to become open-minded about same-sex marriage. I had always been exposed to San Francisco's Castro district, a famous LGBTQ community, as well as its gay pride parade, hosted every year in June (Timberlake). I've grown to respect all couples alike—gay or straight. Same-sex marriage should be legalized because the individuals discriminated against are faced with a violation of human rights, a deprivation of marriage benefits, as well as limitations on love.

Banning same-sex marriage violates the 14th amendment of the Constitution, which guarantees equal protection; however, Proposition 8 contradicts this. Proposition 8 states "only marriage between a man and a woman is valid or recognized in California" (Barnes). Proposition 8 was approved by voters on November 4, 2008, and same-sex marriages stopped the following day. U.S. Circuit Judge Stephen Reinhardt wrote, "Proposition 8 serves no purpose, and has no effect, other than to lessen the status and human dignity of gays and lesbians in California, and to officially reclassify their relationships and families as inferior to those of opposite-sex couples. The Constitution simply does not allow for laws of this sort" (Barnes). On May 26, 2009, the Supreme Court officially banned same-sex marriage; however, the 18,000 same-sex marriages that occurred before May 2009 are still considered valid (Timeline: Same-sex Marriage). This would be considered a loophole in Proposition 8, because if such marriages were legal before the proposition was passed, why not legalize all such marriages to come? The only difference between a married gay couple and a gay couple is the marriage license. Moreover, marriage benefits become unavailable to same-sex couples.

Denying same-sex marriage would restrict marriage benefits for same-sex couples. For example, they would not be able to file joint income tax returns with the IRS and state taxing authorities; visit a spouse in a hospital intensive care unit or during restricted visiting hours in other parts of a medical facility; nor would they receive Social Security, Medicare, and disability benefits for spouses ("Marriage Rights and Benefits"). Straight couples are allowed to receive these benefits once they obtain their marriage licenses, but same-sex couples are not. Even if one is in a same-sex marriage in a state where it is

> **"Same-sex couples should be under the same equal protection as everyone else, receive the same marriage benefits that straight couples do, and not be told whom they can or cannot love."**

legal, or if one is in a domestic partnership or civil union in states that recognize them, one would still be unable to receive marriage benefits as the federal government does not recognize same-sex marriages ("Marriage Rights and Benefits"). This is unfair to all currently married same-sex couples because everybody has a right to these benefits. It does not make sense to deny couples these rights just because their respective partners are not of the opposite sex.

What is the most important component of any relationship/couple/marriage/etc? Love. The only thing that should matter in marriage is love. Some people get married for the benefits, such as the ones stated in the previous paragraph, while some do for reproduction purposes; however, same-sex couples are not getting married for additional benefits; only out of love. An example of a long lasting same-sex couple is Del Martin and Phyllis Lyon, the first same-sex couple to get married in San Francisco. They were together for fifty-five years until Del Martin's death in 2008 (Rachel). An example of a well-known same-sex couple is Ellen DeGeneres, a well-respected talk show host, and Portia de Rossi, who began their relationship in 2004 (Belge). Last, but not least, Neil Patrick Harris, star of the television show *How I Met Your Mother*, and David Burtka have also been together since 2004 (Hartenstein).

I interviewed three people about their opinions on same-sex marriage. Interviewee #1, Max, who is part of the LGBTQ community, said, "You can't control whom you love. Just because you fall in love with someone of the same sex or gender doesn't mean that your feelings are any less genuine or any less valid than the love between a man or a woman." The second interviewee, who is straight, said, "Being in love with someone the same gender as you doesn't make him or her any less human than everyone else." The third interviewee said, "Being in love with a person of the same gender doesn't mean that the love is any less stronger. The one a person falls in love with is a human just like everybody else and shouldn't be labeled with a gender. Honestly, gender just tells you what 'equipment' the person has, so it's invalid."

In a Pew Forum poll conducted in July 2012, statistics showed that people who oppose same-sex marriage are mostly affiliated with a religion (Pew-Forum: Gay Marriage Attitudes). In one of our readings, "Obedience: Ideal in Dogs, Not People,"

Jasmine Fray talks about the Milgram experiment. Fray explains that the "real purpose of the experiment was to see if the participants would follow the orders of the experiment conductor (who represented an authority figure) over their own judgment" (40). Fray then goes on to explain that the results "were precisely what Fromm would have predicted: the overwhelming majority of participants inflicted pain on the actor, disregarding their own ethics and submitting to the authority figure. Even when the actor yelled of heart pain, banged on the wall, and begged" (40). We can use the quote as an analogy for same-sex marriage. The first part of this quote, "inflicted pain on the actor" would stand for people voting against same sex marriage, and the second part of the quote, "even when the actor yelled of heart pain" can symbolize gay people's feelings toward the banning. Religious people see their religion as an authoritative set of guidelines that they have to obey. Therefore, if their religion considers homosexuality a sin, they will obey that. Religion sees homosexuality as wrong because it involves non-procreative sex. Steven Waldman explains in his article, "A Common Misconception," why religious people are against same sex marriage:

> In the case of Judaism, a key Bible passage is the story of Onan, who sleeps with his dead brother's wife but, to avoid giving his brother offspring, doesn't ejaculate inside her. Instead, he "spilt the seed on the ground." God slew him, which some might view as a sign of disapproval. The Catholic catechism decries homosexual acts because "they close the sexual act to the gift of life." Early American antisodomy laws discouraged all forms of non-procreative sex (including, incidentally, heterosexual oral and anal sex). Islam shares a similar view. One Islamic hadith explains that Allah "will not look at the man who commits sodomy with a man or a woman." (Waldman)

The opposition to same-sex marriage would also argue that children of same-sex couples would grow up without one of the gender role models. However, look at it this way: how did gay people grow up? Ellen DeGeneres said, "I was raised around heterosexuals, as all heterosexuals are, that's where us gay people come from…you heterosexuals." Additionally, same-sex couples are most likely to adopt, therefore increasing adoption rates. As many as 127,000 children are waiting to be adopted ("Learn About Children Waiting for Adoption"), and with same-sex couples, these children have more of a chance to be part of a family.

Same-sex marriage should not be against the law. Same-sex couples should be under the same equal protection as everyone else, receive the same marriage benefits that straight couples do, and not be told whom they can or cannot love. Gay people will continue to fight for their rights and they are not going to stop. Another poll conducted by the Pew Forum in July 2012 shows that the silent generation (1928–45) is more likely to oppose same-sex marriage than the millennial generation (1981 or later) is ("Pew-Forum: Gay Marriage Attitude"). I believe this is because the older generation is more conservative, while the younger generation tends to be more liberal. "'Voting as a liberal,' [William O' Brian] said, 'that's what kids do'" ("Keeping Students from the Polls" 71). With this being said, I believe that in the future, people of the millennial generation will continue to foster a growing sense of liberalism, and same-sex marriage will soon be legal. After all, homosexuality is not a choice, but homophobia is.

WORKS CITED

Barnes, Robert. "California Proposition 8 Same-sex-marriage Ban Ruled Unconstitutional." *Washington Post.* The Washington Post, 08 Feb. 2012. Web. 25 Oct. 2012. <http://www.washingtonpost.com/politics/calif-same-sex-marriage-ban-ruled-unconstitutional/2012/02/07/gIQAMNwkwQ_story.html >.

Belge, Kathy. "Ellen DeGeneres & Portia De Rossi." *About.com Lesbian Life.* About.com, n.d. Web. 25 Oct. 2012. <http://lesbianlife.about.com/od/famouslesbians/ig/Famous-Lesbian-Couples/Ellen---Portia.htm>

Fray, Jasmine. "Obedience: Ideal in Dogs, Not People." *Starting Lines 2012.* Santa Barbara: UCSB, 2012. 39–41. Print.

Hartenstein, Meena. "Neil Patrick Harris to Be Dad to Twins with Partner David Burtka, Actor Announces on Twitter." *New York Daily News.* Daily News, 15 Aug. 2010. Web. 25 Oct. 2012. <http://articles.nydailynews.com/2010-08-15/gossip/27072764_1_twins-parenting-skills-neil-patrick-harris>.

"Keeping Students from the Polls." *Writing 1.* Ed. Christopher Warren Dean. Santa Barbara, CA: Alternative Copy, 2012. 71–72. Print.

"Learn About Children Waiting for Adoption." *Adopting.org.* Adopting.org, n.d. Web. 01 Nov. 2012. <http://www.adopting.org/adoptions/learn-about-adoption-waiting-children.html>.

"Marriage Rights and Benefits." *Lawyers, Legal Forms, Law Books & Software, Free Legal Information.* NOLO, n.d. Web. 25 Oct. 2012. <http://www.nolo.com/legal-encyclopedia/marriage-rights-benefits-30190.html>.

"Pew-Forum: Gay Marriage Attitudes." *Pew-Forum.* Pew-Forum, July 2012. Web. 25 Oct. 2012. <http://features.pewforum.org/same-sex-marriage-attitudes/>.

Rachel, Gordon. "Lesbian Rights Pioneer Del Martin Dies at 87." *SFGate.* SFGate, 28 Aug. 2008. Web. 25 Oct. 2012. <http://www.sfgate.com/politics/article/Lesbian-rights-pioneer-Del-Martin-dies-at-87-3198048.php>.

Timberlake, Sean. "San Francisco: The Castro." *SFGate.* SFGate, n.d. Web. 25 Oct. 2012. <http://www.sfgate.com/neighborhoods/sf/castro/>.

"Timeline: Same-sex Marriage." *CNN.* The CNN Library, 18 Oct. 2012. Web. 25 Oct. 2012. http://news.blogs.cnn.com/2012/10/18/timeline-same-sex-marriage/comment-page-1/

Waldman, Steven. "A Common Misconception." *Slate Magazine.* Slate, 13 Nov. 2003. Web. 31 Oct. 2012. <http://www.slate.com/articles/life/faithbased/2003/11/a_common_missed_conception.html>.

Weinger, Mackenzie. "Evolve: Obama Gay Marriage Quotes." *POLITICO.* POLITICO, 9 May 2012. Web. 25 Oct. 2012. <http://www.politico.com/news/stories/0512/76109_Page2.html>.

AUTHOR PROFILE

I am a first-year student from San Francisco. I strongly believe in my essay's topic.

—Debbie Lum

LEARNING AND HUMAN MEMORY

Jerry (Peng Xu) Liu

Instructor: Ilene Miele

> "By better educating future generations, we are contributing not only to their well-being, but also to the well-being of our whole society."

People have been studying the brain and its aspects for thousands of years throughout history; however, it was only recently that we have made the most significant advancements in the field of neuroscience through scientific research. One interesting fact about the brain is that it has actually evolved over thousands of years to arrive at its current state. We are able to see this phenomenon more clearly by examining the different parts of the brain and their functions. Despite our advancements in the area of neuroscience, our current understanding of the human brain and memory is still limited, and there remains much more progress to be made in understanding the process of learning. Because of our insufficient understanding of the learning process, one of the leading issues we face in the society today is the role memorization plays in educating students and the effectiveness of the traditional teaching method.

Ever since I started going to school, it seems that every class section that I have ever attended involved the use of my memory to a certain extent. Whether it be memorizing a poem from a textbook or remembering a certain set of math equations, we are taught to memorize new information every single day in the classroom, sometimes without even knowing the context behind the information we are memorizing. Since the start of the 18th century, this method of learning by memorization has been challenged. Joshua Foer, author of *Moonwalking with Einstein*, states, "Rousseau abhorred memorization, as well as just about every other stricture of institutional education" (192). The 18th century Swiss philosopher is famous for his 1762 treatise, *Emile: Or, On Education*. In the novel, Rousseau created a fictional character that did not learn things from memorization but rather learned everything through personal experience. The treatise also criticized the education system of the time and stated that it was little more than "heraldry, geography, chronology, and language" (qtd. in Foer 192).

Even though the role of memorization in the education system has been met with much criticism over the years, there has also been a wide range of support for memorization. In *Moonwalking with Einstein*, Foer introduces us to "The Talented Tenth," which is a group of high school students taught by American history teacher Raemon Matthews. The Talented Tenth, as Matthews call it, is an elite group of students who are taught to study by using the same techniques that were used in competing for the US Memory Championships. The students in The

Talented Tenth employ extensive use of their memorization capabilities and are required to memorize every single date, fact, and event found in their U.S. history textbook by the end of each year. The students found in The Talented Tenth are also expected to take the rigorous New York States Regents Exam. So far, every single member in the group has passed the exam in the last four years, and, according to Matthews, 85 percent of them scored 90 or better on the test. In the book, Matthews states that making his students memorize "is the difference between only teaching a kid multiplication and giving him a calculator" (190). Matthews himself has won two citywide Teacher of the Year awards.

People have also valued memorization because of various other reasons. For example, many people believe that memorizing information has a constructive effect on a person's brain and that doing things such as rote memorization drills can enhance a person's memorization capabilities. A scientific theory called "faculty psychology" has also been popular among supporters of the traditional school curriculum. The theory states that the human mind is divided into various parts of "mental faculties" and that each faculty could be trained to increase its performance. Many experiments have been done over the years to test this specific theory; some of the researchers include William James and Edward Thorndike. After repeated experimentation was done by both researchers, the results showed that regularly doing memorization drills and tasks did not seem to have a significant effect on a person's ability to remember new information. This served to convince people that doing activities involving memorization in schools is not really beneficial to the students in the long run.

Even though the role memorization serves in school is currently a majorly debated topic, other problems involving the current education system have also been drawing public attention. Some of those problems include the length of class lectures and the size of classes. Because of the various viewpoints people have on the efficiency of the traditional classroom, it is not surprising to see schools implementing other methods of teaching when educating their pupils. One example of non-mainstream teaching can be found today in elite private schools such as Phillips Andover and Deerfield Academy.

In those schools, instead of making the students memorize math equations from a textbook, they are required to derive them by themselves. By doing this, the students will not only be able to better memorize the math equations, but also gain a better understanding of the concepts behind the formulas. Schools such as Deerfield Academy have also been teaching their students in small seminars rather than in a regularly sized class. This often allows more individual attention to each student and serves to facilitate a better learning environment.

Some educators have also been utilizing modern technology as a way of communicating information to students. One example is Salman Khan, founder of the website Kahn Academy. Kahn Academy is an online website where anyone with internet access can find videos that lecture anything from US history to advanced mathematics. In a recent interview with NPR, Khan stated that "It's never been really contradicted that people can pay attention for about ten to eighteen minutes. Afterward, they start zoning out, then they can kind of recheck-in for about ten minutes, then they zone out for an even longer period of time and that keeps going on" (Khan). As a result, Khan made his online lectures in short intervals to utilize a typical person's attention span. Kahn's site has been rising in popularity especially in recent years, with typical users ranging anywhere from middle school students to full-grown adults. This shows that the traditional way of teaching students in a classroom may not be the best or most efficient way to teach after all. His site has been met with much praise and support from both students and educators. Just recently, Kahn Academy has also raised significant funding from organizations such as the Bill & Melinda Gates Foundation.

In today's society, various kinds of teaching methods are used to educate students, and memorization still plays a major role in a person's education. Even though there have been various debates on the pros and cons of different teaching styles, neither one can be said to be definitively better than the other. Personally, I do not believe that memorization should be eradicated from the public education system, nor do I believe that one form of teaching style is better than the other. However, I do believe that each teaching method has its upsides and downsides, and that we could combine the positive aspects of each teaching method to better our current educational curriculum. For example, we could teach students to derive math formulas on their own in public schools and we could also try to use new teaching methods that can better utilize a person's attention span in order to make classes more effective. We could also teach students memorization techniques so they can perform better in classes where memorization is necessary, such as history. Because learning is done for the purpose of self-improvement, finding better ways to teach our children will not only help their academic performances, but also better their personal qualities. By better educating future generations, we are contributing not only to their well-being, but also to the well-being of our whole society.

WORKS CITED

Foer, Joshua. *Moonwalking with Einstein.* New York: The Penguin Press, 2011. Print.

Khan, Salman. Interview by Neal Conan. "Op-Ed: Students Don't Learn From Lectures." *Talk of the Nation.* Natl. Public Radio, 23 Oct. 2012. npr.org. Web. 20 Feb. 2013.

AUTHOR PROFILE

I am a freshman here at UCSB with an undeclared major. During times when I am not burning myself out from researching different majors and careers, I can be found reading books, playing tennis, and surfing the internet (more of the latter). My family resides in Orange County.

—*Jerry (Peng Xu) Liu*

Photo by Loriel Davila

MULTIMODAL
TEXTS

A MOMENT IN TIME

Joyce Liu

Instructor: Ilene Miele

Day 1—

Luminous lights paint the sky with blotches of warm tones while specks of white and gold shimmer in the night sky. The side of the road overlooks the valley of the sleepless city. There are hands around her body that support her while she does her magic. She closes her eyes for a moment and when she opens them, an image of the cityscape appears on her screen. For a moment, the picture fades into blackness, but she pulls the memory back onto the screen for her owner's approval. When a warm glow illuminates the owner's face, she feels a sense of contentment. Afterwards, the image fits snuggly in a folder with thousands of other images.

"She knows her photos spark the emotions of what once was."

A few weeks later, she revisits the warm colors of the night. They take her back to that midnight trip to the narrow road above the city. She remembers her owner's excitement of going on adventures during the transition of one year to another. All those trials and errors until the shot came out perfectly marked her owner's new year.

Day 61—

After a couple of months, she is once again exposed to the calm but icy cold night. Subtle crickets chirp in the background as she closes her eyes. This time, a tripod supports her while she turns the darkness into something beautiful. She waits thirty seconds before all the photons settle into their pixels. The millions of pixels stitch together and form an ominous black sky with wisps of soft white clouds. Then it's sorted into the folder of similar photos. She watches her owner scroll through each image and occasionally delete a few. It felt different this time; her owner wasn't smiling or showing any traces of happiness. Her owner looked quietly along the silhouette of the trees on the screen. She could see the resemblance of the photo in her owner's facial expression. From time to time, her owner would look to the sky and take in the emptiness. She could not understand why her owner looked so sad, but she completed her task. The photo was printed the following week.

Day 222—

She knows each photo has a story to tell. Their importance stems from the subject of the photo and branches into other meanings and correlations. She sees a photo as a seed that houses remnants of memories. The seedling grows alongside its owner; when she matures, the seed matures as well. Throughout life, the seed trigger reminisces of places and things from the past. As more time passes by, the seed begins to sprout and lays its roots in the owner. The memory it provokes becomes a foundation of morals and beliefs, which support and make up who the owner is as a human. Although she might not comprehend why the photos stir her owner's soul, this is the beauty she knows best, the love of life, and what it embodies. She knows her photos spark the emotions of what once was. That is her job after all. All the pixels, tonalities, and contents revive the human memory of the past. Her photos are eyewitness of the past frozen in time. During all this, she is living and reliving each moment.

When she isn't taking snapshots, she sits upon a shelf in her owner's room. Every so often, she sees her prints posted on the walls. As time passes, the walls cover in a vast sea of photos. Each time her owner looks at the photos, she sees the glassy look in her eyes. It is as if her owner is somewhere else in time. The photos seem to teleport her owner to another place, not necessarily a happier time. Some of the photos are cloudy, threaded with sadness from the past, while other photos gleam with bright smiles and sunny days.

Day 365—

A year later, the photos lie in a box with other mementos of the past. They serve as a reminder of how different her life was a year ago. She still sits upon the shelf, but rarely does she ever venture into the world. She has all the time in the world to contemplate and wonder. Yet, she specifically remembers the photos from those two nights. When she retraces her steps through her memory, those nights aren't as cloudy or conflicted. After a period of time, all the bits and pieces of those nights seem to fall into place. The conflicted feelings and uncertainty begin to make sense.

She can see the past more clearly now that some time has passed. The first photo provokes memories of the carefree days and nights she spent exploring new places. It brings back the feelings of curiosity and lighthearted contentment, like the times her owner drove to places like the observatory or mountains to get away from the city. Meanwhile, the second photo fosters a time of sorrow, like the memories of disappointment and regret. She remembers the night when the photo was created; her owner had a thick drape of frustration that blended her with the night.

The more she looks through the photos, she realizes the photos don't hold the memories; they are the spark that lights the memories. Over time, the meanings behind the memories morph as the human begins to grow. A photo doesn't trigger just an individual memory, but rather it branches through other times that hold similar emotions. All the feelings and memories are interlaced in a network of ideas and morals that a person lives by. She comes to a sense of understanding about why she takes photos. The images she produces remind her owner of an earlier time and the importance of the event. They are the seed of remembering and why she exists.

AUTHOR PROFILE

I'm a first year student and pre-biology major with the hope of one day becoming a doctor. I love food, friends, and house music. I was born and raised in the San Gabriel Valley, which is near LA. In my spare time, I enjoy taking photos and exploring my surroundings.

— *Joyce Liu*

ME SPEAKING OUT (SPOKEN WORD)

Kay (Sue Jeong) Lee

Instructor: Roberta Gilman

If I asked you, "who are you?" how would you answer? If I asked you, "tell me about yourself" what would you say? What if you could only choose one word to describe yourself the most? What would that be? An adjective? A noun? Would it be your age or your gender?

Ethnicity, race, or your group? American, Mexican, El Salvadorian, Chinese, Vietnamese, or Korean?

Have you ever paid enough attention to what your ethnicity has to say about you?

Living in America, it seems like people don't really realize how important ethnicity is—where your blood comes from. America is a melting pot. Anyone can be American; you just have to be born here.

> **"It's ironic and frustrating to be a hybrid."**

In Asian countries, your ethnicity is defined by your parents' identity. It doesn't matter where you are born; you follow "the blood."

Again, America doesn't do that. At first, I thought that was really fucked up. Yeah, you can be American, but you are still something else, right? Half polish, half Swedish. Quarter Japanese. Quarter Mexican. Eighth French. Half black. Third Italian. Something else.

So what happens if you can't find your exact identity? No big deal there, I can see that. But it is, indeed, a big deal, for me.

Let me tell you a little bit about myself. I am turning twenty in exactly one week and I was born in Taiwan. Yet my parents are Korean, so I'm Korean. I've been living in the United States for seven or eight years in total now. I went to kindergarten and started elementary school in Palos Verdes (near LA). Then I went back to Korea to finish elementary school and started middle school. Before I could finish middle school, I came back to the States as a freshman in high school. I went to boarding schools in two different states. Pretty complicated, I know.

Four years in high school was definitely the most significant time that built the "me" that I am today. Those four years were a complete blast. I spent great time with amazing people. There were hardly any Koreans in my schools though. Instead, I met people from all over the world: Nigeria, England, Germany, Russia, Italy, Spain, Canada, Malaysia, Morocco, Japan, China, Taiwan, El Salvador, Mexico, Guatemala, Australia, Ethiopia, Vietnam, and I really wish I could name them all.

Here's the thing: no one judged me for where I was from. I was just Kay Lee. In such a special environment, we lived together with open minds and no judgments. I naturally learned how to fit in and became Americanized, to the max.

≈

"FOB" they said. F.O.B: a.k.a. fresh off the boat. That is what they called me here. Now I call myself that too. We call ourselves that. That's what I am: a full-blooded Korean. I have no shame in being a "FOB." I actually have so much pride for my country. But…

≈

But what if…what happens, if I don't feel like a "FOB?"

I'll explain.

≈

Here in America, going to school and living here, I feel so…Korean.

First of all, I just look Korean.

I'm so Asian. My hair is so dark and so straight. My eyes are single-lidded.

I am Korean.

I love kimchi. I love spicy food. I love rice wine, and I love soju. I love karaoke.

I'm sorry; I can't help but feel so Korean.

In Korea, every time I go back home for summer and winter breaks, I feel so…American.

Well, it's embarrassing to say, but I speak good English—at least compared to the people who live in Korea.

Second of all, I live here.

I live here. How else can I explain why I feel so American? I live here. I have been living here. I go to school here. I went to high school here. Do you know what that means? It means that I learned about life—here. I matured—here. I simply grew up—here.

I'm not stuck in conservative ideas.

I'm open-minded. I'm pretty straightforward.

Frankly, people often mistake me for an American.

I'm sorry; I feel so American.

≈

So, who am I? How do I define myself? My home doesn't here feel like home. My home there doesn't feel home either. It's the question of life right here.

≈

Not a native + Not a second generation = Hybrid

I'm a hybrid. I decided to make my own home ground. It's my own hybrid area.

I used to think of it this way: I'm homeless. How pathetic is that? I have two homes but I don't really have a home.

Now I think of it this way: I have two homes. How awesome is that? I have two places to feel connected to.

≈

But listen carefully.

Let's say you feel 80% connected and 20% left out.

What is tough about this is facing the 20%.

What is important is not the number: 30%, 10%, doesn't matter.

It's the fact that this 20% will never disappear, which also means that this 80% will never reach 100%. It's sad.

Here is what happens:

I left Korea, but that doesn't mean it stays the same. It's continuously changing and moving on without me. Every time I go back home, I need to catch up with what I've missed: hot issues, movies and dramas, new fads, changing culture, etc.

Here, I can live here for the rest of my life, but I will always be Korean. There will always be an infinite amount of catching up to do.

No matter where I go, the 20% will remain, lingering there forever.

≈

In Korea, I don't know how they know, but people ask me if I study abroad or if I'm Korean-American. Apparently they can tell that my Korean-ness is somehow imperfect.

My friends ask me what it is like going to school in America. They think it is such a privilege to study in America. Of course it is, but the reality is harsh. It's not easy to study in a second language, get good grades, and try to fit in.

"Do you eat pasta every day? Do you eat steak for dinner? So…you talk with white people?" they ask me.

It just seems impossible to connect with them or find a common topic to talk about.

≈

In America, the 20% is called racism. It's not the kind of racism you think. It's not like, "You are yellow" or "How do you blindfold an Asian? With dental floss!"

It's the racism you feel it in the air that really hurts you.

It's the kind of racism that is unspoken—a social kind of racism.

The best example is slang.

Due to all the catching up I have to do, I continuously have to learn new words, both in Korea and in America.

Once you let people know that you don't fully understand the conversation, you become an outsider, a foreigner, an Asian, no matter how well you speak the language or how good your grades are.

If you want in, you must know what's going on in their language. If you don't understand one word, there immediately comes a transparent wall between you and "the natives."

It feels like the atmosphere is telling me, "Asians are not cool, they are nerds. They are only obsessed with their grades. They aren't cool enough."

For example, let's say you didn't know what "ASAP" meant. It stands for "as soon as possible." It's a very commonly-used phrase, not only for students but also for adults. If people notice that you don't understand these kinds of terms, they will subconsciously change their attitude towards you. They might not even realize it, but you will definitely feel it.

≈

"Ew, how do you eat kimchi? It smells like feet, it's so gross!"

It's one of the healthiest foods you can find. Korean food is highly recommended between professional dietitians and nutritionists for being the healthiest food. How can you eat so much fast food made out of shit?

"How can you tolerate that much hot sauce? You're so Asian…"

We're boss.

"You didn't get an A in math? I thought you were Asian!"

Oh my god, I'm so sorry I got a B in math. I must go die. Perhaps I was adopted.

"I heard Koreans eat dog meat. That is disgusting."

You know how that started? Wars. Brutal wars. People were dying everywhere, there was nothing to eat, and my ancestors made a choice to survive. Not all Koreans eat dogs. We have pets too, and we love our dogs. Other countries eat weird shit too, don't you know?

"The Korean soccer team won bronze in the Olympics! WTF?"

If you didn't know, Korea is a country. It is tiny, but guess what, we have sports teams. In fact, the Korean women's archery team won the gold medal seven times in a row. We actually placed 5th in medal count from 2012 London Olympics after America, China, England, and Russia.

~

It's ironic.

It's ironic how I get so patriotic but I can't fit in.

It's ironic how I love the way I live but still want to be accepted.

It's ironic, the situation.

It's ironic and frustrating to be a hybrid.

Everything is confusing, and it always will be.

There's never going to be a simple answer. But am I alone in my "hybrid-zone"? I don't think so.

So, tell me. Who are you?

WORKS CITED

Fulbeck, Kip. *Paper Bullets*. Seattle: University of Washington Press (2001). Print.

Fulbeck, Kip. "My World." *YouTube*. Web. <http://www.youtube.com/watch?v=ZckwNFCIbA8>)

Trenka, Jane Jeong. *Fugitive Visions: An Adoptee's Return to Korea*. Graywolf Press (2009). Print.

AUTHOR PROFILE

I am first-year biology major. I moved around a lot on the West Coast growing up, but my hometown is in South Korea. Eating delicious food makes me happy. I love to dance and sing. I think I have started to like writing.

— *Kay (Sue Jeong) Lee*

ACCIDENTALLY PURSUING SELF-IDENTITY

Marilou Razo

Instructor: Ilene Miele

> **"**My wall serves as 'memory seeds' so that no matter how busy I am or how much I change I never forget what really matters.**"**

When I moved into college, I started creating the collage that sits before my desk. It started with minor keepsakes that reminded me of home. Among my first decorations were the collage my sister gave me on my graduation day, my little brother's drawing, and the crazy drawing my friend Alice made me. Time went by and the collection began to grow with the addition of the many quotes that line my wall. It started out as a bunch of decorations to make my wall look nice.

However, I noticed that I was very specific about what went on my wall. Not just anything deserved to be on my wall. Many things were rejected, but what all these decorations had in common is that they reminded me of where I had been, where I was at the moment, and where I was going in life. My wall is filled with "memory seeds"; these objects remind me of who I am, and what I value—objects and memory, and I picked them with that in mind.

Mihalyi Csikszentmihalyi, the author of the article "Why We Need Things" states that our identity is constantly changing and that without external objects we cannot pinpoint who we are (2). My decorations above my desk are me. The "Self," or our identity, is something that we create in our mind, so fragile that without these objects as triggers we are lost in the search for ourselves (Csikszentmihalyi 2). My wall is not to be mistaken as something for anyone else, it is for me. My growth and change are marked by these objects; I discover what I stand for through them. This routine decorating soon became an obsession with getting "me" onto something tangible. Colorful was a must at first, but soon began to fade into the background with the acquisition of more meaningful objects. I even bought a postcard solely for the fact that it would add color to my wall. It had a message, which I found extremely cheesy, but I hung it up anyway. Until recently, I crossed out the caption and wrote my own, which reads "El mundo no es de colores, but it could be" which means, "The world isn't great but it could be." That philosophy suited my wall better.

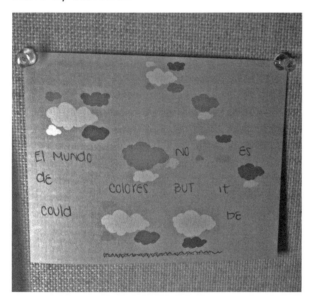

The first quote ever to be nominated to the wall was a "How I Met Your Mother" quote. It reads, "When I'm sad I stop being sad and be awesome instead…'True story,'" by Barney Stinson. My quotes started off being humorous reminders to remind me that no matter what, life is good. Soon they became ideologies and self-empowerment provided by Jim Morrison, Martin Luther King Jr., and many others.

"The chance for greatness, for progress, ends the moment we try to be someone else."
—Faith Jegede

A crazy drawing, my change the world "ticket," and the many quotes that line my wall are among my favorite objects. I have a peculiar way of thinking, hence, the weird drawing. My crazy drawing

reminds me of my appreciation for non-traditional thinking. Many times I forget why I continue to fight this uphill battle. Nothing means more to me than changing the world, and my "ticket" reminds me of that. All the quotes on my wall are radically different; but their similarity is that they serve as reminders. As Csikszentmihalyi says, "Pictures serve as icons of the past, concrete reminders of a life that otherwise would run the risk of getting lost in the labyrinths of memory" (3). These objects on my wall remind me of the beauty of life and my internal liberation from everything. They remind me to strive for humility, to dream bigger and bigger.

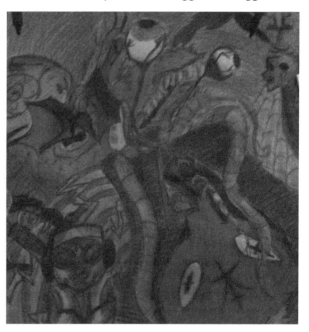

"Expose yourself to your deepest fear, after that fear has no power, and the fear of freedom shrinks and vanishes you are free."
—Jim Morrison

Since I strive for humility, any object on my wall has to have a deeper meaning. It is not enough for it to be aesthetically pleasing. As an extension of myself, it must represent my ideologies—social justice, creativity, humility, freedom from external and internal forces, and the beauty in life—all must be reflected in that object.

"We must rapidly begin the shift from a 'thing-oriented' society to a 'person-oriented' society."
—Martin Luther King Jr.

Objects make it possible for us to look back on a younger self, since the mind is not able to hold the self for very long (Csikszentmihalyi 2). The picture of my piggy connects me to watching cartoons with my little brother and it reminds me of a time when I didn't have as many responsibilities. Objects allow you to point to a certain instance in life and say, "This was a part of me." As Csikszentmihalyi found, "The home contains a symbolic ecology that represents both continuity and change in the life course and thus gives permanence to our elusive selves" (2). My wall reminds me of how I have changed, through the addition of new things but also of what I truly believe. Such as my "ticket" to change the world, it is a part of me that continues and will forever continue. It is the reason I decided to strive for higher education, and it is the force that keeps me going every day.

This collage of objects is a way to express who I am, without the necessity of words. Above all, it is an indirect way of finding out who I am in relation to this crazy life. Objects give their owner wholeness because they help put into context the owner's existence and give one the comfort to keep going. Csikszentmihalyi retells the story of a depressed lawyer who descends into his basement to play the trombone. His trombone helps him cope with the stress of everyday life; it connects him with his college days when everything was spontaneous (2). Many times I place things on my wall that I know are important, but cannot explain why they are important to me. Only with time, as I find out who I am, do I figure out why I give these objects significance.

There are other objects, however, that serve to pave the future, such as my picture of the Peace Corps. It is a possibility that I want to keep in mind as I go through life, which is why it is on my wall. It points to a direction that I can decide to follow, or not, in the future (Csikszentmihalyi 2). The Peace Corps was a definite maybe as I was growing up, but like my identity, it is subject to change. Although the picture is still on my wall, I shy away from that possibility now. Upon coming to college I realized the negative effects that my "good intentions" of going into the Peace Corps may have had on the host country (Illich). The reason I have not taken it down is that although the Peace Corps is flawed, it reminds me of a higher cause and the desire to be of service to others. It is also a constant reminder that one should be careful and mindful of "good intentions."

The crazy drawing, the heart given to me, and my ticket all symbolize my past, present, and future. My wall serves as "memory seeds" so that no matter how busy I am or how much I change I never forget what really matters. Csikszentmihalyi says, "Objects reveal the continuity of the self through time, by providing foci of involvement in the present, mementos and souvenirs of the past, and signposts to future goals" (2). I have indirectly created a timeline where the goals I have reached, my present moments, and my aspirations can all share center stage.

"The objects people see as special in their home point to different directions in time, revealing different aspects of the self that are important, depending on the person's age" (Csikszentmihalyi 3). Objects allow the self to continue on in a tangible way where growth can be seen. For me, these objects constitute the collage that is my wall, and it serves as a friendly reminder of who I am when I am lost. My identity may change with age, and I may add new items that convey a different version of me, but the objects of my past will forever remind me of what meant the world to me long ago.

WORKS CITED

Csikszentmihalyi, Mihalyi. "Why We Need Things." *History from Things*. Eds. S. Lubar & W.D. Kingery. Smithsonian Institution Press. Washington D.C.: Smithsonian Institution, 1993. Print.

Illich, Ivan. "To Hell with Good Intentions." Speech. Conference on InterAmerican Student Projects (CIASP). Mexico, Cuernavaca. 20 Apr. 1968. Web. 13 Mar. 2013. <http://www.swaraj.org/illich_hell.htm>.

Objects and Memory. Dir. Jonathan Fein and Brain Danitz. Ever, 2008. DVD.

AUTHOR PROFILE

I am a first-generation college student from North Long Beach. Growing up my possibilities were limited. My school was constantly underfunded, my peers always seen as future dropouts and I as the "beacon of light." According to the school system, I had "potential." Coming to college my thirst for knowledge has intensified. I have learned to be critical of all that I am taught because that is true knowledge.

I hope to take all that I have learned to become a lawyer who will fight for justice in its purest form and not to become a politician in training.

—*Marilou Razo*

WHO AM I?

Monica Chung

Instructor: Roberta Gilman

This is it, time to create my project. I have gone over the questions that Gray and my classmate asked me. They are good questions because they help me to think and brainstorm. Not only do they make me really think, they also make me dig down deep.

Before I start writing my poems, I decide to go on the internet to look at various kinds of poems. There are haikus, couplets, rhymes, and many other kinds. I don't know which ones to choose; I want to do all of them! However, I won't choose. I want to start typing, so here goes…

One day later

I am done with my poems. This is what happened: I just started typing and I could not stop. There were moments when I had to think for quite a while. As I was typing, I started to discover answers to my question: who am I? It felt like magic. The answers were there as I was writing!

I must say, I am happy and satisfied that I had the opportunity to do this project. In the end, I created several poems. There is one thing I am scared of, though, and that is presenting what I wrote in front of the class. These poems are so personal. However, I realize I must be bold and just have confidence in myself. I want to share what I discovered with my classmates and my professor. I want them to find out what I discovered.

> **"Writing taught me that if we have a question, we should take the initiative to find out the answer."**

Who Am I?

Little Girl in Panama City

She was living in her own little world,

filled with big imagination and big dreams.

Mischievous and sassy

Not shy all the time

Bubbly and smiley

Always laughing and happy,

except when she had to go to school.

She likes to dance.

She likes to play.

She likes her dolls.

She likes to sing.

She likes to dress up.

She likes to fight with her brother.

She likes the time she spends with her family.

She likes TV and Happy Meals.

She likes anything that was fun.

This little girl was me.

I thought nothing wrong of the world

Nor did I really pay attention to it.

Life was good being a kid.

Until one day, something changed everything.

A hunger for money can bring out the ugly in people.

Violence causes scars and consequences.

Yet crooks can't care.

My life was never the same since that one day.

My childhood was taken away.

I became this other girl that wasn't me.

Terrified. Shy. Quiet.

Where Is That Little Girl?

Remainders of my childhood (in LA):

In the beginning, it was tough.

For a while,

poverty and a new beginning made life rough.

People were cruel,

with their negative opinions and views.

Oh! They're not from America.

They're stupid. They're not going to be anything.

It's okay because their negativity was my fuel.

I had this fire inside of me to try hard,

to prove people wrong.

Most of all to make my parents proud

And to give them the life they deserve.

I must say,

the remaining years of being a kid weren't so bad.

I tried my best to not let my past hold me back.

I held my feelings in and tried to let things be.

Teenage Years

Hormones raging as we are aging

To be honest, I thought my teenage years were bad.

Why all of a sudden do I care about what people think?

Why can't I just be me?

Wait a minute?

Who am I really?

To be honest, I really don't know.

I felt like my flame was burning out.

I had so many doubts.

My past came back to haunt me.

All I wanted was to be free.

Free from my past and from teenage life.

Growing up is hard am I right?

I still don't have a sense of who I really am.

I keep asking myself, where is the little girl I was?

She must be somewhere inside hiding

Or is she slowly dying?

Through the View of Another Eye
She's shy and quiet
What a very strange girl she is
Not to mention weak.

Maturity
Who am I?
That question keeps bothering me
Because I really don't know.
But now I have a better sense of it.

My past has changed me,
But it does not have to define who I am.
Yes I am still shy and quiet
An introvert
I still hold things in,
But slowly I am learning to let them go.
I am breaking out of my shell.

It takes time,
But slowly and surely
I am accepting myself for who I am.
I am gaining confidence in myself.
Thanks to a friend and a lot of realization,
I see that I am me.
Beautiful inside and out
Passionate and caring
Strong and not weak, a fighter.
I still have that bubbly, giggly, smiley side of me.
I still have that fire in me.
I may not be exactly the little girl I was,
But that's okay.

It took me this long,
Along with significant people in my life
And a lot of thinking and realization
To finally get a sense of who I am,
if not fully then eventually.
I just have to give it time.

Life has so many surprises.
The ups and the downs
But I try my best to not let the downs hinder me.

Life is like a book filled with chapters.
But not written out for you.
You write it by living your life the way you want to.

Here I am in college.
A fresh start, a new chapter
I'm on fire, I am maturing.
I am learning about myself.
I am discovering many things about life.
It makes me appreciate and be thankful
for the opportunities I had and will have
and the obstacles I overcame and the ones
I have yet to overcome.
I am simply trying to live life to its fullest
I am as happy as my little girl self.

It wasn't until this quarter, really, that I was able to answer my question: who am I? When I first started college, I really wanted to get a full sense of who I was after going through a lot in my life. In my writing class, I learned the significance of three words: specificity, initiative, and discovery. These three words weren't just words; they led me on this path of discovering a part of who I am even though it took time and I had to let myself remember certain things. Writing taught me that if we have a question, we should take the initiative to find out the answer. We have to think outside the box. If we take the initiative and express our curiosity with specificity, we can discover many things. I had to learn to be bold because I am usually a quiet person, never speaking what I feel or think. Writing helped me find my expressive self and that's who I am.

AUTHOR PROFILE

I am on a journey of learning more about myself and coming to terms on what I've been through. Some of my dreams and goals are to discover more about myself, give my parents the life they deserve for the sacrifices they made, go to medical school or grad school, and volunteer in third world countries. Most importantly, I want to live life to its fullest. I am grateful to have my parents and my friend Lydia supporting me. I am also grateful for Professor Gilman's amazing life lessons. The challenges I faced in her class made me think outside the box and led me to a path of discovery. Lastly, I am thankful for a significant person who made an impact in my life and who inspired me. Thanks Geoff for seeing the real me and helping me realize who I truly am.

—*Monica Chung*

Photo by Leo Vargas

WRITING 2

Photo by Leo Vargas

TEXTUAL
CARNIVALS

THE SEX PISTOLS

Meagan Reece

Instructor: Christopher Dean

> **"**Considered dangerous to the very fabric of society and banned across the country, the Sex Pistols show us that by having do-it-yourself ethics, violent passion, and the willingness to stick it to the man, both music and society can be revolutionized in one fell swoop.**"**

Destroyed hotel rooms, thousands of loose women, drugs available at any time, and anarchy seeping from every pore—this was the live fast, die young attitude of the Sex Pistols. Their anti-establishment music inspired more than a generation—it started a revolution. Vocalist Johnny Rotten, guitarist Steve Jones, drummer Paul Cook and bassist Glen Matlock, who was later replaced by punk icon Sid Vicious, not only transformed the youth, they created the essence of punk music, crushed societal boundaries, and made their way to the top of the charts. Considered dangerous to the very fabric of society and banned across the country, the Sex Pistols show us that by having do-it-yourself ethics, violent passion, and the willingness to stick it to the man, both music and society can be revolutionized in one fell swoop.

The Sex Pistols had humble beginnings, starting as a band called The Strand originating in London (Strongman 96). Steve Jones and Paul Cook were two of the founding members, playing on instruments they had stolen and hanging out at two local shops called Acme Attractions and Too Fast to Live, Too Young to Die (Strongman 96). These two shops would single-handedly pave the way to achieving the punk look, and would later be pivotal in bringing Sid Vicious into the band (Robb 84). This was the first way in which the Sex Pistols would transform the youth—through fashion, and the statement that the punk look would make. It was known as "anti-fashion," and it caught on like wildfire in the punk sphere. Their leather jackets, motorcycle boots, ripped jeans, and spiked hair were not just fashion statements, they were an identity that was embodied by the music of the Sex Pistols. This identity was one of challenging mainstream society, as well as one of anti-establishment ideals, which were at the heart of the punk movement. The idea was to turn fashion upside down and to turn the ugly into the desired. There were many do-it-yourself elements to anti-fashion, as the clothing was modified using safety pins, metal studs, buttons, and patches. By turning fashion on its head, anti-fashion was an attack on the mainstream, the powerful, and the fashionable (Strongman, 96). The Pistols' message carried through to their clothing, showing the world that they could not be controlled or stopped.

The youth loved the Sex Pistols and desired the exhilarating rush of their music rather than the safety of popular music of the time, while mainstream media and musical critics took the opposite side, demonstrating to the masses a violent distaste and hatred for punk music.

Bernard Brook-Partridge, a member of the Greater London Council and chairman of the Arts committee stated that "Most of these [punk] groups would be vastly improved by sudden death. The worst of the punk rock groups I suppose currently are the Sex Pistols… I would like to see somebody dig a very, very large, exceedingly deep hole and drop the whole bloody lot down it" (Gimarc 49). But this growth of the punk attitude in the youth only added to what the "essence of punk" is—a disregard for the establishment and resistance to tyranny in any form, especially in the media and politics. This view of punk as an ideology started through the Pistols' lyrics. For example, while discussing their career as a band in "Great Rock 'n' Roll Swindle," they state "They all drowned when the air turned blue, 'cos we didn't give a toss/ Filthy lucre ain't nothing new, but we all get cash from the chaos." These lines of lyrics clearly show the punk mentality making a statement. It is saying that even though mainstream society discouraged them and tried to run them out, because they "didn't give a toss" and continued down their own path, they are flourishing and succeeding. Also, in their song "God Save the Queen," they state "Don't be told about what you want, don't be told about what you need/ no future, no future, no future for you." This line completely embodies the essence of punk, in claiming that you need to go your own way in fighting against the establishment and tyranny, or else there will be "no future" but the bleak one that "the man" wants from you. The things the Sex Pistols preached to their audience helped create the idea of punk, and aided in bringing their message to the masses.

Another way the Pistols created the essence of punk music is through their own actions. If they were going to sing about anarchy, mocking the English royalty, destroying everything, and being the "antichrist," they had to live this no-holds-barred lifestyle themselves. Cue drug use, drama, and detrimental media appearances. Sid Vicious, the replacement bass player for Matlock in early 1977, was the face of drug use in the punk sphere (Robinson). When Sid first joined the band, his excitement at being a big pop star made him giddy and childlike. To him, his new "status meant press, a good chance to be spotted in all the right places, and adoration" from others (Robinson). However, as time went on, he met a

woman named Nancy Spungen, an emotionally disturbed drug addict and sometime prostitute from New York (Robinson). She is thought to be responsible for introducing Vicious to heroin, creating "the emotional codependency between the couple [that would] alienate Vicious from the other members of the band" (Lydon 147). Sid's drug use caused him to do the most outlandish, or as some view it, punk things seen to this day. He carved "gimme a fix" into his chest with a razor, hit audience members in the head with his bass, simulated oral sex onstage, and spat blood in a woman's face all while under the influence of heroin (Klein).

Further, the Pistols as a band crashed the Queen's Jubilee in 1977 by performing on a private boat chartered down the River Thames. They passed right by Westminster Pier and the Houses of Parliament in order to make a mockery of the Queen's procession, which was planned for two days later (Strongman 98). The event ended in multiple arrests; however, the band members were safely hustled away from the police. The Pistols also defaced the portrait used of the Queen for her Jubilee as the cover art for their single "God Save the Queen." Elizabeth II's eyes and mouth are symbolically covered by the single's title as well as the band name, making a mockery of royal political prowess as well as of the monarchy itself.

Aside from drug use and drama, the band's media appearances did much to establish the attitude of punk. When appearing on the *Today* TV show in 1976 hosted by Bill Grundy, their uncensored mouths and wild attitudes got the Pistols into nationwide trouble. Grundy was known for being a drunk and felt that he had no time for this upstart band; therefore, he treated them with disregard and contempt. He tried to get them to swear on air and Jones, realizing Grundy's plan, "launched into a stream of F-words" (Coon). This episode of rebellion against a TV host and complete disregard for etiquette of any kind landed the Pistols on the front page of the news, bringing the music and attitude of punk rock to the masses. After the incident they were dropped from their record deal with EMI, who had "buckled to internal pressure," yet they honored their "40,000 pound contract in full" (Coon). This display of punk attitude served to show all who were watching what it means to be a punk. The Pistols wouldn't just sit politely as someone insulted them; they stood up for themselves and showed society what punk really is: a revolution against "fucking rotter[s]" like Grundy who were out to try and control their music and ideals (Strongman 152).

The Sex Pistols' music also served to crush normal societal boundaries. What is normal to see in society is bands and musicians singing about love or going out, or in the 70s, acid trips, peace, and "letting it be." But that is the opposite of what the Sex Pistols sang about. Their song "God Save the Queen" was met with a mixture of love and hate—hate so strong that it caused a riot against the band members themselves. In "God Save the Queen," they state that the Queen is "A fascist regime," that "She ain't no human being," and that "Tourists are money, but our figurehead is not what she seems." Clearly this feeling was not one expressed by the majority of citizens, as Johnny Rotten and his producer, Chris Thomas, literally had to fight for their message. They were "violently attacked by supporters of the Queen, with John being slashed several times. Paul Cook was also set upon with an iron bar" (Coon). However, because the Pistols are who they are, they went on undeterred and released a few singles like "Pretty Vacant" and "Holidays in the Sun," as well as *Never Mind the Bollocks*," their "one and only true album" (Coon). These songs also gave a voice to a generation of youth in England who grew up with a bleak view regarding the government. They lived in the wake of post-industrial Britain in a time low in jobs and low in hope, making rebellion an escape from the world around them. Normalcy and the "right" way of doing things were not things the Pistols were concerned about—they wanted to do what they wanted, and breaking down the walls of society was just one part of their agenda.

With "God Save the Queen" on the charts at number two and their album "*Never Mind the Bollocks*" having pre-release orders so high it immediately charted at number one, the Sex Pistols successfully brought punk and all that goes along with it to the masses (Coon). Their fashion, attitudes, lifestyles, media appearances, lyrics, and much more all rolled together created what we know today as punk. The revolution they created is still alive and thriving in today's world, as the Pistols' part in the first wave of punk started an avalanche of punk rock bands, inspiring groups like The Damned, The Buzzcocks, The Clash, Joy Division, the Fall, and later, The Smiths (Nolan). With a sound that has been imitated but never surpassed as well as unrelenting vision, the Sex Pistols kicked society's ass all the way to the top, and are to this day still saluted by punks worldwide because of their willingness to challenge the norm and their ability to inspire through their incredible music.

WORKS CITED

Coon, Caroline. "The Sex Pistols: Biography." *Sex Pistols Official Website*. Universal Music Company, n.d. Web. 23 Oct 2012.

Gimarc, George. *Punk Diary: The Ultimate Trainspotter's Guide to Underground Rock 1970–1982*. New York: St. Martin's Press, 1994. Print.

Klein, Howie. "Sex Pistols: Tour Notes." *New York Rocker*. 1978: n. page. Print.

Lydon, John. *Rotten: No Irish, No Blacks, No Dogs*. London: Hodder and Stoughton, 1993. Print.

Nolan, David. *I Swear I Was There: The Gig that Changed the World*. London: Independent Music Press, 2006. Print.

Robb, John. *Punk Rock: An Oral History*. London: Elbury Press, 2006. 84. Print.

Robinson, Charlotte. "So Tough: The Boy Behind the Sid Vicious Myth." *PopMatters*. N.p., 09 2006. Web. 23 Oct 2012.

Strongman, Phil. *Pretty Vacant: A History of UK Punk*. Chicago: Chicago Review Press, 2008. Print.

AUTHOR PROFILE

I'm a third year English Major at UCSB and am a total music junkie finding my fix through writing about music and working for a music website.

—*Meagan Reece*

ARE MEDIA AND LEARNING COMPATIBLE?

Blanca Lopez

Instructor: Daniel Wuebben

> **"**The ease of access and numerous sites available on the Internet—such as Facebook and YouTube—greatly distract students from what is being taught. Hence, I believe that the use of the Internet must be prohibited in a classroom setting.**"**

The Internet, like any revolutionary invention, has been the subject of many recent debates. The Web has a great potential for spreading knowledge because of its massive volume of readily available information. But, according to writer Nicholas Carr, this characteristic of limitless material is changing us into "scattered and superficial thinkers."[1] By default, I must add, we are becoming scattered and superficial students. The use of computers in college classrooms is detrimental to student attention and the retention of information. The ease of access and numerous sites available on the Internet—such as Facebook and YouTube—greatly distract students from what is being taught. Hence, I believe that the use of the Internet must be prohibited in a classroom setting.

Before analyzing the distracting effects of computers in a classroom setting, we must consider those disrupting effects at large. The increasing amount of websites and their information provide an immense expanse of possible diversions from both work and entertainment alike. According to a recent web server survey conducted in May 2012, about 662,959,946 sites exist on the Internet; actually, this number is down from 676,919,707 in April 2012.[2] With this many available websites, it is hardly difficult to see why so many people wander from site to site indiscriminately. Within these millions of webpages is still a bigger threat to our attention and focus: hyperlinks. These hyperlinks are words or images that link one document to another document or image, and web pages are laden with them. In 2006, WebsSiteOptimization.com, "found that the average web page contained 474 words, 281 HTML tags, and 41 links, 10 of which pointed outside the domain."[3] This means that while reading an online article, readers are given the overwhelming choice to skip to another line or paragraph of the text or leave the page entirely. The Internet is aptly nicknamed the "Web"; hyperlinks connect one bit of information to an infinite number of other bits of information in a complex, tangled web. Carr explains that the numerous links divide our attention and

---

1 Nicholas Carr, *The Shallows: What the Internet is Doing to Our Brains* (New York: W. W. Norton & Company, 2010), 112.

2 Netcraft, Netcraft Ltd, last modified May 2 2012, http://news.netcraft.com/archives/2012/05/02/may-2012-web-server-survey.html.

3 Website Optimization, last modified May 31 2011, http://www.websiteoptimization.com/speed/tweak/average-web-page/.

therefore "strain our cognitive abilities, diminishing our learning and weakening our understanding."[4] We are forced to forge a path between all of the distractions while attempting to concentrate on the content of the webpage. Transferring our attention from one subject to the next and from one page to another can indeed be beneficial to activities that require multitasking. However, reading, for example, is no such task. Full attention is vital in developing a fuller understanding and deeper thinking. Otherwise, we are left with superficial thoughts and knowledge.

Apart from making us more distracted, the Internet has rendered us more impatient. The speed with which the Web gives us information is virtually instantaneous. We can navigate from one page to another in a matter of seconds. And we can have multiple browser windows open at the same time, an entirely new subject is one swift motion of the hand away. Gone are the times when we had to move from book to book or from shelf to shelf. Thus we have grown accustomed to being given what we want as soon as we decide we want it. Again, we see that reading is negatively affected. When we read online, we merely scan and skim the text. Carr mentions a study that tracked eye movements of volunteers as they read online articles. It was found that the volunteers' eyes skipped "down the page in a pattern that resembled, roughly, the letter *F*."[5] Online, people do not read in the traditional way of reading line by line. Instead they skip around trying to find the text's importance or entertainment. Furthermore, "fewer than one in ten page views extend beyond two minutes"; it appears that if people do not find something valuable in the few seconds it took them to skim, they quickly move on to something else.[6] The more we become accustomed to the rapid flow of information, the more challenging it may be for us to be patient when something forces us to slow down.

Computers, accompanied with Internet, can indeed be a valuable tool in the classroom. Many students type faster than they write, allowing them to take notes more efficiently. Additionally, the Web can be used to research a professor's specific point in order to gain a better understanding. But in reality, most students do not visit sites that supplement the in-class information. PalatnikFactor.com, a blog devoted to online marketing, found that in 2007, some of the top websites visited by college students were Facebook, MySpace, ESPN, and EBay—none of them educational sites.[7] This does not necessarily occur because the class material is boring, but because the Internet provides slightly more engaging endeavors. Students can update statuses, comment in blogs, or shop online—all behind their screens. Answering emails and playing games take precedence over writing notes and listening to the professor. Students force themselves to attend to their flashing email reminders while attempting to focus on the professor's lecture before they check the weather.

Online games may be even more hazardous than any other activity because they demand more attention. A game requires the participant to concentrate solely on playing. Reading an article, on the other hand, needs less concentration, especially with the current trend of skimming, and allows attention to at least be shared. This tendency to simultaneously have multiple sites open occurs even beyond the classroom walls. The Pew Internet and American Life Project conducted research in 2006 that found that many college students had online games open together with schoolwork, such as when writing papers.[8] The game, or any other website, wastes much time, prolonging, for instance, the writing process. Even worse, it motivates the student to work faster in order to return to the game. The result is shoddier and sloppier work. This trend of mixing academic tasks and recreational activities also reflects our developing impatience. The student, either in class or while completing homework, turns to something on the Web that provides instant gratification when the lecture or homework assignment is moving too slowly to sustain interest.

---

4 Nicholas Carr, *The Shallows: What the Internet is Doing to Our Brains* (New York: W. W. Norton & Company, 2010), 59.

5 Nicholas Carr, *The Shallows: What the Internet is Doing to Our Brains* (New York: W. W. Norton & Company, 2010), 130.

6 Nicholas Carr, *The Shallows: What the Internet is Doing to Our Brains* (New York: W. W. Norton & Company, 2010), 4.

7 Pablo Platanik, Platanik Factor, last modified October, 9 2007, http://palatnikfactor.com/2007/10/09/top-10-sites-visited-by-college-students-men-vs-women/.

8 Steve Jones, Pew Internet &American Life Project, Pew Research Center, last modified July 6, 2003, http://www.pewinternet.org/Reports/2003/Let-the-games-begin-Gaming-technology-and-college-students/2-Gaming-Comes-of-Age.aspx?view=all.

The inattentiveness and impatience the Internet encourages is most dangerous and toxic to learning and education. Essential components of learning are the preservation and memorization of information. We know how to spell because we memorized the alphabet and the order of letters in thousands of words, and we preserved the helpful grade school tip to sound out a word when we have no idea how to spell something. The difference between obtaining an A+ and a C– on an exam is how much information a student retains. Similarly, an expert is not born knowing everything about a subject; he or she memorizes all of the information. Memorization does not stand alone either. Memory consolidation requires attention. According to the website "The Human Memory," the consolidation process begins with attention. This is so because attention produces a memorable experience, which then causes neurons to fire much more frequently. The higher frequency of neurons increases the probability that the experience or event is encoded as a memory.[9] And paying attention, to begin with, requires our conscious choices. Many times, we have found ourselves in a situation where more than one person is talking. To absorb anything being said, we must choose only one person to focus on. This dilemma is present every time students use computers during class. They have to decide whether to pay attention to a lecture or their newest email, with the latter usually winning. If they are able to attend to more than one task, their attention and retention are shallower. In fact, a professor at Colorado State University, Diane Sieber, found that students who use computers in class on average do 11% worse on exams than their peers.[10] The entire learning process ultimately stems from our attention. Therefore, the distractions of the Internet hurt learning because they restrict information attainment and retention.

Although it will be difficult, the best way to contend with the Internet's negative effects will be to prohibit the use of computers in class. Disposing of the Internet in classrooms and lecture halls is not ideal; a great deal of money was spent to install it,

and professors themselves may access the Web for teaching purposes. But, the instructor should notify the students that computers are not allowed in class. This will greatly reduce distractions and increase attention, memorization, and, essentially, learning.

BIBLIOGRAPHY

Carr, Nicholas. *The Shallows: What the Internet is Doing to Our Brains.* New York: W. W. Norton & Company, 2010.

"The Human Memory." Luke Mastin. Last modified 2010. http://www.human-memory.net/processes_encoding.html.

Jones, Steve. "Pew Internet & American Life Project." Pew Research Center. Last modified July 6 2003. http://www.pewinternet.org/Reports/2003/Let-the-games-begin-Gaming-technology-and-college-students/2-Gaming-Comes-of-Age.aspx?view=all.

Lovett, Haley A. "Finding Dulcinea." Dulcinea Media, Inc. Last modified September 9 2010. http://www.findingdulcinea.com/news/education/2009/march/Students-Using-Laptops-in-Class-Do-Worse-on-Tests.html.

"Netcraft." *Netcraft Ltd.* Last modified May 2 2012. http://news.netcraft.com/archives/2012/05/02/may-2012-web-server-survey.html.

Platanik, Pablo. "Platanik Factor." N.p. Last modified October 9 2007. http://palatnikfactor.com/2007/10/09/top-10-sites-visited-by-college-students-men-vs-women/.

"Website Optimization." N.p., Last modified May 31 2011. http://www.websiteoptimization.com/speed/tweak/average-web-page/.

AUTHOR PROFILE

I am the first in my family to go to college and am studying zoology. After college, I hope to pursue a career in wildlife conservation. Although my family is originally from Mexico, my siblings and I were born and raised in the small town of Lompoc, California.

—*Blanca Lopez*

---

9 The Human Memory, Luke Mastin, last modified 2010, http://www.human-memory.net/processes_encoding.html.

10 Haley A. Lovett, Finding Dulcinea, Dulcinea Media, Inc., last modified September 9, 2010, http://www.findingdulcinea.com/news/education/2009/march/Students-Using-Laptops-in-Class-Do-Worse-on-Tests.html.

WHY NOT? THE UNKNOWN POTENTIAL OF THE PROPER USE OF COGNITIVE ENHANCEMENT

Bradley Afroilan

Instructor: Ilene Miele

"Research on cognitive enhancers, like Adderall and Ritalin, is a worthwhile investment, but it is a difficult investment to get subsidized because of the generalizations that cognitive enhancement damages health, challenges academic integrity, and threatens personal identity."

In May of 2010, Kyle Craig, a thriving student at Vanderbilt University "stepped out in front of a passenger train and ended his life at the age of 21" (James, 2010). Friends and family considered Kyle Craig as a very social kid, and his mother saw him as a "bright light" (James, 2010). What could have made this aspiring young man take his own life? While Craig appeared happy, his secret use of the drug Adderall, normally used to treat patients suffering from ADHD, led to his untimely demise. As a result of trying to keep up with his friends, Craig used Adderall in order to stay focused on his studies and even "[took] more, mixing it with alcohol" just to party (James, 2010). However, Craig's abuse was more serious than even he knew; his abuse lead to psychosis, or as Frank K. Berger from the National Library of Medicine states, a "loss of contact with reality" because he could not enjoy life like he used to in the past (Berger, 2012). Imagine being in this position: doing so well, but wanting to do so much more. Would you risk your life by taking a drug that might kill you just to keep up with others? While most people after hearing stories about people like Kyle Craig probably say no, the question is why not?

The way news stations portray these incidents instills the idea in people that cognitive enhancement can only lead to negative experiences. However, law school professor Henry Greely of Stanford University states that studies show that Adderall and Ritalin "increase executive functions…in most healthy people" (Greely et al., 2008). This issue is definitely split because one side states its danger and the other side states its potential, which will never be known unless research can be done. Research on cognitive enhancers, like Adderall and Ritalin, is a worthwhile investment, but it is a difficult investment to get subsidized because of the generalizations that cognitive enhancement damages health, challenges academic integrity, and threatens personal identity. Consequently, these negative notions about cognitive enhancement heavily influence society's decision to not use these enhancers, even though these enhancers can lead to a new potential in human society.

While research on cognitive enhancement is a worthy investment, there are many negative notions about the issue that prevent research. Researchers Lynn Hagger of the University of Sheffield and Gareth Hagger Johnson of the University College of London state that research on the drug Ritalin back in the 1960s is the closest thing we have to a study done on cognitive enhancement, which is defined as "methods to improve the psychological functioning of individuals who are not ill" (Hagger and Johnson, 2011). Ritalin is primarily given to patients suffering from ADHD in order to allow them to focus on given tasks and be calmer. However, Ritalin and other cognitive-enhancing drugs like Adderall have shown to also increase focus in individuals who do not suffer from ADHD. Unfortunately, there has not been a lot of research done on cognitive enhancement because of the media's coverage of incidents like what happened to Kyle Craig. As a result, philosopher Nick Bostrom at the University of Oxford states that "there is scant data at the current time on such 'ecological effects' of cognitive enhancers" (2010). Researchers of cognitive enhancement do not know what the effects of these drugs, like Adderall or Ritalin, are. Perhaps patients would respond like Kyle Craig, perhaps not.

In regard to academics, Adderall and Ritalin are prohibited because Bostrom (2010) states that school authorities claim that "such drugs enable users to gain an unfair advantage, and that therefore the rules ought to be changed so as to prohibit them." Since school authorities believe that these drugs create an imbalance in common classrooms or on major tests like the ACT and SAT, these drugs are considered illegal. Furthermore, Hagger and Johnson (2011) state that cognitive-enhancing drugs have "potential effects on personal identity, which is a core aspect of self." As seen in the case of Kyle Craig, many students abuse drugs because they have so much pressure from family, friends, and, most of all, themselves. As a result of competition and trying to keep up, many students go to unnecessary lengths to meet the expectations of others, even if it means endangering their lives by the use of drugs. Unfortunately, since research has not been done, students do not know the outcome of taking these drugs, and they are at the mercy of the drugs. They may succeed and do very well in school and social life, but there is also the possibility that they can develop a psychological disease which can affect their normal interaction with other people. Sometimes, it is not even the child making the decision to use the drug; sometimes children "are taking enhancing drugs at the behest of achievement oriented parents" (Greely et al., 2008). Bostrom (2003) asks "are we really prepared to sacrifice on the altar of consumerism even those deep values that are embodied in traditional relationship between child and parents?" Parents forcing children to take cognitive-enhancing drugs is like turning them into just an object, a product that took time and money to create. Consequently, because of these negative connotations about cognitive enhancement, the general public does not want to partake or have any research done. However, the world will never know the potential of these enhancements unless research is allowed.

While there are many negative notions that influence the perspective of cognitive enhancement, if this perspective shifted, more people would try these drugs. It is generally accepted that if something can make us better, we should capitalize on the opportunity because it will put us in a better position in life. Even though there are all these negative reviews of Ritalin and Adderall, these drugs can enhance people by "improving their abilities to focus their attention, manipulate information in working memory and flexibly control their responses" (Greely et al., 2008). Just because something negative about the issue exists does not mean that human society should not do research. In regard to the negative ideas that surround children taking cognitive enhancing drugs, some parents may find it "easier to love a child who thanks to enhancement is bright, beautiful, healthy, and happy" (Bostrom, 2003). All parents want to give the best to their children because the parents want them to succeed in life. Even though it seems that children do not have a voice in the drug-taking decision, they do know the difference between what is right and wrong. They know that cheating is wrong, but if school authorities state that "enhancement is not regarded as cheating, children may regret being enhanced later in life" (Hagger and Johnson, 2011). If the children did not enhance at a young age, even when the cognitive enhancers were considered conventional, they could feel as if they missed out on a large opportunity later in life.

In conventional terms, some parents will go to great lengths and may even hire personal tutors for the child or put them into a private school. These two are also forms of enhancement because tutors and private schools can give many advantages to the child, such as personalized learning plans or free resources like college counseling. However, why is it that tutors and private schools are appropriate and legal? It is because they are considered "conventional…such as education, mental techniques, neurological health initiatives, external information technology, and epistemic" (Bostrom, 2010)? The way students, parents, and most people view cognitive enhancement depends completely on whether or not society deems them appropriate or inappropriate, conventional or unconventional. Even though education may be conventional, Norman Daniels, a bioethicist at Harvard University, states that education is "already an enhancement technology, merely another of the ways in which 'our uniquely innovative species tries to improve itself'" (as cited by Hagger and Johnson, 2011). Education may be socially accepted, but that is because any good set of rules can restrict what is appropriate and what is inappropriate. Cognitive enhancements are unconventional "largely due to the fact that they are currently novel and experimental rather than to any problem inherent in the technologies themselves" (Bostrom, 2010). However, if research is allowed and it finds that cognitive enhancement can safely increase cognitive functions of the mind, just like "oral contraceptives, IVF, and even the telescope," which were once controversial but now accepted, these enhancers will be more accepted by the public (Bostrom, 2010). Once society sees that research on cognitive enhancement shows positive results, society will accept the use of them. However, if society "[allows] status quo bias to affect our attitudes towards enhancement [it] could result in our missing out on valuable goods" (Bostrom, 2010).

The main concern for research is to clear the slate of negative experiences of cognitive enhancement. Research on cognitive enhancement must be regulated "in order to ensure that the public is protected from the worst harms of irresponsible enhancement use" (Bostrom, 2010). It is such a controversial issue that it must be regulated carefully so that the test subjects, as well as the individuals who have decided to partake, are safe. Even though the research may be deemed safe by society, the last decision always comes down to the individual. Cognitive enhancement would be like smoking cigarettes—the government approves of them, but it is up to the individual to decide whether or not

he or she will smoke. In addition, there are benefits to cognitive enhancement that would give an incentive to people who want to make them legal. All the money that is made off of cognitive enhancement "would be invested in providing medical necessities for the least well off, and the remaining funds would be allocated to finance education" (Dubljevic, 2012). All this money would go to those who cannot afford medical aid, and it would go to education, another form of enhancement that in today's day and age desperately needs funding. The key word here is moderation because even though there is regulation, there will still be many people who will be against the use of these drugs.

If research is a success, there will be plenty of people who will accept and use the drugs, but there will still be many opponents. Ritalin and Adderall were originally only for patients suffering from ADHD to help them focus, but these drugs also could help people who are healthy to focus even more. Many people who oppose the research on cognitive enhancement, and the use of these drugs, may argue that the use of these enhancers would create a larger inequality. However, even without cognitive enhancement, natural selection "may have favored a balance between different personality traits, some helpful and some harmful, depending on the environment and situation" (Hagger and Johnson, 2011). Unfortunately, by natural selection, someone is always better than someone else. Even though Ritalin and Adderall were originally for patients suffering from ADHD, these drugs can open a new field for people who do not have ADHD.

The opponents of cognitive enhancement drugs, specifically believers of Christianity, may be against the drugs because researchers would be "playing God, messing with nature, tampering with our human essence, or displaying punishable hubris" (Bostrom, 2010). However, researchers could discover and unlock new potentials in the brain which can make a new society, a "post human society" (Bostrom, 2003). This society would no doubt be more advanced and more mature than our current society in many different ways. These 'post humans' would be "smarter than us, that can read books in seconds, that are much more brilliant philosophers than we are, that can create artworks, which, even if we could understand them only on the most superficial level, would strike us as wonderful masterpieces" (Bostrom, 2010). This seems like a wonderful concept and is completely possible because there have been many past medical breakthroughs that have improved human life, such as with pain relievers. Just like pain relievers, cognitive enhancers like Aderall and Ritalin would make our brains better. In regard to a change in personality, it may not be as serious of a case like with Kyle Craig's psychosis if the research and tests are regulated properly. In fact, Bostrom states that we "may favor future people being post-human rather than human, if the post-human beings would lead lives more worthwhile than the alternative humans would lead" (2010). Hopefully, if research is done correctly and in moderation, these post-humans will be smarter than us and better than us. They might be able to cure malignant diseases like cancer and AIDS and may have answers to questions that even the smartest people cannot answer. However, we will never know unless research is done. There is a potential society that can exist just because of research in cognitive enhancement.

While there is a split perspective on the issue of cognitive enhancement, it is a worthy investment because a whole new society may arise from this research. However, regulation is necessary for this cognitive enhancement research to be done because it still is a controversial issue. As time goes by and research is done, cognitive enhancement will hopefully be socially accepted. It will definitely take some time to be accepted, but eventually many people will accept the use of Ritalin and Adderall as part of the status quo. However, there still will always be a few problems surrounding cognitive enhancement like opponents of drugs and those who abuse them. In regard to science and research, "the pursuit of knowledge (as represented by cognitive enhancement) is a legitimate claim" (Hagger and Johnson, 2011). This research is in the name of knowledge for knowledge's sake because if we never try, then we will never know the possibilities.

REFERENCES

Berger, F. K. (2012, March 7). *Psychosis.* Retrieved from http://www.ncbi.nlm.nih.gov/pubmedhealth/PMH0002520/

Bostrom, N. (2003). Human genetic enhancements: A transhumanist perspective. *The Journal of Value Inquiry, 37*(4), 493–506. Retrieved from http://www.springerlink.com/content/r45507622j852433/fulltext.pdf

Bostrom, N. (2010). Smart policy: Cognitive enhancement and the public interest. *Contemporary Readings in Law & Social Justice, 2*(1), 68–84. Retrieved from http://web.ebscohost.com/ehost/pdfviewer/pdfviewer?sid=1ffb6737-5a0b-46de-95b8-a95cfb63d266@sessionmgr11&vid=2&hid=7

Dubljevic, V. (2012). Principles of justice as the basis for public policy on psychopharmacological cognitive enhancement. *Law, Innovation & Technology, 4*(1), 67–83. Retrieved from http://web.ebscohost.com/ehost/pdfviewer/pdfviewer?sid=e26698a9-0b4f-46ac-b2fb-8e5abc5e881a@sessionmgr14&vid=2&hid=21

Hagger, L., & Hagger Johnson, G. (2011). Super kids' regulating the use of cognitive and psychological enhancement in children. *Law, Innovation & Technology, 3*(1), 137–166. Retrieved from http://web.ebscohost.com/ehost/pdfviewer/pdfviewer?sid=446294cf-1abd499a-8059-43da0f7d5161@sessionmgr15&vid=2&hid=126

James, S. D. (2010, November 10). Adderall abuse alters brain, claims a young life. *ABC News.* Retrieved from http://abcnews.go.com/Health/MindMoodNews/adderall-psychosis-suicidecollege-students-abuse-study-drug/story?id=12066619

AUTHOR PROFILE

My name is Bradley Afroilan, and I am an eighteen-year-old freshman here at UCSB. I am majoring in sociology and hopefully will also major in psychology. I am from San Jose, California. I like to run, play guitar, and play with dogs.

—*Bradley Afroilan*

THE WESTERN SNOWY PLOVER: THREATENED BY HUMANS, PREDATORS, OR ITSELF?

Peter Cross

Instructor: LeeAnne Kryder

"As a chick, the Western Snowy Plover is vulnerable to human beings, predators, and exotic plant species. Therefore, the most important factor in restoring the Western Snowy Plover population is enabling as many chicks to reach adulthood as possible."

ABSTRACT

The Western Snowy Plover is a threatened species with a steadily declining population. This decline is mostly due to the fact that this species nests on very open areas on the beach; it is constantly vulnerable to predators and human influences. Out of all the ages, the chicks are most susceptible; in fact, most of the declining population is in the chick population. In this paper, I go into detail of why the Western Snowy Plover's chick population is declining and how that affects the net population decline as well.

INTRODUCTION

On the beaches of the University of California Santa Barbara (UCSB) lives the Western Snowy Plover (*Charadrius alexandrinus*). These small gray and white birds are about six inches tall, and are commonly seen running rapidly on the beaches close to Manzanita Village. In 1973, the Western Snowy Plover was listed as a threatened species by the United States Fish and Wildlife Services (USFWS). Why is it that such an agile, swift-running species, which would not even let me get within the proximity of 10 meters, is declining in population to the point of being threatened? The answer lies in three major points: the introduction of non-native species, intervention of human beings, and predation by other bird species. Other factors, such as age, parental care, nesting habits, and reactions toward humans and other predators also contributed to these three key reasons.

METHODS

I did most of my research online, looking up academic journals through the UCSB library database. The studies I read were not necessarily on the Western Snowy Plover population at UCSB but on the populations at other beaches in California. In order not to be too close to the lagoon, I decided to conduct my observations at the beach southwest of the Manzanita dormitories of UCSB. I visited this location three times this weekend: the first visit was at noon on the twelfth of October, the second visit was at three o'clock p.m. on the thirteenth of October, and the third visit was at seven o'clock p.m. on the fourteenth of October. I sat at the same spot for all three days and recorded all my information from observations and databases in a notebook.

I observed the interactions between the Western Snowy Plover and humans, looking at how humans disturbed the Western Snowy

Plover's habitat and how the Western Snowy Plover reacted to human beings. I also looked at the plants and seaweed on the beaches and how the Western Snowy Plovers interacted with them.

RESULTS

Colwell, McAllister, Millett, Transou, Mullin, Nelson, Wilson, and LeValley (2007) state that "many plovers nested in fine, sandy substrates of ocean-fronting beaches amidst sparse debris fields of dried brown algae, shells, dead vegetation, driftwood, and occasional garbage" (p. 379). In beaches open to recreational use by humans, these nests are located right where humans walk, run, and lie down. However, when I went to the beach southwest of the Manzanita dormitories of UCSB, I was unable to find any nests in the sand.

Predators of the Western Snowy Plover consist of Common Ravens (*Corvus corax*), American Crows (*C. brachyrhynchos*), Gulls (*Carus*), Turkey Vultures (*Cathartes aura*), Double Crested Cormorants (*Phalacrocorax auritus*), and Canada Geese (*Branta canadensis*). There is a spread of exotic plant species, such as the European Beachgrass (*Ammophila arneria*), in the habitats of these Western Snowy Plovers as well. At the beach of UCSB, I saw a multitude of patches of Brown Algae (*Phaeophyceae*), which is actually a native species to the beach. These algae were dispersed everywhere, and I was unable to find any exotic species.

The Western Snowy Plover's behavior changes with age and the way it is raised. Colwell, Hurley, Hall, and Dinsmore (2007) found that "by 10 days of age, there was a 90% chance that chicks approached by a human would run away" (p. 643). This is consistent with my observation at the UCSB beach, for I was unable to get within 10–15 meters of an adult Western Snowy Plover. However, studies also showed that when approached by predators, most chicks didn't flee but froze; Colwell, Hurley, Hall, and Dinsmore (2007) found that "nearly all (33 of 34) chicks lay motionless in response to the approach of a potential avian predator" (p. 643). Unfortunately, I was unable to observe this for myself because I did not see any avian predators approach Western Snowy Plover chicks during my visits.

Colwell, Hurley, Hall, and Dinsmore (2007) found that "brooding also played a role in a chick's survival. Overall, chicks that fledged were brooded less on average (35% ± 2%) than those that did not survive (69% ± 5%; $F_{1,285} = 6.3$, $P = 0.01$)" (p. 643). In this same study, it became evident that the Western Snowy Plover has longer brooding periods than most other plovers. While other plovers, such as the piping plover (*Charadrius melodus*) and the Semipalmated Plover (*Charadrius semipalmatus*), do not brood after 14 and 5 days respectively, the Western Snowy Plover can brood up until its chick is a fledging. During my visits at the beach, I also observed an adult Western Snowy Plover brooding its young.

DISCUSSION

The nesting habits of the Western Snowy Plover are a key reason why the species' population is declining. Since the Western Snowy Plover builds its nest on the ocean-front sands of the beach, it is vulnerable to many avian predators, such as the Turkey Vulture. Furthermore, the Western Snowy Plover chicks immobilize themselves in the presence of a predator. These two factors make a Western Snowy Plover chick an easy target; this is one reason for the decline in population of the Western Snowy Plover.

Even in the absence of these predators, many beaches are occupied by human recreational activity. This either leads to the destruction of eggs and nests or to the migration of the Snowy Plover into other, less suitable habitats.

The exotic plant species also inhibits the Western Snowy Plover from making a standard nest. This inhibition leads to a decline of breeding, which leads to a decline in population; however, in the area I observed, I did not see any exotic plant species; all I saw was the brown algae, which is a native species at this beach. Despite the presence of these native species, I did not see any Western Snowy Plover nests on the beach. This is most likely a result of human inhabitation forcing the Western Snowy Plover to build nests elsewhere unnaturally.

The Western Snowy Plover's long brooding period also contributes to the decline of the population. Simply stated, it is much easier for an avian predator to spot an adult Western Snowy Plover brooding with its chicks than to just see the smaller chicks themselves. When an avian predator descends to hunt, the parent will flee instinctively. The chicks, having been sheltered for so long, become confused and immobilize themselves, and as a result are consumed by these avian predators. Due to these long brooding periods, chicks do not escape from parental care, and this lack of independence makes the chicks a more susceptible target to predators. This explains the fact that the chicks that fledged were brooded less on average than those that were not.

Throughout this research, it became evident that the Western Snowy Plover became threatened due to the vulnerability of its chick population and to its ocean-fronting nesting habits. As a chick, the Western Snowy Plover is vulnerable to human beings, predators, and exotic plant species. Therefore, the most important factor in restoring the Western Snowy Plover population is enabling as many chicks to reach adulthood as possible. Once the Western Snowy Plover has fledged, it is generally able to escape danger and to survive.

When matured, these birds are swift and cautious. However, a one-sided caution by the Western Snowy Plover is insufficient at times. We humans must also be cautious of our environment; we must watch where we are stepping when walking on the beach, for this is where the Western Snowy Plover builds its nests.

REFERENCES

Brindock, K. M., Colwell, M. A. (2011). Habitat selection by western snowy plovers during the nonbreeding season. *Journal of Wildlife Management,* 75(4), 786–793.

Colwell, M. A., McAllister, S. E., Millett, C. B., Transou, A. N., Mullin, S. M. Nelson, Z. J., Wilson, C. A., LeValley R. R. (2007). Philopatry and natal dispersal of the western snowy plover. *The Wilson Journal of Ornithology*, 119(3), 378–385.

Colwell, M.A., Hurley, S. J., Hall, J. N., Dinsmore, S. J. (2007). Age-related survival and behavior of snowy plover chicks. *The Condor*, 109(3), 638–647.

Mullin, S. M., Colwell, M. A., McAllister S. E., Dinsmore, S. J. (2010). Apparent survival and population growth of snowy plovers in coastal northern california. *Journal of Wildlife Management*, 74(8), 1792–1798.

AUTHOR PROFILE

This is an essay I wrote after multiple visits to the beaches at UCSB. It focuses on my observations of the Western Snowy Plover. I am currently a student at UCSB, and I was enrolled in Dr. Kryder's 2LK class. Although my major is undeclared, I love writing, and I am considering a career in journalism.

—Peter Cross

Photo by Marisol Jimenez

WRITING 2

SERIOUS
INQUIRY

WHAT EFFECTS DO SEXUALLY DEGRADING LYRICS HAVE ON YOUNG PEOPLE'S IMAGE OF MODERN GENDER ROLES AND SEXUAL POLITICS?

Zoe Kam

Instructor: Leslie Hammer

> **"**The ready availability of uncensored lyrics and videos has definitely led to the premature sexualization of childhood.**"**

INTRODUCTION

Rap and hip-hop have been the dominating musical favorites among America's youth for at least the past thirty years. Although frequently criticized for its often virulently degrading lyrics, rap music represents a hugely influential, multi-billion dollar industry. Indeed, the fact that the rap industry is so powerful among American youth is a cause for much worry among much of older, more conservative America. The sexually degrading lyrics of modern hip-hop must have some visible effect on American youth. This paper seeks to find the effects that degrading lyrics have on modern gender roles and sexual politics, especially as perceived by young people. I hypothesize that sexually denigrating lyrics in popular music have caused a premature sexualization of childhood, a stereotypical misogynistic characterization of women, and the creation of a "sexual economy of illicit eroticism" (Miller-Young, 2008, p. 264).

THE SEXUALIZATION OF CHILDHOOD

Few would dispute that American youth are becoming sexualized at increasingly younger ages. Teen pregnancy has become a nationwide dilemma that is affecting people across all race and class boundaries. Even if not engaging in the act of sex, almost all youngsters are exposed to sometimes quite blatant sexual themes in the media. This exposure can be seen in the way that teens are dressing and behaving—in the clothing styles and dance moves that have become provocative to the point of indecency.

Rap music cannot be blamed directly for the increasing sexualization of childhood, but it is safe to say that the popularity of this music in the last 30 years has coincided with an extreme sexualization of mainstream society. Hip-hop culture (culture that mirrors the lifestyle that rappers present in their music—careless promiscuity, explicit dancing, alcohol and marijuana use, extravagance) has definitely influenced the lifestyles of American youth. Munoz-Laboy, Weinstein, and Parker (2007) argue that much of American youth actually construct their gender identity through hip-hop culture (p. 615). The researchers conducted in-depth interviews with many young clubbers, who spoke casually of promiscuity, groping on the dance floor, and sexually explicit explanations of what goes on at clubs (Munoz-Laboy, Weinstein, and Parker, 2007, p. 619–623). Keep in mind, these were not normal 21+ clubbers. In fact, the mean ages were 17.9 for men and 15.3 for women (Munoz-Laboy, Weinstein, and Parker, 2007, p. 618). To an onlooker, these people seem far too young to speak with such experience on sexual matters. It can be assumed that the music played in these clubs was hip-hop and that lyrics like Ludacris' "How Low" (2010) were specifically directing their behavior:

> She could go lower than I ever really thought she could
>
> Face down, ass up
>
> The top of your booty jiggling out your jeans, baby pull your pants up (Ludacris, "How Low," 2010)

The consumers of music like this are largely, if not entirely, young people like those interviewed at the clubs. It can be assumed from there that the ease with which sex is obtained and disregarded by these youngsters is highly influenced by the sexual nature of the lyrics of the music and also by the lifestyle that the lyrics recommend. Their gender identities are constructed by hip-hop culture, as are their perceptions of how healthy sexual interactions should occur.

Children have also been increasingly sexualized by the lyrics of rap music and by the mere fact that it is playing almost everywhere at all times. One need only step into a restaurant, a dorm room, or just turn on the radio to hear one of the many popular rap songs. This music has pervaded mainstream society. At this moment, six rap songs are on Billboard's Top 20 Chart (2012), an impressive number considering the relatively recent birth of the genre. A huge portion of young people are exposed to this music, whether they seek it out or not. The problem lies in the fact that the pornographic nature of the lyrics and the videos is almost not at all censored. The difference between "clean" and "explicit" versions consists of changing the word "bitch" to "chick" and "nigga" to "gangsta", although it is argued that explicit versions are much more popular, and that though the profane word is replaced, the listener is still aware of what word is supposed to be there (Hunter, 2011, p. 21). Even some music videos that are past soft-pornography and are clearly in the domain of real porn are available for viewing on web sites like YouTube ("Make it Nasty" by Tyga is one recent example). The ready availability of uncensored lyrics and videos has definitely led to the premature sexualization of childhood.

THE STEREOTYPICAL MISOGYNISTIC CHARACTERIZATION OF WOMEN

> Imma sip Moscato and you gon' lose them pants
>
> And Imma throw this money while you do it with no hands
>
> Girl, drop it to the floor, I love the way your booty go
>
> All I wanna do is sit back and watch you move
>
> And I'll proceed to throw this cash (Waka Flocka, "No Hands," 2011)

Although the lyrics to this chart-topping song by Waka Flocka may not seem to be virulently misogynistic, its subtle themes of power and control nicely illustrate the true problems with rap music with regard to women. Waka Flocka describes a scene in which a female is not only dancing for him, but is also rewarding him with sexual favors, while he sits, watches, judges, and decides whether or not to "throw this cash" on her, virtually debasing her to the status of a stripper. This is where the true misogyny lies—not just in regarding women as "bitches" or characterizing them by their behinds—but in the subtle control that rappers exert over their female characters and in the female eagerness to please the rapper.

Views like this are dangerous when they settle into the minds of young people. They present women as objects that find worthiness in their ability to perform sexually. The closest that a woman can get to being humanized is being treated like a stripper. When this idea finds its way into young men's minds, violence and objectification of women are inevitable.

This pervasive idea can be seen illustrated in modern dance culture. Dancing styles of young people today are no longer innocent partnerships; they represent powerful gender inequalities (Munoz-Laboy, Weinstein, Parker, p. 625, 2007). Although both members take part in the dance, "grinding" involves the male mimicking sexual penetration of a woman, usually vigorously or violently, furthering the idea of male domination. It can be assumed that the music incites the dancing, therefore that the lyrics incite the type of dancing. The lyrics like those by Ludacris mentioned above create a male-empowering identity for young men and an objectification of women as something to either be rubbed or gazed upon.

The newest development in rap music that is worrisome to those trying to reverse misogynistic views of women is the growing number of women who have accepted the image assigned them by hip-hop culture and who actually portray themselves as such. Virtually all young party-going women are okay with the debasing dance form of grinding. Preteen girls have even been noted as identifying themselves as "freaks" (Stokes, 2007, p. 175) and "bytches" (Stokes, 2007, p. 177). Of course, this willingness of everyday teenagers to represent themselves negatively can be connected to the fact that many female hip-hop role models have also embraced the image.

Singer Rihanna's lyrics represent a quiet acceptance of abuse and a submission, even adoration, of male dominance:

> Just gonna stand there and watch me burn
>
> Well that's alright because I like the way it hurts
>
> Just gonna stand there and hear me cry
>
> Well that's alright because I love the way you lie (Eminem feat. Rihanna, "Love the Way you Lie," 2010)

Newest female rap sensation, Nicki Minaj, represents a full female immersion in misogyny. In almost all of her songs, Minaj objectifies herself and her sexual relations. Rather than using her power over popular culture as a female model of strength and independence, Minaj further debases herself and all women:

> Somebody point me to the best ass-eater
>
> I tell him "Pussy clean!" I tell him "Pussy squeaky!"
>
> Niggas give me brain [oral sex], cause all of them niggas geeky (Big Sean feat. Nicki Minaj, "Dance (Ass)," 2011)

THE CREATION OF THE SEXUAL ECONOMY OF ILLICIT EROTICISM

Finally, rap music has created what Mireielle Miller-Young calls the "sexual economy of illicit eroticism" (Miller-Young, 2008, p. 264). This is the idea that in male–female interactions, both parties are mutually dependent on one another, exchanging different parts of their sexualities in order to both benefit from the interaction. Unlike mainstream views of relationships (where both parties mutually receive love and support) in these relationships, both parties gain image and access. What this economy promotes is hypermasculinity and hypersexuality. There is a "dependence on black women, especially their sexualized bodies, by black men in authenticating their claims and representations of manhood." (Miller-Young, 2008, p. 264). Though the rappers call their women "ho's," they clearly depend on these "ho's" to maintain their manly status. In this way, the female does have power in the rap world—her hypersexuality undergirds male hypermasculinity. Females can also be seen as gaining from the situation; they "mobilize their sexualities in the marketplace of desire for their own interests of access, opportunity, mobility, and fame." (Miller-Young, 2008, p. 264).

Why is this economy a problem? It produces gender identities through the commodification and manipulation of sex—identities which are then consumed and recorded by youth. Although the economy is mutually beneficial, it simultaneously creates manipulative and unhealthy gender roles.

CONCLUSION

Many defenders of rap music will argue that the lyrics are truly harmless and that young people listen to hip-hop for its musical value and not as real life advice. I do not mean to assert that young people go to rap music (or any kind of music for that matter) directly looking for advice on how to live their lives. However, many rappers stand as role models to young people. When these impressionable teens hear Drake calling women "bitches" and insist on treating them like sex objects, it becomes much more acceptable and even "cool" for them to do the same. The casual degradation of women and the fact that young people are very receptive to the demands of popular culture creates a situation in which music does indeed play a powerful role.

Snoop Dogg, a huge rap superstar, has been quoted as defending misogyny in his music, saying, "We're talking about ho's that's in the 'hood that ain't doing—that's trying to get a nigga for his money," (Moore 2007). This outlook is precisely what has led to the stereotype of African-American women. Rappers justify their lyrics by even further debasing black women—they're not talking about collegiate women or white women, but "ho's that's in the 'hood," creating a distinction between the women and allowing for one group to be abused but not the other.

"Because commercial rap is so formulaic in both lyrics and videos, it communicates a specific gender ideology that supports the culture of consumption. Music videos and lyrics communicate sexual and gendered 'scripts' where males and female characters act out life's dramas. Young people internalize these highly repetitive scripts and often use them to understand their own and others' lives." (Hunter, 2011, p. 31). The sexually denigrating lyrics of modern rap have led to the extreme transformation of sexual politics and gender roles in young people's eyes, as seen through the premature sexualization of childhood, the stereotypical misogynistic characterization of women, and the creation of a sexual economy of illicit eroticism.

REFERENCES

Adams, T. M., Fuller, D. B. (2006). The words have changes but the ideology remains the same: Misogynistic lyrics in rap music. In Editor Unknown, *Journal of Black Studies* (pp. 938–957). Thousand Oaks, CA: Sage Publications, Inc.

Big Sean (featuring Nicki Minaj) (2011) Dance (Ass). *Finally Famous*. G.O.O.D. Music/Def Jam Records.

Billboard. (2013, May 25). Hot 100. Retrieved May 25, 2013, from Billboard.com website: http://www.billboard.com/charts/hot-100

Eminem (featuring Rihanna) (2010) Love the way you lie. *Recovery*. Interscope-Geffen-A&M.

Hunter, M. (2011). Shake it, baby, shake it: Consumption and the new gender relationship in Hip-Hop. In Editor Unknown, *Social Perspectives* (pp. 15–36). Berkeley, CA: University of California Press.

Ludacris (2009) How low. *Battle of the Sexes*. DTP/Def Jam Records

Miller-Young, M. (2008). Hip hop honeys and da hustlaz: Black sexualities in the new hip-hop pornography. In Editor Unknown, *Meridians* (pp. 261–292). Bloomington, IN: Indiana University Press.

Moore, T. (2007, April 15). Filthy, degrading lyrics paying huge dividends. *New York Daily News*. Retrieved from http://www.nydailynews.com/

Munoz-Laboy, M., Parker, R., Weinstein, H. (2007). The hip-hop club scene: Gender, grinding, and sex. In Editor Unknown, *Culture, Health, and Sexuality* (pp. 615–628). Abingdon, UK: Taylor & Francis, Ltd.

Waka Flocka Flame (featuring Roscoe Dash and Wale) (2010) No hands. *Flockaveli*. 1017 Brick Squad/Warner Bros./Asylum.

Stokes, C. E. (2007). Representin' in cyberspace: Sexual scripts, self-definition, and hip-hop culture in black american adolescent girls' home pages. In Editor Unknown, *Culture, Health, and Sexuality* (pp. 169–184). Abingdon, UK: Taylor & Francis, Ltd.

AUTOR PROFILE

I am a first year at UCSB majoring in comparative literature with a minor in history. I am a member of the gospel choir and the English club. My favorite pastimes are singing and creative writing.

—*Zoe Kam*

NOT THE AVERAGE OUTING

Jaime So

Instructor: Wendy Hurford

"As a passenger on the raft, all she could do while riding a rapid was hold on for dear life, duck low, and hope that her navigator got them through alright."

It was August of 2009 when my mother, Beverly, packed up all of her essential outdoor gear and embarked on the adventure of a lifetime. For sixteen days she left me and my sister in the less-than-capable hands of my father as she went on a rafting trip through the Grand Canyon on the Colorado River. Every year, the beautiful Grand Canyon of Arizona attracts hundreds of thousands of visitors from across the globe, and for good reason. It's a wonderfully scenic place with towering vermillion rock walls, historical sites, abundant wildlife, and numerous cascading tributaries to explore. The best way to experience all that the canyon has to offer is to travel through the canyon's interior on a boat trip down the Colorado River. Rafting the Colorado River is an unpredictable and thrilling experience unlike any other in the world. Although Beverly's personal experience was amazing, she noticed many unsettling problems that threaten recreation on the Colorado. I found two articles that effectively explained the issues that Beverly noticed while rafting the river. The articles "A River Runs Through Them" by Michael Tennesen and "Straight Flush" by Sid Perkins explain the negative effects that dams, such as the Glen Canyon Dam, have on the Colorado River environment. Beverly's rafting party started their journey right beneath the Glen Canyon Dam, and just about every issue can be traced back to the dams on the Colorado. The additions of dams such as the Glen Canyon Dam, have significantly changed the Colorado River landscape, and subsequently, the rafting experience for recreational river travelers like Beverly and her group.

Beverly's rafting party consisted of six rafts and fifteen people total, many of which were veteran adventurers who had rafted down the Colorado River before. They were all required to attend an orientation by a National Parks ranger prior to embarking on their journey through the canyon. In the orientation, the ranger explained safety procedures and rules about sharing campsites with other river travelers. Here is where the dams pose a problem for recreational river travelers as well as river ecology. First of all, dams trap sediment that would usually flow down the river, and they add to riverside beaches and sandbars (Perkins 152). Also, water released from the dam fluctuates according to energy demand, as the dam is used to generate hydroelectric power for surrounding urban areas; instead of water levels fluctuating seasonally, they rise and fall within a twenty-four hour period (Perkins 152). This causes excess erosion on the beaches that line the river, and this is important because, "The riverside landforms are important for several reasons. Ecologically, they provide habitat for wildlife and vegetation as well as spawning grounds for fish. The fine-grained features also serve as campsites for the multitude of rafters and hikers passing through the Grand Canyon" (Perkins 152). Finding a sandbar suitable for parking six rafts and having sleeping space for fifteen people would be hard enough even without the excess erosion. With even less space for the many travelers who pass through the Canyon on a regular basis, park rangers have to make a point to tell them all to take extra care to be considerate of other people's needs for camping space.

The erosion of riverside beaches and sandbars also affects the non-natural features that make the Grand Canyon unique. For example; "the sediments safeguard hundreds of archaeological sites along the waterway, protecting them from the forces of erosion and the prying eyes of vandals or artifact collectors" (Perkins 152). Most of the trip down the river involves exploring the inside of the canyon on foot, away from the boats, and some of the most interesting things to see while on a hike, aside from natural phenomena, are historical sites. One of the sites Beverly visited was the granaries of Nankoweap. The granaries are ancient stone brick structures that were built right into the canyon walls by Native Americans. On another hike, her group encountered mining supplies left by prospectors over a hundred years ago. If the river continues to erode the riverbanks in this way, such fascinating landmarks and artifacts may be in danger. Recently though, scientists have been trying to remedy this problem by releasing enough water from the dams to cause floods periodically and redistribute sediment to the river's beaches (Perkins 53). Only time will tell if this method will effectively restore essential sandbars. These man-made floods could also help to ease the rapid problem on the Colorado River.

The rapids are the most thrilling part of the trip down the Colorado River. The ever-changing conditions on the river make the rapids more unpredictable and treacherous every year. Beverly's rafting party did not include any hired guides; everybody there was an experienced outdoor adventurer. Each of the six boats was navigated by a skilled member of the group that had been rafting down the Colorado

before. Every rapid needs to be scouted before anyone tries to ride through it. Scouts try to scope out the safest paths to take through the rapid. To make it through rapids safely, the boat must surf over the rapids and try to avoid getting stuck in holes, eddies or on rocks. Rescuing people from flipped rafts is quite an ordeal. One boat goes through a rapid at a time while some members of the group stay on the shore with lifelines, and other boats that made it through before wait at the bottom of the rapid to catch the capsized boats and their passengers. If the first boat to go down a rapid flips, then its passengers basically have to float helplessly down the river until the other boats catch up to them. Luckily, Beverly's raft made it through the entire trip without flipping. Her boat was the only one in the group to accomplish this. She said about her navigator that, "One couldn't ask for a better boatman," which was great for her because she had to trust his abilities completely. As a passenger on the raft, all she could do while riding a rapid was hold on for dear life, duck low, and hope that her navigator got them through alright.

The addition of dams has not made navigating the rapids of the Colorado River any easier; in fact, it has contributed to making them even more extreme. "In the pre-dam era, many floods were large enough to scour landslide debris from the channel and restore river flow. Boulders can more easily hold their position during today's weaker floods" (Perkins 152). Due to the lack of large seasonal floods, boulders that find their way into the river from landslides riddle the Colorado's famed rapids and make them especially treacherous (Perkins 152). The last rapid that Beverly's group went down was a newer rapid created by these special circumstances. It was the most intense rapid that the group faced. One boat was violently jarred and it catapulted one of its occupants into a hole that Beverly described as a "washing machine." By the time the other members of the group were able to fish him out, the rushing water had stripped off all of his clothes, including his heavy-duty hiking boots. Only his lifejacket stayed on, and he probably owes his life to that. Beverly described riding the rapids as one of the most terrifying experiences of her life, and after hearing the story about her group-mate, I certainly believe her.

Falling into the river while riding a rapid certainly would not be a pleasant experience. In August, the temperatures in the canyon are typically around the high nineties, or even into the one hundreds, every day (Perkins 152). Swimming in the river to cool off is out of the question though because the water temperatures vary between forty and fifty degrees Fahrenheit, far too cold to be comfortable even in ninety-degree weather (Perkins 152). This is one of the side effects of the Glen Canyon Dam. "Whereas the river below Lake Powell once ran hot in the summer months and nearly froze in winter, its water now comes out of the bottom of the Glen Canyon dam, where it's chilled to the mid-40s and only rises to the low 50s" (Tennesen 43). Before the installation of Glen Canyon Dam, the river reached temperatures as high as eighty degrees Fahrenheit during the summer (Tennesen 43). To battle the heat, Beverly's party was equipped with very large pump water guns that they frequently shot at each other. Many of the tributaries that feed into the Colorado are thankfully unchanged and unharmed by the dam's debilitating effects. Beverly's most vivid memories of her trip involve one of these tributaries; a creek that runs through a narrow side canyon called Elves Chasm. The water in Elves Chasm is a bright opaque turquoise color that is caused by the water's alkalinity. For the adventurers, hiking through the chasm involved much climbing over red sandstone boulders and trekking through the odd colored water. Here the water was a comfortably warm temperature, and the members of the group stopped many times to frolic in the turquoise water and slide down small waterfalls.

I may have made it sound like the dams have completely ruined the river rafting experience, but that could not be further from the truth. As of right now, rafting down the Colorado River is still an unforgettable and wonderful experience. Although she shared with me all of the events of her trip, Beverly said that even all that she told me:

> does not even come close to capturing the true experience. We all came off of that river adventure with our different stories and perceptions. I can tell story after story of the shenanigans, humor, fear, and camaraderie of this group but words can't even come close to describing the experience. You have to be there, do it, become part of the white water raft crew and live it yourself to fully understand what it was like to make this journey. I would do it again and again and again! And if life does give me the opportunity to do so it will be a different experience but no less spectacular or wonderful.

However, if the negative side effects of the dams along the Colorado continue to go on unchecked for much longer, then recreation along the river, and the river environment itself, could be in danger. The Colorado River and Grand Canyon of Arizona deserve to be respected and preserved so that people may continue to enjoy their wonder.

WORKS CITED

Perkins, Sid. "Straight Flush." *Science News*, Vol. 167 Issue 10, p. 152–153. 5 March 2005. Print.

Tennesen, Michael. "A River Runs Through Them." *National Parks*, Vol. 80 Issue 1, p. 40–45. Winter 2006. Print.

AUTHOR PROFILE

Jaime So was born in Santa Rosa, California and grew up in the San Francisco Bay Area and Sonoma Wine Country. All members of her family are avid outdoorspeople, and she loves to spend her free time hiking, skiing, and camping. She graduated at the top of her class from Analy High School in Sebastopol and is now a first year Biology major at University of California, Santa Barbara.

—Jaime So

WHY DO THE TERMS IN SENATE BILL 1070 LEAD TO RACIAL PROFILING?

Melissa Carlos

Instructor: Leslie Hammer

> **"**Although Arizona intends to target immigrants of different races, the terms in SB 1070 are left undefined and lead to racial profiling.**"**

INTRODUCTION

Racial profiling has always existed in the United States. Whether we do it unconsciously or consciously, we judge people by their physical appearance. Often, we misjudge people by thinking they behave a certain way when in reality they can be the complete opposite. In recent headlines, Arizona has implemented Senate Bill 1070. Critics of this law say that a section of it contributes to racial profiling and causes law enforcement to single out a certain group of people. Senate Bill 1070 has become national news, and it is one of the strictest anti-immigration laws in effect. Arizona Governor Jan Brewer signed SB 1070 into law on April 23, 2010, with the intent to control the number of undocumented immigrants in Arizona (Williams, 2011). The bill requires law enforcement to stop people whom they suspect to be undocumented, and check their legal status (Corlett, 2011). The controversy behind the law is that law enforcement stops people based on their physical appearance, thereby racially profiling people. Why do the terms in SB 1070 lead to racial profiling? Although Arizona intends to target immigrants of different races, the terms in SB 1070 are left undefined and lead to racial profiling.

THE CONTROVERSY

This bill has led to a nationwide controversy. For example, J. Angelo Corlett (2011) comments on SB 1070, saying that "Police officers can detain and demand papers from anyone they have 'lawful contact' with, but since the law defines illegal immigrants as trespassing while in any part of the U.S., some believe that this gives the police the freedom to question people who are otherwise not breaking the law or engaging in suspicious activity and that this might lead to police abuses" (p. 2). In other words, Corlett is stating that law enforcement officials are open to making their own assumptions as to who looks suspicious. The police can abuse their power by stopping an innocent person based on their looks. Whether a person looks suspicious or not, law enforcement can stop whomever they want and demand to know a person's legal status. Corlett (2011) also adds, "For until law enforcement officers get to know facts about a person's 'race, ethnicity, or national origin,' all they really amount to is officers' perception" (p. 2). Corlett (2011) describes that since officers don't know about a person's background, they perceive them as bad because of what they have been exposed to. According to SB 1070, police officers need to stop people that look like undocumented immigrants, but how is an officer to judge what an undocumented immigrant looks like? Since police officers are exposed to criminals and often think of brown people as criminals, they are going to stop people of color. This may lead to an abuse of their power because they may stop people based on racial stereotypes and false perceptions.

WHAT THE EXPERTS SAY

A critic of racial profiling, Kirk Miller (2013), states, "The notion that police officers may make decisions based on the racial characteristics of citizens threatens the idealistic principles of fair and equal treatment before the law" (p. 33). SB 1070 suggests racism and unequal treatment for undocumented immigrants. This is unfair because law enforcement can stop someone during his or her daily activities and without a plausible excuse. Just by looks, law enforcement officials can stop people and ask them for identification even if the person didn't do anything wrong. Miller (2013) also adds, "Racial profiling presents a fertile arena to examine police policy and practices, because it exists at the intersection of crime control efforts and questions of police procedure, fairness, and accountability" (p. 33). Miller describes that not only is racial profiling an issue, but it also leads to questioning of police policy and their regulations. Law enforcement policies change, and sometimes they are unfair toward racial minorities. Racial minorities receive unfair treatment from police officers because of an unfair assumption that they are all criminals. The terms in SB 1070 lead law enforcement to misjudge people of color and to perceive them as criminals.

Another author, India Williams (2011), states that "Moreover, there are numerous categories of lawfully present aliens who will not have readily available documentation to demonstrate that they are lawfully present" (p. 273). Williams (2011) continues by stating, "The United States also pointed out that its citizens are not required to carry identification, and some citizens might not have easy access to a form of identification that would satisfy the requirement of section 2(B)" (p. 273). In other words, Williams illustrates that this bill affects everyone because since officers must stop people based on looks, people that are legally in the country are also affected. The ambiguity of this bill leaves

officers targeting legal citizens and therefore disrupting the daily lives of citizens. Williams (2011) adds, "The fact that someone is a racial minority cannot alone justify the ordinary criminal stop simply because law enforcement authorities believe that racial minorities are prone to break the law" (p. 274). Williams (2011) goes on to say that racial minorities are targeted because racial stereotypes make all racial minorities seem like criminals when in reality they are not all criminals. Law enforcement must detain people that look like racial minorities because they perceive them to be criminals and people that must be undocumented immigrants in the United States. That may not be true because not all racial minorities are undocumented, and so SB 1070 leads to racially targeting one specific group. Williams (2011) quotes the Supreme Court stating, "[T]he likelihood that any given person of Mexican ancestry is an alien is high enough to make Mexican appearance a relevant factor in making an immigration stop" (p. 274). This statement is an example of racial profiling because the Supreme Court is suggesting detaining only people with Mexican features, and that alone is a plausible reason to stop someone. The Supreme Court is targeting only one certain race and singling them out. Just because someone "looks Mexican" should not be a reason to stop someone.

Moreover, Rodney E. Hero (2010) states that immigrants shape the development of American policies. Hero writes, "The development of this ethno racial order in the United States is a key contextual factor shaping the way that immigrants are incorporated into contemporary American politics" (p. 453). Senate Bill 1070 was influenced by the influx of Mexican immigrants in Arizona. Hero (2010) also writes, "It is well established that both race/ ethnicity itself and immigration have major impacts on American politics; at the same time, politics has an impact on both race/ethnicity and immigration policy" (p. 455). He once again reiterates that immigration impacts the policies in America. Senate Bill 1070 is intended to control the immigration population in Arizona, but it targets only one group of immigrants. This causes unequal treatment from law enforcement and therefore leads to racially profiling people. The increase of Mexican immigrants has caused the Arizona government take extreme measures to pass SB 1070.

FROM A DIFFERENT PERSPECTIVE

Although SB 1070 leads to racial profiling, supporters argue that Arizona needs to control the number of undocumented immigrants in its state. Many people cross the Arizona/Mexico border illegally, and some of those undocumented immigrants disrupt the people living by the border. The Arizona government has a right to protect its citizens in any way they see fit, and they have a right to implement their own immigration laws. Others assert that leaving the bill under ambiguous terms also allows law enforcement to determine on their own who they should stop and check for legality. The beliefs of others are that the terms are open for interpretation and allow for a broader group of people to be stopped. Although law enforcement does only stop people with Hispanic features, the bill allows them to catch a wide range of undocumented immigrants. Some may argue that law enforcement only stops people based on their color and not by their race.

J. Angelo Corlett (2011) describes that law enforcement is not practicing racial profiling and states, "So strictly speaking, not only is *racial* profiling not taking place in law enforcement, it ought not to, that is, so long as it is conceived in popular terms" (p. 2). Corlett (2011) continues by stating, "What *is* really happening is *color* (and/or other morphological) profiling, which is believed by many, erroneously, to indicate the 'race' of a suspect" (p. 2). So in other words, the author is saying that law enforcement doesn't stop people by their race, but by the color of their skin. She indicates that law enforcement doesn't stop people based on their race, because race is biological, and police officers instead stop people based on their appearance. Although Corlett presents a valid argument, India Williams (2011) states, "Moreover, section 2(B) of Senate Bill 1070 is ineffective policy because it transforms state and local police into immigration agents, undermining their ability to form the community relationships they need to do their jobs effectively" (p. 280). She illustrates that law enforcement should have another focus, instead of stopping people they think are undocumented immigrants. Police officers are not immigration agents, and should therefore do their jobs by protecting the community. A police officer's job is to protect the citizens in the community and not to act like immigration agents.

CONCLUSION

Although the Arizona government doesn't intend to target only Mexican immigrants, the terms in SB 1070 lead to racial profiling and even lead to the detaining of legal citizens. The fact that law enforcement can stop someone just solely based on their looks doesn't achieve the goal that they intend to achieve with SB 1070. SB 1070 undermines racial minorities through racial profiling.

REFERENCES

Corlett, J. (2011). Profiling color. *Journal Of Ethics*, *15*(1/2), 21–32. doi:10.1007/s10892-010-9093-8

Hero, R. E. (2010). Immigration and social policy in the united states. *Annual Review Of Political Science*, *13*(1), 445–468. doi:10.1146/annurev.polisci.041608.135744

Miller, K. (2013). The institutionalization of racial profiling policy: An examination of antiprofiling policy adoption among large law enforcement agencies. *Crime & Delinquency*, *59*(1), 32–58. doi:10.1177/0011128708328863

Williams, I. D. (2011). Arizona senate bill 1070: State sanctioned racial profiling? *Journal Of The Legal Profession*, *36*(1), 269–284.

AUTHOR PROFILE

My name is Melissa Carlos, and I am a first-year here at UCSB. I come from a small city in Los Angeles County, and my racial background inspired me to write on this topic.

—*Melissa Carlos*

THE TRUTH ABOUT WAL-MART

Corine Toren

Instructor: Auli Ek

> **"Although Wal-Mart allows its consumers to enjoy its 'always low prices,' the franchise proves to be disadvantageous to society."**

While Wal-Mart is known to have utilized unconventional labor tactics in order to provide consumers with "always low prices," they continue to remain one of the leading retail companies in the world. Although Olsson's article "Up Against Wal-Mart" confirms that Wal-Mart's success results from their illegitimate labor practices, Semmens refutes Olsson by justifying Wal-Mart's strategies in his article "Wal-Mart is Good for the Economy." However, Jacobs' article "Living Wage Policies and Wal-Mart" proves that Wal-Mart's expansion harms the economy and eliminates jobs that pay above minimum wage. Although each author offers insight about their perspective of Wal-Mart's impact, their evidence validates that Wal-Mart is detrimental to society.

Karen Olsson's (2009) article, "Up Against Wal-Mart," credits Wal-Mart's prosperity to its unethical policies. Throughout her article, Olsson describes the harsh conditions Wal-Mart employees endure (p. 346). Wal-Mart's illegal labor practices originally began at the opening of the first Wal-Mart franchise. Sam Walton, the founder of Wal-Mart, bought his first franchise store in 1945. After learning business strategies from other big franchise chain stores, such as Sears, Walton concluded that those stores "distributed goods to stores most efficiently, lowered prices to generate a larger volume of sales, and in the process generated a lot of cash to finance further expansion" (Olsson, 346). From that point on, it became Wal-Mart's priority to cut costs. Moreover, Walton paid his first employees under minimum wage at the time, which continues to be a problem for full-time employees at Wal-Mart stores today. For example, 22-year-old Jennifer McLaughlin, a full-time Wal-Mart employee, must provide for herself and her family with a Wal-Mart salary. Although Jennifer only makes about $16,800 per year, she is considered a highly paid worker. In addition, she must rely on Medicaid for her 1-year-old son because Wal-Mart would deduct $85 from her paycheck for medical insurance (p. 346). Jennifer complains that Wal-Mart employees are underpaid and the store is understaffed. Therefore, Jennifer and her colleagues have sued Wal-Mart for their violation of the wage and labor laws.

As a result of employee complaints, a Wal-Mart in Oregon was tried and found guilty for forcing its workers to work overtime for no extra pay. Additionally, they are also guilty of sex discrimination because they deny promotions and equal pay to women. More than two-thirds of Wal-Mart's employees are women. However, less than

10% are given the privilege of becoming managers, and those that are lucky enough are paid less than men (p. 347). In former manager Carolyn Thebes's testimony, she claimed that in an attempt to keep their payroll low, Wal-Mart supervisors often deleted hours from their time records and chastised employees who maintained that they worked overtime. As a result of Wal-Mart's abuse, employees from 100 stores in 25 states began to form unions (p. 348). In response to the unions, Wal-Mart attempted to formulate strategies in order to prevent the uprisings, but in doing so Wal-Mart violated the Federal Labor Law by interrogating their workers or firing them for supporting the union (Olsson, 2009).

Although the notorious allegations expressing that Wal-Mart mistreats its employees remain prominent, Semmens (2011) defends Wal-Mart's labor practices. He clarifies that the franchise benefits the country and boosts the nation's financial system. In his article, Semmens (2011) explains that people continue to perceive Wal-Mart in a negative light, even though the franchise provides its consumers with good quality and low-priced products. In response to the accusations claiming that Wal-Mart mistreats their employees, Semmens (2011) asserts that Wal-Mart provides many jobs throughout the nation, and workers are not forced to choose Wal-Mart as their employer (p. 9). Despite the harsh work conditions and poor environment, many people still desire to work at Wal-Mart. At the beginning of their employment, they are given responsibilities and requirements that they must fulfill, and if they are uncomfortable completing their tasks, they can leave at any point (Semmens, 2011).

Furthermore, Semmens (2011) continues to manifest Wal-Mart's potency by proving that the company's prosperity creates rivalry tensions between other leading companies. Wal-Mart is a successful franchise that has over $9 billion of profits per year (Semmens, 2011, p. 10). Other franchises, dubbed "losing companies," blame powerful businesses such as Wal-Mart for their lack of profitability in the competitive business world (Semmens, 2011). Moreover, Semmens (2011) contends that nobody forces people to walk into a Wal-Mart store. He explains that Wal-Mart is skilled at "accurately interpreting consumer needs and efficiently serving them" (Semmens, 2011, p. 9). Wal-Mart generously

provides quality products for a lower price for their consumers to enjoy. Therefore, products sold for lower prices allow more items to be manufactured and merchandised, thus improving the nation's economy. Beside Wal-Mart's dedication to the country, the company also donates millions of dollars to charitable institutions within the communities that Wal-Mart has served. As a result, Wal-Mart is a company that devotes itself to provide the best for their customers and to benefit the nation's economy (Semmens, 2011).

While Semmens attempts to prove that Wal-Mart is beneficial to the economy, Jacobs (2008) illuminates Wal-Mart's negative impact on the country. Many communities around the country have been concerned with the way Wal-Mart operates its stores, manages its employees, and the effect it may have on smaller businesses. Multiple cities have passed laws that require big franchise stores, such as Wal-Mart, to be a certain size. In Chicago, community groups Grassroots and ACORN attempted to persuade the Chicago City Council to pass the Big Box Living Wage Ordinance, which asserts that merchandising stores that profit more than $1 billion per year and are larger than 90,000 feet must pay their employees a minimum of $10 an hour (Jacobs, 2008, p. 9). Unfortunately, Mayor Richard Daley vetoed their request. If Wal-Mart employees received $10 per hour, their yearly salary would be raised by $1,020 to $4,640 per year, and the average Wal-Mart consumer would need to spend less than one percent more than they currently do (Jacobs, 2008, p. 9). Steve Hoch, an employee at the Wharton School wrote, "The standard argument by the retailer is that they can't afford to do it, but if everybody has to, then the playing field is level" (Jacobs, 2008 p. 10). Similarly, Wal-Mart claims that they cannot afford to pay their employees more money due to the competitive business environment, while Costco, another large franchise, can afford to pay their employees a minimum of $10 an hour and succeed in the business world (Jacobs, 2008).

In order to demonstrate Wal-Mart's harm on society, Jacobs (2008) examines a study from the University of California, Berkeley Center for Labor Research and Education. At the University, researchers conducted a study in order to discover the impact of Wal-Mart's expansion on the country. In their first study, the researchers concluded that the establishment of new Wal-Mart stores hinders citizens from acquiring jobs that pay above minimum wage. Additionally, Wal-Mart expansions are detrimental to competing businesses, such as grocery stores, because their wages decrease by 1.5% (Jacobs, 2008). Every time a new Wal-Mart store opens in a county, the average retail earnings in the county fall by 0.5 to 0.9 percent (Jacobs, 2008, p. 9). The healthcare provided by these retail companies are 5 percentage points less than they are supposed to be without the existence of a Wal-Mart store in their county (Jacobs, 2008). The study concludes that the effects of a new Wal-Mart store lowers employee wages and is harmful to other retail businesses (Jacobs, 2008).

Although Wal-Mart allows its consumers to enjoy its "always low prices," the franchise proves to be disadvantageous to society. In her article, Olsson delineates Wal-Mart's mistreatment of their employees and attributes the company's success to its unlawful labor practices. Semmens, on the other hand, questions Olsson's assertions, claiming that Wal-Mart benefits the economy by providing jobs and quality goods for a lower price. After examining a research study, Jacobs triumphantly refutes Semmens and demonstrates that Wal-Mart expansions negatively impact rivalry industries, while harming the nation's economy in the process.

REFERENCES

Jacobs, K. (2008). Living wage policies and wal-mart. *Social Policy, 38*(2), 6–10.

Olsson, K. (2009). "Up against wal-mart." In Graff, G., Birkenstein, C., & Durst, R., *They Say/I Say: The Moves That Matter in Writing* (342–355). New York: Norton.

Semmens, J. (2011). "Wal-Mart Is Good for the Economy." *The Freeman, 55.* Retrieved from http://www.fee.org/the_freeman/detail/wal-mart-is-good-for-the-economy#axzz2ScObDLQi.

AUTHOR PROFILE

I am currently a first year student at UCSB from Los Angeles, California. I am a Communication major, and I hope to pursue a career in writing in the future, either writing novels or screenplays. I love to write, and I am very excited to continue learning and writing at UCSB.

—*Corine Toren*

MUSIC AND STRESS: THE EFFECTS OF LISTENING TO MUSIC AND REDUCTION OF STRESS LEVELS

Gordon Deng

Instructor: Christopher Dean

> **"With so many genres of music, there is notably a special soothing power that emanates from music's ability to resonate harmoniously with each and every specific person in the world."**

ABSTRACT

This study sought to understand and validate the relationship between listening to music and stress reduction. Participants who were part of this study answered survey based questions. They were mainly gathered from the social networking site Facebook, but also included students from Professor Christopher Dean's Writing 2 class. Because of the high number of participants who listened to music while engaged in stressful activities, it was believed that music reduces negative stress levels.

INTRODUCTION

This study seeks to determine whether or not listening to music reduced negative stress levels. Stress is a major concern that has gained increasing levels of attention throughout the years because practically anything can induce negative stress; stress affects people of all ages, from infant children, to young students, to old adults. However, music stands as a possible remedy in alleviating stress and its symptoms because of its ability to calm and relax the body and mind. Thus, it is believed that music plays an important role in reducing negative stress levels.

REVIEW OF LITERATURE

In today's busy world full of work and jobs to complete, our lives are full of stress; people do whatever they can do reduce stress levels. One way many people reduce their stress levels is by listening to music. With so many genres of music, there is notably a special soothing power that emanates from music's ability to resonate harmoniously with each and every specific person in the world. Music may have the ability to chime in with people's emotions, but how exactly does music reduce stress levels? The key element lies in music's ability to induce changes in emotion.

The brain is the central processing component of our stress sensation and perception, but there are many parts of the brain that affect our perception of emotion. Because the brain consists of many parts, music must affect a greater majority of these parts in order to induce a change in emotions. As stated by Yehuda (2010), music has the ability to affect our nervous system—the communication network in our body. Yehuda (2010) explains that with the help of Magnetic Resonance Imaging technology (MRI), anyone concerned with the functions of the brain can see the effects of music on specific regions of the brain. Results from Yehuda's study showed that the region of the brain associated with the control of hormones—the hippocampus—was highly stimulated by music when participants were placed under an MRI while music was playing in the background (Yehuda 2010). Music was also stated to induce the release of dopamine and serotonin from their respective receptors in the brain; these two neurotransmitters are associated with arousal and good moods (Yehuda 2010). These findings by Yehuda provide a valuable basis for music and its ability to relieve stress.

In an experiment by Kushnir et al. (2012), they sought to analyze the changes in stress of pregnant women who listen to music before their cesarean section. Child bearing is regarded as one moment in a woman's life where she experiences astronomical levels of stress, making this study extremely reliable in collecting data on music and stress reduction. It was found that women who listen to preferred music before their cesarean sections reported higher levels of beneficial emotions during and after their operation whereas the control group, women who did not listen to music, reported a decline in positive emotions (Kushnir et al. 2012). Women who also listened to music before their cesarean section stated that the operation felt less threatening, and therefore, less stressful (Kushnir et al. 2012). While child bearing represents only one form of stress, and undoubtedly an extremely big and real one, this study supports the validity of music and its potential ability to reduce stress levels.

While music may have the ability to change the stress levels of individuals, there are also more specific factors of music and its ability pertaining to this ability. One finding by Mornhinweg (1992) connected the relationship between music familiarity and stress levels. Resulting data supported the notion that unfamiliar music helps relax individuals more than unfamiliar music does (Mornhinweg 1992). This conclusion helped confirm two key points. The first point defended the notion that music has the ability to reduce stress levels in individuals. This is significant because relaxation is a major step forward in stress reduction. The second point supports the notion that music may be a universal

stress reliever. The fact that unfamiliar music had a greater calming effect than did familiar music supports the idea that any type of music possibly contains stress-alleviating effects. Mornhinweg's 1992 study ultimately supports the notion that all music, in all its varying complexity, contains the ability to reduce stress levels because the need to listen to familiar music may not be a beneficial factor. In another study by Sandstorm and Russo (2010), it was concluded that music was better at reducing the heart rate of participants than white noise alone. A high heart rate is another indicator of a stressful moment, positive or negative; this is a clear indication that music must be a possible key variable in alleviating stress. These facts further support the hypothesis that music has the ability to reduce stress levels.

METHODS

All data and statistics were collected from survey-based questions. In this particular survey, the online tool *Survey Monkey* was used to create and distribute the surveys; *Survey Monkey* created a hyperlink and that hyperlink was distributed through a private event page on Facebook. Participants mainly consisted of personal Facebook friends, but also some students from Professor Christopher Dean's Writing 2 class. There were a total of 80 participants, aged 18 to 25; 23 identified as male, 55 female, and 2 transgender. Only 35 of the 80 participants were from UCSB as there were far more non-UCSB students on the personal Facebook friends list than there were UCSB students. This survey began with an informed consent statement. Participants who clicked next on the page agreed to its terms and conditions. Next, the survey asked participants about their demographics (such as age, ethnicity, and household income). Following the demographics page, participants answered questions about their mood, stress levels, musical tastes, and music listening frequencies. One question asked on average how many hours per day a participant listens to music while another asked for an estimate of their total stress levels throughout the day. The resulting data was then analyzed, and, with the help of *Survey Monkey*, transposed into graphs and other related graphics.

RESULTS

After answering questions on the demographics page, the survey asked participants, "On a scale of 1–7, how happy are you feeling? 7 being the most happy, and 1 being the least happy." The answer with the greatest number of selections was 5 with 37.7% of total answers, followed by 4 with 22.1%, 6 with 19.5%, 3 with 10.4%, 7 with 7.8%, 2 with 2.6% and 1 with 0.0%. Next, participants answered a similar question, but in regard to stress levels, with 7 being the most stressed, and 1 being the least stressed. 28.6% of participants answered with a 6, 24.7% with a 5, 15.6% a 3, 13.0% a 2, 25.2% a 1, and 3.9% a 7. These baseline questions show that there is indeed a certain degree of stress among participants.

When asked on average how many hours of music participants listened to a week, 58.9% of all participants who answered this question stated over five hours a week, followed by 17.8% who stated 2 to 3 hours, 12.3% 4 to 5 hours, 9.6% 1 to 2 hours, and 1.4% who listened to music less than 1 hour a week. When asked "After listening to music, I feel less stressed," 48.1% of all participants who answered this question agreed that, after listening to music, they felt less stressed; additionally, only 5.2% of participants either disagreed or strongly disagreed

with this statement while 94.9% either felt neutral, agreed, or strongly agreed with the same statement.

In terms of stress levels throughout the days of the week, participants felt least stressed on Friday and Saturday, with 70.6% and 79.4% of total selections made, respectively (participants were allowed to select more than one day of the week). In line with these results, participants felt equally stressed Sunday to Thursday, averaging 52.96% of the total number of selections made. Conversely, participants felt least stressed on Friday and Saturday, with 15.5% and 9.9% of total selections made, respectively.

When faced with the statement "I listen to a wide range of music genres," 40.5% of participants agreed, 33.8% strongly agreed, 16.2% were neutral, 9.5% disagreed, and 0.0% strongly disagreed. Specifically, when asked in a free response question about their favorite music genres, 14 expressed interests in rock, 13 in hip-hop, 13 in R&B, 12 in popular music, and 8 in alternative, to name a few. Also notable, only 19 participants did not express interest in more than one music genre. Of the 72 participants who answered the next question, 59.7% either agreed, or strongly agreed with the statement, "when I listen to music, I prefer to listen to my own playlist as opposed to others."

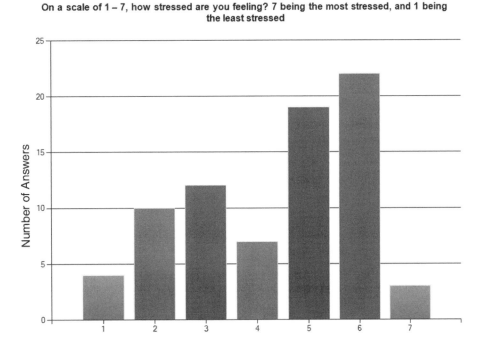

Figure 1. Baseline Stress Levels of Participants. This chart illustrates the distribution of participants' self-reported stress levels, ranging from 1 (low) to 7 (high).

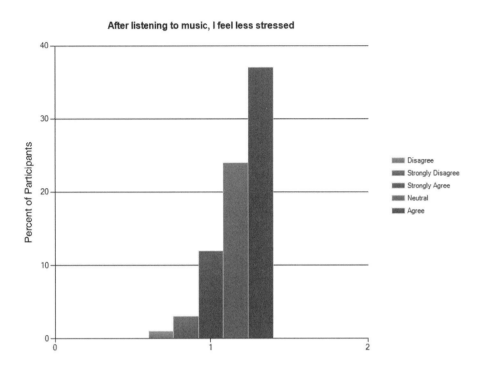

Figure 2. Agreement Levels with the Statement "After listening to music, I feel less stressed." This illustration depicts participants' feelings about the above statement.

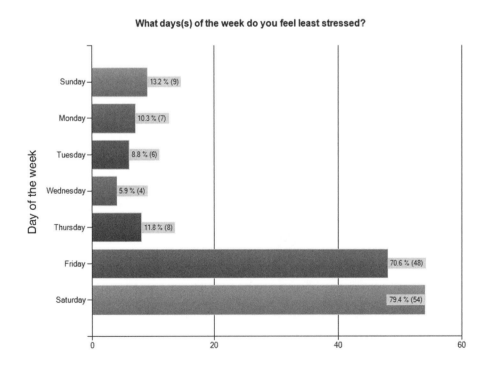

Figure 3. Days Participants Feeling the Least Stressed. This above illustration depicts the percentage of all sections made by participants of their most stressed day(s) of the week.

Participants also answered questions about listening to music while doing other activities. When asked if participants listened to music before they slept, 36.1% of those who answered stated yes, 26.4% stated no, and 37.5% stated sometimes. 48.6% of participants stated they do not listen to music while showering or bathing, while only 18.1% stated yes, and 33.3% sometimes. However, when posed the statement "I listen to music when I exercise," 65.3% stated yes, 20.8% sometimes, and 13.9% no.

When posed with the statement "I listen to music through noise isolating/canceling earphones and/or headphones," 54.9% of participants who answered stated sometimes, while 26.8% stated all the time, 15.5% never, and 2.8% uncertain. 47.2% of participants also expressed that they preferred to listen to music loud enough so that they can hear others with ease, followed by 27.8% who preferred playing music loud enough so that it was difficult to hear others around them. Participants also expressed familiarity with noise isolation or canceling headphone/earphone technologies. When asked if participants use these technologies, 54.9% of

participants who answered this question stated they sometimes do, while 26.8% do all the time, 15.5% never, and 2.8% were uncertain.

On the last page of the survey, participants were asked the free response question, "What contributes most to your stress?" Of the 59 participants who answered this question, 34 answered with elements revolving around school, exams, and homework. The second biggest stress contributor indicated were relationships, life, and other personal issues in general, with 10 participants who answered within this category. Finally, when asked "How do you tend to deal with your stress?" of the 58 participants who answered this question, 9 stated they listened to music, which was also the largest category of total responses. Trailing music was sleep with 8 answers, exercise with 6, and some sort of recreation with 5. These final two questions, coupled with the results from the entire survey, depict a strong correlation with music and its potential ability to alleviate stress levels. While there are certainly limitations to these results, they are nonetheless cohesive and viable.

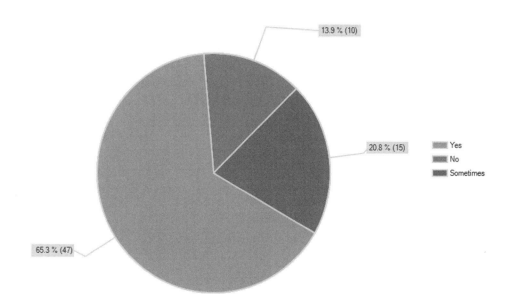

I listen to music when I exercise

13.9 % (10)

20.8 % (15)

65.3 % (47)

Yes
No
Sometimes

Figure 4. Participants' Agreement with the Statement "I listen to music when I exercise." This illustration depicts the percentage and number of participants who either do, do not, or sometimes listen to music while exercising

DISCUSSION

This study sought to verify the correlation between listening to music and its ability to reduce negative stress levels. The hypothesis of this study states that listening to music would decrease levels of negative stress. After gathering the results, it seemed that this hypothesis is quite valid; listening to music does decrease levels of stress.

Validating this hypothesis first required a baseline of stress levels. It is quite clear that participants had higher levels of stress than not. When asked how stressed participants were feeling, 66.3% of participants who answered the question indicated they were in the 4–7 range. This meant that the greater majority of participants indicated they were stressed. Because all of the participants were college students, it is not strange that so many participants indicated high levels of stress. These participants are bombarded with tasks such as exams and homework while also needing to balance their personal lives and relationships, as stated by participants in the free response section of the survey. While this does mean that there obviously was stress in our participants, it was not safe to say all of their stress was negative. However, it was safe to assume at least some degree of their stress was negative, as college education is an important issue and was not taken lightly by our participants.

With a baseline stress level established, results from participants' answers about their music listening habits and frequencies shed much light on music's ability to reduce stress levels. Because participants indicated there was a high level of stress present, it made sense that participants indicated that they listened to many hours of music. Almost 60% of participants indicated they listened to over 5 hours of music a week. It can be deducted that participants may listen to music to reduce their stress levels. However, it must be noted that not all students listen to music to reduce stress; students may just listen to music for pure enjoyment, and not for the specific purpose of reducing stress. Nonetheless, if it were true that participants listened to music to reduce their stress, and for those who actually did, results indicated that 63.7% of participants who listened to music either agreed or strongly agreed that after listening to music, stress levels were reduced.

Conversely, only 5.2% disagreed with the same notion. So, if at all were participants listening to music to reduce stress, and those who did, verified that, in their opinion, music does in fact reduce stress levels. To further support this claim, results show that over 50% of participants indicated they listen to more music when they were stressed, while only a little over 10% did not. If participants who were stressed find relief in listening to music, it would makes sense for these particular participants to listen to more music in order to gain the stress reducing effects from listening to music. These results and correlations are a strong indication that music can in fact reduce stress levels.

The relationships between listening to music, stress, and activities may shed further light on music's potential ability to reduce levels of stress. A generally low stress activity, such as showering, may not require listening to music. As such, only 48.6% of participants indicated they listened to music while showering. On the other end of this spectrum, 65.3% of participants indicated that they listened to music while exercising. In context, the contrast between showering and exercising is a relatively lower stress activity and relatively higher stress activity as there is less pressure placed on an individual while showering. There may be a need to listen to music while exercising due to the minor negative stress generated from the lack of oxygen or muscle pain commonly related with exercising. Therefore, it would make sense that more participants listened to music while engaging in a higher stressed activity than a lower stressed activity. Results indicated that 26.4% of participants do not listen to music before sleeping, while 36.1% did, and 37.5% sometimes did. This supports the assumption that music may be needed to help reduce stress. Sleeping with high levels of stress may be difficult, and therefore, if music does alleviate stress levels, it would prove beneficial to listen to music before sleeping. This result coincides with the initial base stress levels of participants—that there exists a high stress level among participants. Therefore, if participants, in fact, do change their music listening behaviors in relation to what activity they were doing, these findings may help conclude that music does in fact reduce stress levels.

Limitations to the Study

Although initial results do indicate music's potential ability to reduce stress, there are nonetheless many limitations to this study that must be addressed. The first limitation that needs to be addressed was the demographics of the participants who took this survey. The population was not the best representation of UCSB as there were too many females—68.8% females to 28.8% males. The ethnicity was also not spread out either; Asians consisted of 83.8% of the surveyed population. This survey also failed to explicitly state the differences between current and possible future stress. Therefore, the results may only indicate conclusions, but not specifically conclude solid assumptions. This study also does not express the distinct characteristics of stress as there are many form of stress—positive and negative stress—because the survey never explicitly asked for participants to categorize their stress. Free response answers only allow participants to express their stress in a negative or positive light, but none were categorized explicitly. Lastly, not all questions in the survey were answered. Therefore, important information may have been omitted, resulting in possible skewed data.

CONCLUSION

Articulating the data provided a base with strong support for hypothesis of this study. It was hypothesized that if listening to music reduced stress levels, then participants would self-report reductions in stress levels after listening to music. Concluding data showed that 63.7% of participants agree or strongly agreed that listening to music reduced stress levels. In addition, 54% of participants expressed that they listened to more music when stressed. The data results gathered from these participants are all valid because they represent a group with a relatively high stress level before taking the survey. Participants also expressed that listening to music as a top alleviator in reducing stress levels. Nonetheless, beyond the strong correlations found in this study, similar studies in the future must be made to further support this study's hypothesis and other similar hypotheses. There needs to be a greater distinction between the different types of stress and music's effect on each type of stress. Conducting a study in this manner will result in stronger and more conclusive deductions revolving around music's possible ability to reduce levels of stress. However, from this study and participants alone, there is still strong evidence that supports music's ability to reduce stress levels. This study supports the notion that listening to music does in fact contain an ability to reduce negative stress levels.

REFERENCES

Kushnir, J., Friedman, A., Ehrenfeld, M., & Kushnir, T. (2012). Coping with preoperative anxiety in cesarean section: physiological, cognitive, and emotional effects of listening to favorite music. *BIRTH*, *39*(2), 121–127. doi:10.1111/j.1523-536X.2012.00532.x

Mornhinweg, G. C. (1992). Effects of music preference and selection on stress reduction. *Nursing Journal of Holistic Medicine*, 101–109. doi:10.1177/089801019201000202

Sandstrom, G. M., & Russo, F. A. (2010). Music hath charms: The effects of valence and arousal on recovery following an acute stressor. *Music and Medicine*, 137–143. doi:10.1177/1943862110371486

Yehuda, N. (2011). Music and stress. *Journal of Adult Development*, 85–94. doi:10.1007/s10804-010-9117-4

AUTHOR PROFILE

I am a freshman attending UCSB as a first-generation college student. I am from San Francisco, CA.

—*Gordon Deng*

STUDENT PHOTOGRAPHY

Photo by Loriel Davila

Photo by Shannon Mirshokri

WRITING 2

EXPLORING
GENRES

THE DIMENSIONS OF GENRE: TWITTER AND POLITICAL SPEECHES

Kelley Coe

Instructor: Kristy Slominski

"The connection of Twitter and political speeches lies not only in the point that both genres force the authors to boldly reveal their personal identities, but also the substantial fact that many politicians use Twitter as another way to communicate with the people."

Genre contains the overarching complexities of writing: it targets an audience, conveys a certain purpose, and forms around its limitations and location. A booming genre like Twitter has certain concrete boundaries, like a maximum amount of 140 characters per tweet, while the genre of political speeches has rhetorical limitations, like political correctness. Both genres, though, still allow the writer much freedom to reveal their intent. Genres are guidelines to format writing but do not dictate the content. The key to being successful in a genre is the ability to find a personal voice in the midst of the criteria and rules that accompany each genre—to stick to the conventions without losing one's identity.

At times, limitations force writers to conform their styles to fit the genre's conditions. Twitter is a genre that makes writers concise and clear solely because of its character limit. Besides this restriction, Twitter is virtually limitless; anyone can post statuses, photos, or website links to their followers. A critical point of Twitter is how many followers one has—the more followers, the bigger the audience. The main template that Twitter has when one goes to tweet is: "What's on your mind?" And that's essentially how Twitter evolved into a public diary, where self-expression is welcomed and expected.

The ultimate success in the world of Twitter comes from receiving some sort of response so one knows that the tweet was relatable or entertaining. This is where "retweets" and "favoriting" come in—retweeting and/or favoriting a tweet shows that it had an effect on someone, and the reader wants to share it with others as well. In the Twitter world, there are famous accounts with thousands of followers, like "Student Pains." This particular account is full of college humor tweets that most students can easily relate to. For example, on October 10, 2012, Student Pains tweeted, "'Your homework tonight is to read pages 57–112' Nice, no homework." That tweet alone received 197 retweets and 55 favorites in 35 minutes because it's funny and completely relatable. This is proof of Student Pains' success, and with more exposure through retweets, it will continue its success with an increase in followers and gain more recognition. With these pointless statements that express the majority's "pains," Twitter allows for a connection to exist between many people, both in reality and in cyberspace, adding to its popularity.

On the other hand, political speeches are lengthy, detailed, and rife with rhetoric in order to make the public feel connected to the speaker. When NCBLA, The National Children's Book and Literacy Alliance, interviewed Thomas LaFauci, former speechwriter for Joe Biden, about speech writing, LaFauci said:

> [Speechwriting] is language that can make us see ourselves in a new, more focused light; language that reveals something about who we are and what we stand for as a people; language that unmasks a mystery or consoles us in times of tragedy or trouble. A great inaugural speech should reach into our collective soul to touch what is most human in the human spirit. ("Our White House: Looking In, Looking Out")

This proves how greatly rhetoric, syntax, and diction affect a speech, and how a speechwriter must keep the audience in mind. With political speeches, success is evident when the audience feels like they have a connection with the speaker, and when they believe that they have found a strong, trustworthy leader.

Speechwriters must be aware of the issues at hand while maintaining a humanistic and charismatic tone for the public to relate to. With such an extensive targeted audience, the speech must accomplish many factors to be considered successful. Many believe Franklin Roosevelt's first inaugural speech to be one of the greatest political speeches in American history. He reveals himself and his goals for his presidency in the most humbling way—he dug out America from the pits of the Great Depression. Roosevelt says in his 1933 inauguration, "Happiness lies not in the mere possession of money; it lies in the joy of achievement, in the thrill of creative effort. The joy and moral stimulation of work no longer must be forgotten in the mad chase of evanescent profits... We do not distrust the future of essential democracy. The people of the United States have not failed" (Bartleby.com). The rhetoric of this powerful political speech filled Americans with the pride that they had lost in the midst of financial decline. The success of political speeches derives from when an audience as a whole feels a sense of hope and pride after the speech is over. This genre is one of the most influential ones because of the power it can project over large numbers of people at once.

Successful political speeches must strategically mask any negative aspects of the topic at hand in order to boost morale. Roosevelt may have felt uncertain or frightened about taking on the presidency in such tumultuous times, but the genre of political speeches does not call for leaders to show their weakness. Admitting fear would have been a failure for Roosevelt, for the audience would feel unsure and suspicious. Former president George W. Bush had to play the role of a fearless American leader when he addressed the 9/11 attacks. In such a time of distress and turmoil, the American people looked for a father figure—for a president to tell them that the nation would fight back and avenge the deaths of hundreds of innocent citizens. Bush's top speechwriter, Michael Gerson, wrote with a comforting conviction. In the address to a joint session of Congress after the attacks, Bush stated, "This generation will lift the dark threat of violence from our people and our future. We will rally the world to this cause by our efforts, by our courage. We will not tire, we will not falter and we will not fail" ("Top Bush Speech Writer Resigns"). His word choices and phrases, like "dark threat of violence" and "we will not fail," are what make this speech successful. Those words made Americans confident and patriotic, ready to back up their president with the decision to fight back. In general, this particular genre hides all aspects of negativity in order for the audience to feel hope, and in this case, uplifted, not disheartened. Political speeches enhance optimism and positivity to inspire listeners.

The connection of Twitter and political speeches lies not only in the point that both genres force the authors to boldly reveal their personal identities, but also the substantial fact that many politicians use Twitter as another way to communicate with the people. This is especially crucial during election time, when candidates are fighting to prove themselves to the nation. On August 30, 2012, Mitt Romney tweeted, "Our economy runs on freedom, not government. It's time we put our faith back in the American people #BelieveInAmerica #RomneyRyan2012." With well over a million followers, Romney's tweets showed his views and instilled hope in his supporters. His followers could have spread this message to their followers by either using the same hashtag or retweeting it. The ability to "go viral" is the main attraction to Twitter for running candidates—millions of people can be reached daily at an unparalleled rate.

In this 2012 election, both President Obama and Governor Romney used Twitter more than ever to express their ideals, and more specifically, their identities. They also used it to point out the other candidate's flawed plans and theories. It essentially helped them in their campaigns to promote themselves and demote their opponent. With this Twitter fame, it can be deduced that this added onto both candidates' success, more so for President Obama. This can be shown through the number of followers they had at the end of the election—Obama with 24,155,699 and Romney with 1,730,081. Obama is obviously very much ahead, which means that his message reaches out to almost 23 million more readers than Romney's. President Obama's campaign staff utilized this powerful tool and tweeted on October 8, 2012, "FACT: Unlike President Obama, Romney has no plan to end the war in Afghanistan and bring our troops home." This tweet is strong and aggressive; it cuts straight to the point and jars the reader with the capitalization of "fact," followed by a powerful political sentence. The instantaneous rate of information that can be shared to the public through this new genre has become another vital portal for politics.

Twitter and political speeches may have many similarities with self-expression and the necessity of being concise and rhetorical, but there is a striking difference: Twitter is a two-dimensional world with just texts that are 140 characters or fewer, whereas political speeches start out as two-dimensional entities, but become three-dimensional once spoken. This can be seen through how both genres convey humor. The power of speech, along with its gesticulations, inflections in voice, and environment, are all factors that Twitter can never partake in. For example, in President Obama's speech at the Al Smith dinner, he made the audience laugh approximately 17 times in a matter of eight and a half minutes. In one of his best jokes, he slyly stated, "Earlier today I went shopping at some stores in Midtown. I understand Governor Romney went shopping for some

stores in Midtown" (Kurtzman). He smiled when people laughed and looked to his left at Governor Romney with a knowing look on his face. For Twitter, the only tangible reaction is through a gain in followers or through retweets and favorites. Like in the Student Pains example, sarcasm has to be obvious and the tweet has to be a quick joke for the reader to pay any attention to it. Humor is difficult to accomplish through mere two-dimensional textual portals. In comparison, though, favorites and retweets are Twitter's version of applause, laughter, and cheering—proof of success for both genres.

Twitter and political speeches achieve success in different ways, but both call for the writer or speaker to expose their personal identity and intentions. One is through a concrete, textual portal, while the other relies on chemistry with the audience and the ability to read a speech convincingly. The successes of both genres can be measured in the same way—how the audience reacts. Reaction is the measurement of success, but success begins with the author's intent.

WORKS CITED

Gordon, Kelsey (KelseyNgordon). "I have heels higher than your standards." 9 Oct 2012, 10:29 p.m. Tweet.

"Inaugural Addresses of the Presidents of the United States." *Bartleby.com*. Bartleby Bookstore, n.d. Web. 10 Oct 2012. <http://www.bartleby.com/124/pres49.html>.

Kurtzman, Daniel. "Obama Al Smith Dinner Speech 2012 Transcript." n.pag. *About.com*. 5 Dec 2012. Web.

Obama, Barak (BarackObama). "FACT: Unlike President Obama, Romney has no plan to end the war in Afghanistan and bring our troops home" 8 Oct 2012, 5:12 p.m. Tweet.

Romney, Mitt (MittRomney). "Our economy runs on freedom, not government. It's time we put our faith back in the American people #BelieveinAmerica #RomneyRyan2012" 30 Aug 2012, 5:49 p.m. Tweet.

Student Pains. "'Your homework tonight is to read pages 57–112' Nice, no homework." 10 Oct 2012, 8:10 p.m. Tweet.

"Top Bush Speech Writer Resigns." *ABC Good Morning America*. ABC, 25 Jun 2006. Web. 10 Oct 2012. <http://abcnews.go.com/GMA/Politics/story?id=2116251&page=1>.

"Writing Political Speeches: An Interview with Thomas LaFauci, former speech writer to Senator and Vice President-elect Joseph Biden." *Our White House: Looking In, Looking Out.* National Children's Book and Literacy Alliance, n.d. Web. 10 Oct 2012, <http://www.ourwhitehouse.org/writing_lafauci.html>.

AUTHOR PROFILE

I'm originally from Los Angeles and am a freshman at UCSB. Music, sports, and academia comprise most of my life as a student. Travelling is an essential part of who I am. Fortunately, it has been easy for me to travel, as my mother is a flight attendant. I love writing; it serves as my creative outlet.

—*Kelley Coe*

EXPLORING GENRES   The Dimensions of Genre: Twitter and Political Speeches

THE IMPORTANCE OF LITERACY PRACTICES IN COMPUTER SCIENCE

Michael Sprague

Instructor: Michael Joiner

> "A developer can write code that does not adopt any literacy practices and is barely readable by a human being, but if the resulting program meets the specifications of the initial design, it is considered a success."

When writing software, there are numerous literacy practices that a developer should implement in order to both solve the problem efficiently and to write code that is readable by others. This paper will present each literacy practice with a simple, cumulative example to demonstrate the effectiveness of the corresponding practice in designing or writing software. The following practices have been gathered through experience, lecture observation, and the conducting of an interview with a computer science professor, Phil Conrad, at UC Santa Barbara. Writing pseudocode, using visual aids, inserting comments, and adopting naming conventions are literacy practices that are critical in the process of creating code that is readable and maintainable by colleagues.

One of the most important literacy practices in software development is writing pseudocode, an informal description of the structure of a program. During the initial planning stages of creating software, a developer will often utilize pseudocode to organize thoughts and create a basic sketch of an implementation for the program. This process can be thought of as analogous with brainstorming and outlining for writing a paper; the writer does not need to worry about syntax or semantics, they only need to worry about getting their "point" across. Pseudocode is primarily used when a computer scientist is introducing a concept or solving a difficult problem. During an interview, Professor Conrad referred to pseudocode as a critical means to both write code and communicate with peers. For instance, consider the following scenario: a programming team at a hypothetical company named Froogle is tasked with creating software to count the total amount of money piled upon the desk of the CEO. In an initial project-planning meeting, the lead developer might write the following pseudocode on the whiteboard to sketch the steps to describe the program to his or her colleagues:

1. Start with the stack of cash and initialize the total amount to zero
2. Go through each dollar bill
3. Add the bill's value to the total amount
4. Repeat steps 2 and 3 until there are no more bills left
5. Display the total

In this case, creating pseudocode allows the team to clearly understand the main purpose of the program and to consider its design. If the lead developer had not explained this to the team, then each individual would have a different idea of the program's function. In addition, this technique allows different sections of the project to be delegated to different developers. For example, the least experienced developer might be tasked with implementing step five, since it is the simplest, but the lead developer might take on tasks two to four, since they are more complicated. In practice, pseudocode is an extremely effective way for developers to hash out program designs and abstract concepts with peers without having to worry about getting bogged down by the specifics of communicating with the computer.

Visual aids such as graphs, flow charts, or class hierarchies are crucial literacy practices used to design a program. Flow charts and graphs can be drawn on paper, a whiteboard, or on a computer to help visualize abstractions that are (or will be) used in development, especially within larger projects that require numerous abstractions. Developers often represent data structures, methods of efficiently organizing and storing data in a computer, with different graphs or flow charts to assist themselves or other developers in understanding and implementing a program that utilizes the data structure. For example, the lead developer at Froogle might draw the following data structure diagram for a list to suggest a means of storing the different denominations of dollar bills that are stacked on the CEO's desk:

$5	$10	$1	$20	$5	$50	$1	$5	$10

The graphic above allows developers to understand the way that the money will be stored internally. Each square represents a location in memory that stores one bill, and each bill is arranged in the order that they were picked up from the desk. Since there are multiple ways to store numbers in a computer, this visual aid clarifies the internal implementation of the data used in program to a developer. In addition to data structures, Professor Conrad also emphasized the use of class hierarchy diagrams to design reusable code. The purpose of a class hierarchy diagram is to break up the code into abstractions that can be reused in other programs, akin to interchangeable parts of a car. Just like how a mechanic can remove the engine of one car and with some modification insert it into another compatible car, a software developer can use one piece of code and insert it into another program. For example, a developer at Froogle could copy the algorithm that counts the total dollar bills and place it in a different program to count the total number of words in a document. In general, the use of visual aids by programmers is critical in effective design and creation of software. Visualization allows the developer to reach levels of abstractions and devise clear solutions to complex problems that would not otherwise be possible.

Another important literacy practice used in programming is commenting code. The purpose of a programming language is to create a means of communication between the developer and the computer. However, it is not without friction. Comments allow programmers to insert annotations in the code that are directed at other programmers, but ignored by computer. Comments serve a variety of purposes ranging from code planning to debugging. For example, during an interview, Phil Conrad equates his use of comments in code to headings or paragraphs in an essay; comments are used not only as a guide to any reader of the program, but also as an outline to the writer. Consider again the example of the money-counter program under development at Froogle. When a developer starts to write the program, he might begin by writing comments loosely based upon pseudocode that was written previously to act as an outline:

```
# Define a function to compute the total cash
that is sitting on the CEO's desk
# It takes in a list of numbers (the dollar bills)
and prints the total sum to the screen:
# 1. Initialize the total amount to zero
# 2. Go through each dollar bill and do the
following:
# 3. Add the bill's value to the total amount
# 4. Once we have counted every bill, we display
the total
```

The comments written in this example are more structured and context specific to the programming language than the pseudocode previously written. This Computer Science literacy practice breaks down the solution of the problem for the programmer in a more specific way than pseudocode.

Comments are an integral part of software development that both help the developer get started in the beginning of the writing process and allow the developer to communicate with future readers of the program.

In Computer Science, a naming convention is a literacy practice that denotes a set of guidelines that a programmer should follow when naming functions, variables, or identifiers. This is similar to the idea of comments because the computer is indifferent to any naming schemes that the programmer implements. Akin to common writing conventions for different genres, developers use different naming conventions depending on the programming language and context. When possible, a developer should write meaningful names for identifiers because it makes the code easier to read and maintain by other programmers. For example, a programmer at Froogle could write an implementation for the money-counting problem in the following way:

```
# Define a function to compute the total cash
that Mike has gotten from his students.
# It takes in a list of numbers (the dollar bills)
and prints the total sum to the screen:
def printTotalCash(bills):
# 1. Initialize the total amount to zero
totalAmount = 0
# 2. Go through each dollar bill and do the
following:
for eachBill in bills:
# 3. Add the bill's value to the total amount
totalAmount = totalAmount + eachBill
# 4. Once we have counted every bill, we display
the total
print totalAmount
```

Because of the use of proper naming conventions and comments, the above code reads logically to other programmers and almost makes sense in plain English. Consider a counterexample where equivalent code is written without proper naming conventions or comments:

```
def ts(bs):
t = 0
for b in bs:
t += b
print t
```

While the above code would function identically to the previous code, it is exceedingly more difficult for a developer to understand the purpose of the program. If a programmer wanted to add a feature to this program or if the above code did not work correctly, it would take him longer to understand the code and thus longer to implement any changes. The implementation of standard naming conventions by programmers is critical in writing software that is maintainable and understandable by other developers.

Using literacy practices in creating software is analogous to using literacy practices in writing papers, with one major exception: they each have vastly different goals. The author's main purpose of writing a paper is typically to present the audience with information deemed important by the writer and to convey his analysis of the material to the reader. However, a software developer's main purpose does not relate to the reader of the program, but instead, it relates to the user of the program. A developer can write code that does not adopt any literacy practices and is barely readable by a human being, but if the resulting program meets the specifications of the initial design, it is considered a success. To the contrary, if an academic paper is illegible, then the paper will be considered a failure. This means that every literacy practice in Computer Science is optional and each is widely debated upon. For example, Professor Hardekopf stated the following in lecture: "Let's be real. How often do people comment their code? And even if they do, how long does it really stay up to date?" Ben Hardekopf rarely uses any comments and does not adopt standard naming conventions in the code that he gives to students to use for a base for projects. Imagine if a history professor assigned a reading for the class that only used abbreviations and had a nonsensical sentence structure! Ideally, the use of comments in code provides clarity for the reader and allows for issues or incorrect implementations to be identified with ease. However, because code is constantly being changed and rewritten by other developers, comments do not always stay relevant. Imagine if the money-counting program at Froogle was changed to begin at one hundred dollars, but the developer did not take the time to update the comment:

```
# 1. Initialize the total amount to zero
totalAmount = 100
```

Not only is the above comment incorrect, it is also misleading! Developers need to take care to update comments when they change a program; otherwise, they may leave future programmers confused at the implementation. However, because the use of software development literacy practices does not affect the outcome of the resulting program, practices are often used sparingly and incorrectly in real-world situations.

A software developer should adopt common literacy practices to aid in effective communication with peers. The use of pseudocode allows the developer to organize his or her thoughts and to create a basic sketch of a potential implementation for a given program. This pseudocode can be used with the addition of visual aids to work with other developers to come up with an efficient solution to the problem. Once an implementation has been devised, a programmer can outline the code using comments to help guide the reading and writing of the program. While the developer is writing the code, he or she will most likely adopt a set of naming conventions to create code that is understandable by other programmers. Literacy practices such as writing pseudocode, using visual aids, inserting comments, and adopting naming conventions are all critical in the process of creating code that is readable and maintainable by other developers. Moreover, although Computer Science literacy practices are optional, the advancement of software development would not be possible without effective communication. Thus, literacy practices are a necessity for collaboration, and without them modern technology would not exist.

WORKS CITED

Conrad, Phillip. Personal Interview. 6 February 2013.

Hardekopf, Ben. Programming Languages. University of California, Santa Barbara. 7 February 2013. Lecture.

AUTHOR PROFILE

I'm a third year computer science major and avid software developer.

—*Michael Sprague*

EATING DISORDERS IN BALLET FOR THE MEDICAL AND PSYCHOLOGY DISCIPLINES

Mackenzie Keil-Long

Instructor: Kendra Sarna

> **"**When it comes to ballet, psychologists are fascinated with dancers' reactions towards eating disorders.**"**

When you watch ballet dancers, you may admire the way they can gracefully move around the stage. Perhaps, you even have hint of jealousy at the thinness of the dancers' body. Yet, you should consider how these dancers have achieved these slender bodies. Many academic fields have considered this as well and have found that eating disorders are rampant in the dancing world in order for dancers to attain their "perfect" bodies. Although authors have looked at the eating disorders of ballet dancers, each field looks at this problem in a unique way. A psychology paper by Jaime Kaplan entitled "Recreational Ballet Students: The Mirror Image of Professional Ballet Aesthetics?" found that ballet dancers at different levels have similar opinions on the ideal body image. Joseph Toro, Marta Guerrero, Joan Sentis, Josefina Castro and Carles Puertolas wrote a medical paper titled "Eating Disorders In Ballet Dancing Students: Problems and Risk Factors," which discovered that ballet students do not have a greater risk of developing eating disorders than other girls the same age. Although both authors focus on eating disorders in ballet dancers, the findings of Toro et al. help identify and treat eating disorders in ballet dancers, while Kaplan's findings simply reinforce what has already been found.

The medical field completes research or experiments to expand knowledge on the physical body. Its inquiries remain within the physical body and not the brain. Toro et al.'s article focused on whether ballet dancers have a greater risk of developing eating disorders than the general population and found those risk factors. The authors questioned ballet dancers and a control group of the general adolescent population to find signs of eating disorders, such as body image. The authors discovered that dancers did not show a greater risk than the general population. However, upon further investigation the authors found that there were risks that can cause eating disorders. When using sources, primary sources dominated the article's main argument. Primary sources encompassed nearly the entire paper; eight out of the ten pages were for primary sources and their discussion. Primary sources are the sources created by the author, while secondary sources are those previously researched by others. It is important for an experiment to have high amounts of primary sources because it shows that this paper has new information. Toro et al.'s primary sources were those found from their experiment and questionnaires, such as the girls' eating behaviors and personality traits. The conclusion focused on their experiment's findings. For example, dancers eating behaviors show risk factors, like lower BMI and pressure from classmates to change their weight (Toro et al. 46). However, secondary sources appeared as well. The authors cited various studies stating eating disorders' presence around the world from the 1980s to the early 2000s. These statistics showed how eating disorders are fairly common in ballet around the world. Many of these statistics came from older studies, making one wonder if they can still hold true. The assessment had many citations since the tests they used, the EAT-26, CIMEC, and CETCA, were not of their own creation. The citation of these tests helps the paper's reliability and the authors' credibility. The conclusion was the only time the authors discussed the older studies' conclusions, stating that ballet students' personality traits were from their "drive for thinness and perfectionism" (Toro et al. 41). When citing the paper, its main focus was on its own research and not research done in the past. This is important because the authors are trying to show what they have discovered and the secondary sources only highlight that they have done their research.

Psychology papers focus on mental functions and their connection to physical actions and outside stimuli. When it comes to ballet, psychologists are fascinated with dancers' reactions towards eating disorders. Kaplan asked recreational and preprofessional ballet students about their attitudes towards perfectionism and their drive for thinness. The author found that the two groups did not have significant differences with ideal body image or BMI. Both had a desire for a small body and believed that the "ideal ballet body" should not be changed (Kaplan 97). This paper had a mixture between primary sources and secondary sources. It began by citing definitions of different eating disorders, such as Anorexia Nervosa and Bulimia Nervosa, and the various symptoms, including that "most of these women see themselves as fat or overweight when they are not" (Kaplan 94). The paper then discussed past research on why thinness has become important in the ballet community, which is primarily from the creation of a perfect ballet image that emerged over the last sixty years (Kaplan 94). Kaplan also discussed past studies relating dancers to eating disorders, such as a twelve-year-old

dancer who found she was praised more when she had lost weight, and other papers finding that eating disorders in ballet are not a new phenomenon (94). The second half of the paper was filled with primary sources, mostly the statistics and answers found in the dancers' questionnaires. The primary sources were mainly used to draw the author's conclusion. However, using past studies allows the author to show that this is a fairly common finding and strengthens her own findings. So in a way, the author used her own sources in a combination with background sources to draw her conclusion. In this paper, the author focused on the mind of the dancers. The author began with an overall impression of anorexia, stating how it is associated with starvation and bones. She continued by saying "To ballet dancers, these familiar associations are often hidden by what they perceive as the more important concerns of success, beauty, and perfection" (Kaplan 93). This tells the reader that, at least in the dancer's mind, perfection is more important than health. The questionnaires also found that many of the dancers fell within the drive for thinness and perfectionism subscales (Kaplan 97). This showed what the dancers strive for in their mind.

Each paper has its own strengths and weaknesses, but when focusing on whether the paper is finding further knowledge and preventing future eating disorders, the medical paper is clearly superior. Both papers set out to find eating disorders involved in ballet, so it can be considered as common knowledge that eating disorders play a major role in ballet schools. Both referred to past studies that confirmed this idea. Yet, Kaplan's paper merely confirmed that eating disorders are an epidemic for ballet dancers. We already know that some ballet students have eating disorders, and the fact that Kaplan found this correlation in different levels of ballet dancers does not help treat the problem. For example, Kaplan found that her study "…suggests that the ballet subculture may have a greater influence over all students than type of studio environment" (97). It only states that this is an instance where the disease is more prominent, which does not help treat the disease. This affirms a fact, but does not explain what causes the disease. The medical article is clearly stronger in finding ways to prevent the disease by both its research methods and discovering various risk factors. The medical paper compared two groups that have completely different environments: the general public and dancers. Toro et al. found that ballet dancers are not different from regular adolescents in their personal body image (46). It is very important to compare the experiment group to a control group. That way, the results are not influenced in a selective view. Kaplan's research used two groups involved in ballet. She discussed how this is important since "thinness in the dance world is not equivalent to thinness in the larger society" (Kaplan 94). Instead, she states how dancers must be compared to someone in the dancing world in order to get a good percentage of body fat (Kaplan 94). This seems like a good idea, however, her paper later discovered that there was no significant difference between the two dance groups in ideal body image, BMI, etc. (Kaplan 97). Since Kaplan used two similar groups, she found that there was no major difference between the two. If she had chosen two different groups to compare, like Toro et al., then she would have found more differences between the groups. Dancers do not have a "normal" body type, so comparing them to what is normal to a non-dancer can help find what symptoms we should look for. Toro et al. found their results through a non-distorted sample group, since they used two separate, nonrelated groups. Toro et al. also looked into the different risks that cause the ballet dancers to have eating disorders. Instead of focusing on the problem, the medical article tried to find the causes so that we can prevent it. However, in order to prevent the disease, we have to discover what is causing it. Toro et al. found that the risk factors that could potentially cause dancers to have an eating disorder are: lower BMI; lower age of menarche (menstrual cycle); more pressure from classmates to change their weight; greater desire to reduce size of body parts; and greater dedication to physical exercise, "spending almost 10 times longer on sports activities than controls" (94). The authors found how the results can suggest preventions. They thought dancers' concern level for their bodies should be monitored for presence of depressive symptoms prior to dance studies. They also thought coaches should avoid criticism about the body, weight, and food, and act with care. Finally, students should be observed since exposure of the body in

public and other stressful experiences cannot be avoided for the dancers (Toro et al. 48). Finding the risk factors and possible solutions is important in helping treat the disease. Medical personnel already know the symptoms to watch for, but discovering the common risks factors can help personnel keep dancers away from stresses.

With that being said, I am not claiming that the Kaplan's paper did not have its own strengths. The paper did confirm that there is a problem with ballet dancers in their mental body image. While questioning the dancers, she found that many did not believe that the "perfect ballet body" should be changed and is reasonably obtainable (Kaplan 97), which is ironic since they harm themselves to achieve it. She also found that both groups had a desire for a small body type (Kaplan 97). Without knowledge of this problem, there would be no need to find a solution. However, as I stated before, this paper focuses the dancers' eating disorders and does not help further prevention of this problem. It only confirms that there is a problem. Another strength is that Kaplan's paper discovered that eating disorders are not only apparent on one level of ballet, but can appear at many different levels. With the knowledge that the eating disorders are not fixed on one particular group of ballet dancers, people can widen their search for symptoms of eating disorders in many different groups. Thus, a group of dancers at risk will not be overlooked. The paper allows us to know that both groups have a problem. Yet, the drawback of this strength is that we cannot know how at risk these dancers are for eating disorders without a control group. Without a control group, results can over-exaggerate or under-exaggerate the problem. We cannot be sure whether or not these girls have a normal and healthy lifestyle if we compare them to someone who is living a similar lifestyle. Dancers could eat less when compared to someone who eats regularly. Yet perhaps, when compared to other dancers, they eat the same amount. When only looking at the small picture, results can be misinterpreted.

The medical paper is not perfect in all of its aspects since it does not focus on the medical field. The paper focused only a little on the effects of eating disorders on the dancer's bodies. Excluding the BMI test, the tests were geared towards the mind of the dancers and control group rather than their bodies, which is the focus of medical papers. It is difficult to say how this particular article can help advance the medical field since it focuses little on the physical body. However, disciplines are not isolated from one another. The article's findings may not advance the medical field, but eating disorders affect the body, so finding a solution to a disease that harms the body is a breakthrough. Toro et al. helps advance the prevention of eating disorders in ballet dancers. The article reveals risks of the disease and discusses ways that dancers also offset eating disorders, such as eating more calories because of their active lifestyle (Toro et al. 46).

Whenever I think about ballet, there are two instances that appear in my mind. Neither involves actual dancing, but instead focuses on the pressure from coaches for dancers to lose weight. A documentary explained how a dancer was blatantly called fat by her coach pinching her back. Another was how a dancer's coach compared her body to a sack of potatoes. I thought this was odd since both of these girls were extremely skinny. To me, it seemed like these coaches had some disease where they saw everyone else as fat. Yet, those comments caused both of the dancers to develop eating disorders. That is why I wanted to look into this topic; I wanted to know if those types of situations were common among dancers or if they were rare instances.

Both disciplines are important to consider when looking into this topic. The medical field looks at the dimensions of the body from many different angles. It can consider which proportions are best for the dancer's performance, best fit the "perfect ballet body," and are healthiest or most dangerous. Psychology focuses less on the physical body and more on the dancer's mental body image. The dancers have low BMI, but some consider themselves to be overweight. The drive for the "perfect ballet body" can cause the dancers to develop other psychological diseases than eating disorders, such as anxiety or depression (Toro et al. 47). So this idea needs to be fixed before the problem becomes out of control.

When writing her paper, Kaplan only looked at what the "perfect ballet body" entails, but Toro et al. went further. Toro et al. did not state what the perfect ballet body was, but they discussed symptoms of the dancers that showed similar characteristics. The authors were able to find the effects of this image, which is important for the prevention of the disease. Understanding where this image comes from helps us, the readers, better understand the standards that these dancers are striving for. If we do not know what image dancers want, then we will not be able to notice the change in dancers' bodies. Plus there is the word "perfect" which relates to the dancers strives for perfectionism, which occurred in both of the papers.

Toro et al. was able to find risks to help prevent eating disorders in ballet dancers, whereas Kaplan reinstated the idea that eating disorders occur in ballet. It is important to have studies reaffirm other studies' findings since the original discoveries may be wrong or misinterpreted. However, these types of studies do not advance the subject. Toro et al. found something new in the correlation between ballet dancers and eating disorders. In fact, they even state, "To our knowledge, this is the first time results of this nature have been found" (Toro et al. 46). When I first researched ballet dancers and eating disorders, Kaplan was the ideal piece because it affirmed the idea that eating disorders exist in the ballet world, while providing background information on eating disorders. Yet, Toro et al. introduced an entirely new idea. Toro et al. did not give a lot of background information, but they discovered that our belief of eating disorders in ballet may be completely wrong. Although that was not the answer I was originally looking for, it advances the subject and prevention, which is more important than confirming my view. Toro et al. found information that can help prevent the problem and further our knowledge on the relationship between ballet dancers and eating disorders.

WORKS CITED

Kaplan, Jaime F. "Recreational Ballet Students: The Mirror Image Of Professional Ballet Aesthetics?." *Psi Chi Journal of Undergraduate Research* 14.3 (2009): 93–98. Academic Search Complete. Web. 20 Feb. 2013.

Toro, Joseph, Marta Guerrero, Joan Sentis, Josefina Castro, Carles Puertolas. "Eating Disorders In Ballet Dancing Students: Problems And Risk Factors." *European Eating Disorders Review* 17.1 (2009): 40–49. Academic Search Complete. Web. 20 Feb. 2013.

AUTHOR PROFILE

I am a freshman at UCSB. I live in Claremont, California and was born in Boston, Massachusetts on August 6, 1994. I have a mother, an older brother whom I am very close with, and a German father. I also have two cats, Chickie and Moo-Moo, and a dog, Chelsea. I play soccer, and I love to travel.

—*Mackenzie Keil-Long*

A FINE BALANCE BETWEEN INTERPRETATION AND IMPLEMENTATION

Julie Moorad

Instructor: Vincent Rone

Withholding criticism and ignoring differences are racism in its purest form. Yet these cultural experts fail to notice that, through their anxious avoidance of criticizing non-Western countries, they trap the people who represent these cultures in a state of backwardness. The experts may have the best of intentions, but as we all know, the road to hell is paved with good intentions. (Good Reads)

"It is important, especially when discussing religion, to realize that there cannot necessarily be one correct interpretation or belief. That is why when analyzing the evidence that is brought up in these papers, one must consider biases, as well as the interpretations of those that are quoted."

When issues arise surrounding morals and religion, the debate becomes heated. To question the way in which another group of people live their lives seems wrong, but if morals are being infringed upon, is it not in some ways the responsibility of outsiders to step in? Yet, there is a line between being helping and overbearing which needs to be maintained. Thus, it is the responsibility of citizens to understand cultural practices in context. For example, how women are affected by today's view of Islamic culture and in turn whether intolerance should be tolerated. The article "Please, Go Wake Up!" written by Marc De Leeuw and Sonja Van Wichelen analyzes and responds to the ideas behind the film *Submission* by Ayaan Hirsi Ali. They approach the topic through a feminist lens with an emphasis on the effect of mass media on the cultural values of a society. In contrast, the essay "Does the Qur'an condone domestic violence?" by Sadia Kausar, Hussain Sjaad, and Mohammad Mahzer Idriss addresses the various interpretations of the Qur'an and their effect on Islamic law and practice. With a background in law, religion, and sociology, these authors offer an essay that touches upon social issues. Although feminist studies scholars and lawyers probably approach topics from different standpoints, their essays are more similar than one would think.

It is up to the discretion of the writer how formal or friendly their writing is. For some, inserting their opinion using "I" is unheard of, while for others it is a go-to method. Kausar et al. were much more formal than De Leeuw and Wichelen. They begin their essay by stating that they, "the authors" (De Leeuw 326), do not condone violence against women. This is as personally revealing as their essay gets, since through the rest of the piece they maintain a very academic tone, channeled toward law scholars. On the other hand, De Leeuw and Wichelen approach their audience in a much more familiar way, using "us" to equate themselves with the audience. Since their topic about the outlooks of people from Denmark is more personal, it is truly necessary to connect with their audience through the writing. Although their approaches may differ, both of these essays utilize evidence from different disciplines to analyze how cultural values surrounding morality and justice are enacted and viewed.

While their focus may be the same, Kausar and De Leeuw's writing styles contrast easily, as demonstrated through their choice of evidence, as well as their presentation. Kausar's essay is quite formal in its structure and tone. She presents three interpretations from Ulama (Islamic Scholars) of verse 4:34 from the Qur'an. Some condone domestic violence against women who have been "disobedient," while others' translations include nothing of the sort (Kausar 98). In her analysis, she interprets the verses and defines their key terms: disobedience, guarded, and beat lightly. She then elaborates on the terms throughout the rest of the essay. By defining and emphasizing certain words, she makes her point clear while backing up her arguments with evidence from the various interpretations. Her points are made even stronger by utilizing multiple Ulama's interpretations, instead of simply one. Beside these pieces of evidence, the bulk of Kausar's essay is an analysis of the terms, making the reader at times question the authority that she has.

In contrast, De Leeuw pulls evidence from multiple sources including sociologists and anthropologists, as well as direct quotes from Hirsi Ali. Much of the evidence is drawn straight from the film, as well as from articles written about it. *Submission* demonstrates that women are victims of domestic violence; in the film, their bodies are painted with verses from the Qur'an, suggesting that the Qur'an is what legitimizes this violence. In explaining the succession of vignettes about four women, De Leeuw highlights the tone, scenery, and words of the narrator. Observations make up a majority of the evidence provided, thus their points are a bit biased. Yet he does acknowledge that one of his sources is controversial, calling it "a controversial article in a respectable weekly journal" (De Leeuw 326). His recognition that some of his sources are biased helps the reader keep a more open mind about the information. What De Leeuw does effectively is present quotes in smaller snippets, instead of larger chunks, so the evidence is easily digestible and his points are therefore more coherent. Evidently, both scholarly papers use similar techniques, yet the most differentiating aspect is in how they direct their readers' interpretation.

It is important, especially when discussing religion, to realize that there cannot necessarily be one correct interpretation or belief. That is why when analyzing the evidence that is brought up in these papers, one must consider biases, as well as the interpretations of those that are quoted. When interpreting the Qur'an, there is not a single interpretation that appeals to all, but merely a few that most agree upon. Thus, it is a good decision on the part of Kausar to include multiple interpretations of the Qur'an. In the introduction, she acknowledges that she cannot limit evidence in order to not offend people: "This chapter will contain some Islamic views that will not be seen positively by others, but they are nevertheless dominant views and need to be understood as such (if not entirely accepted)" (Kausar 98). Kausar recognizes that peoples' views differ and that that will affect how they view her paper, yet that does not keep her from excluding or including certain information.

It is important to distinguish between evidence from a source and the author's opinion. While Kausar acknowledges differences and analyzes according to the interpretations, De Leeuw struggles in differentiating his opinion and analysis from the evidence he provides:

> The depiction of the Koranic verses on the semi-naked bodies suggest as if the "root of evil" (here five verses from the Koran) can be exactly localized, isolated, and eventually, dismissed... Moreover, it dismisses the work of Islamic feminists that have long been countering these masculinist discourses... (De Leeuw 328)

While this quote does indeed analyze the differences between written religious documents, the lack of a citation makes the author's personal point of view unclear. While this is obviously a challenging topic to write about since so much of it is up for interpretation, it is the author's utmost responsibility to make their writing clear and to support it with strong evidence or interpretations of that evidence. They must also take into consideration that their reader does come with their own personal beliefs, and thus write to cater to multiple groups of people.

It is necessary for the author to utilize evidence effectively to guide the reader to their point of view.

Both essays suffer from the inability to be completely unbiased, which in some ways benefits their arguments by allowing some readers to seemingly "stumble" upon their intended point. However, they lose the ability to convince someone who is utterly opposed to their ideas to accept their points. For example, if one does not agree with the interpretation from the Ulama that Kausar presents on page 98, and her subsequent explanations of the terms within, then it is unlikely that they will agree with her general conclusion about the use of violence in Islamic societies. In contrast, De Leeuw's perspective seemingly allows the reader to come to their own conclusions by simply stating the events that occurred surrounding Hirsi Ali's film. However, upon closer inspection, it is obvious that De Leeuw is stating his opinion quite directly, almost forcing the reader to accept it. He engages the audience to form this sort of trust between them and himself. He implements rhetorical questions to entrap the audience: "Would a narrative of suppression by Muslim women told in fluent Dutch have a different effect on a Dutch audience?" (De Leeuw 329). After he poses the question, De Leeuw goes on to prove his point even further. These essays demonstrate the difficulty that religious studies scholars face when writing a paper to convince someone of a point of view that may be in conflict with peoples' inherent beliefs.

Both of these sources focus on the ethical and moral issues to which Islamic women are subjected, yet they differ in the personal aspect that they include or lack. Kausar's essay is very impersonal and talks about written works as opposed to personal beliefs. At times, it is so dense one must read through it multiple times, but the content is indeed there. De Leeuw's piece focuses much more on how *Submission* was constructed and thus affected views on Islamic culture. While the use of headers clearly indicates which direction he is going, his evidence is at times a bit unclear. He assumes that the reader knows who some of these people are. It can be assumed that they are scholars, but they are referred to without any introduction. For example, he simply states, "As Leila Ahmed suggests…" (De Leeuw 333). As the audience, we literally have no idea who this person is, unless we know her from some outside context. With no explanation, the value of this evidence becomes overshadowed by the reader's confusion. Overall, the personal approach that De Leeuw uses is much friendlier to the reader, but Kausar is much more convincing and authoritative in her delivery of evidence, which is the most important aspect to an academic paper.

WORKS CITED

De Leeuw, Marc, and Sonja Van Wichelen. "Please, Go Wake Up!" *Feminist Media Studies* 5.3 (2005): n. pag. *Academic Search Complete*. Web. 22 Oct. 2012.

Good Reads. N.p., n.d. Web. 8 Dec. 2012. <http://www.goodreads.com/author/quotes/46245.Ayaan_Hirsi_Ali>.

Kausar, Sadia, Sjaad Hussain, and Mohammad Mahzer Idriss. "Does the Qur'an condone domestic violence?" *Honour, Violence, Women and Islam*. Ed. Mohammad Mahzer Idriss and Tahir Abbas. New York: Routledge, 2011. 96–113. Print.

AUTHOR PROFILE

I'm from Berkeley, California. I love spending time with my friends, playing sports, and going on adventures.

—*Julie Moorad*

ANIMAL RIGHTS

Megan Talbert

Instructor: Joel Gruber

> **"**The purpose is not to prove facts, but to introduce the audience to new ideas and ethical ways of thinking.**"**

Animal rights and their lawful and ethical standing are commonly disputed, leading to publications from distinct disciplines. The article "Animals and the Law: Property, Cruelty and Rights," written by Jerrold Tannenbaum, discusses aspects of law associated with animal rights. Within the book *The Ethics of Animal Research: Exploring the Controversy*, the chapter "Ethics and Animal Research," written by Bernard E. Rollin, takes a philosophical standpoint on this controversy. With similar purposes, each author approaches the topic in strikingly different ways, focusing on different conventions and types of evidence to support their ideas.

The word choice within Tannenbaum's article is of a much higher level, including words such as: "infringe," "despotic," "Anglo-American," and "chattel." The text is formally written by a professor, which creates the informational tone. It can be assumed that the reader already has a basis of knowledge in this area because it would take a conscious effort to find this article within a database. Therefore, the author can write an informational article without compelling information since the audience is already interested. The title is divided into three straightforward parts that address the contents of the article: Property, Cruelty, and Rights. Since this title has no appealing aspects, it can be assumed that the reader intends to research at least one of these major topics. This defines the audience as a group of educated people interested in the subject. By analyzing the author's purpose and audience, the conventions used can be determined. Due to the audience's interest in the subject, subheadings and different size text allows the reader to navigate through the abundance of information.

Tannenbaum approaches his topic with examples and definitions to create a deeper meaning for the word "property" in relation to animal rights laws. Tannenbaum states that "animals are classified by the law as property," and he uses a variety of types of evidence to support his point that "what the law means by 'property' is not what many people appear to understand" (Tannenbaum). He uses an anecdote to describe the common misinterpreted definition of property. "The boy was playing soccer with his friends in the back yard... The boy ran into the neighbor's lawn to retrieve the ball...'This is my *property!*' [the neighbor] screamed. 'Get off of my *property!*' ...'Well, this ball is my *property!*'" (Tannenbaum). Tannenbaum acknowledges that both the boy and his neighbor view their "property" as something "they have the right of control." Under this definition, if something is not your property, permission is needed for you to use it. In addition, he adds another anecdote to further identify this incorrect definition of property under the law.

He explains that the modern understanding of the word property is derived from eighteenth century English law. William Blackstone wrote, "there is nothing which so generally strikes the imagination, and engages the affections of mankind, as the right of property" (qtd. in Tannenbaum). Tannenbaum infers that the reader is familiar with Blackstone, without stating why this man's beliefs have authority. Assuming the reader is not familiar with Blackstone, this evidence is ineffective. According to Tannenbaum, Blackstone believed property was something "one man claims and exercises over the external view of the world." Under this definition of property, Tannenbaum recognizes this would mean the law "must afford animals with very little protection and, indeed, must have a very low regard for them." If this definition of property were valid under the law, animal owners would have the right to treat their animals in any manner. After defining the common definition of property, Tannenbaum is now able to state that property "refers to priority of certain kinds of rights of possession or use," and when someone owns property, they are "more entitled to possess or use it than anyone else, and that if someone else attempts to take it from me or to deprive me of my use or enjoyment of it, the law will recognize my priority—by giving it back to me." This definition clarifies the difference between the use of the word "property" in modern times and under the law. This helps the author build up to his statement that "all conditions placed on the ability of people to possess, use, or dispose of their animal property were based on human interest" (Tannenbaum). Therefore, the author has thoroughly defined "property" so the reader will comprehend that animal cruelty laws were designed to protect animal owners. Then the reader can contemplate how they view property and how it has changed.

Within Tannenbaum's article, he includes sections of the law to demonstrate its advancement, though he fails to effectively address his own opinions. Since this is an academic text and the law is indisputable, he may have intended to reveal minimal opinions. He does state his idea that, "Whatever they might originally have been intended to do, cruelty laws today clearly are intended at the very least to protect animals" (Tannenbaum). Then he proves that these cruelty laws "merely: create legal duties to animals," through anecdotes and excerpts of laws from the Mississippi and Louisiana Supreme Court (Tannenbaum). According to the Louisiana Supreme Court, "A horse under its master's hands, stands in the relation of the master analogous to that of the child to the parent" (Tannenbaum). He uses this excerpt to address that a person had the same rights over their animals and children because both are their property, and cruelty laws apply to both. This directly supports his idea because laws made under a Supreme Court are indisputable. For further support, he uses the thoughts of a famous philosopher, which is ineffective because it is from a separate discipline. Even if the statement is convincing and supports Tannenbaum's claim, it is not as effective as it could be if he used his own words to convey his own opinions.

"Ethics and Animal Research" is one of many chapters in a book designed to give the reader knowledge in many aspects of the subject. Therefore, it is not expected that the reader will already have a vast amount of knowledge about the discipline, so the word choice the author chose is fairly common, including: "abolitionist," "propaganda," and "ideology," which establishes the audience as a group of fairly educated people interested in animal experimentation. The author wants to interest the reader so they can reflect on how they have seen ethics in relation to animal experimentation in their own lives, defining the reflective tone of the essay. Furthermore, the author's purpose is to hook the reader's attention so they will read the entire chapter and want to get involved. In addition, the author's audience and purpose determine the conventions. There is only a chapter title followed by a paragraph format, with no sub-headings. Since it is a compilation of information and ideas, paragraph format is an effective way to construct this piece.

Using supporting evidence, Rollin approaches his topic by introducing the idea that people previously lacked ethical values. He uses an anecdote containing emotional appeal to describe the lack of ethics associated with animal testing. There was a film created by the Foundation for Biomedical Research in which the question, "*Will I Be Alright Doctor?*," which is also the name of the film, was "uttered by a frightened child before undergoing surgery." The physician then replied, "Yes, you will be alright if these anti-vivisectionists leave us alone to do what we need to do with our animals" (Rollin). Although the author fails to state the year this film came out, it addresses that ethics had not always been considered in animal testing. Rollin then elaborates with the fact that between 1975 and 1985, there was no written evidence supporting harmful procedures on animals. This is because science "at most provides society with facts relevant to making moral decisions," but science does not and cannot make these "moral" decisions (Rollin). He states this to demonstrate that science is not particularly associated with ethics, because they cannot be considered facts; instead, they are based upon the moral judgments of the people. He uses this evidence to build up to his idea that statements such as "killing is wrong" cannot be considered fact; they are driven by emotions. This helps to support the anecdote about the movie *Will I Be Alright Doctor?* This anecdote uses emotional appeal to create sympathy for the girl, forcing the weaker audience to support vivisection. The anecdote fails to state what kind of surgery is being performed. Maybe it is only a minor surgery, simply removing a mole or ingrown toenail? The reader must consider why this information was left out; the anecdote forces the viewer to believe the child is dying, which may not be the case. If the girl were simply having a toenail removed, the author's argument would be much less powerful. The viewer would most likely believe that animals should not be harmed to study this process, since it is not potentially harmful or deadly to the child. Though it is a weak argument, this anecdote helps the author to further develop the rest of the piece by showing the reader how ethics were viewed prior to today.

Within Rollin's chapter, he dominantly supports his ideas through reasoning and thoughts from other philosophers. Rollin states, "one could not find a morally relevant difference between humans and animals that justified excluding animals from what I call the 'moral arena'". He supports this claim by stating that since animals don't have a language

or voice, some people think animals are less valuable than humans (Rollin). He argues against this by declaring that this difference "could not bear the moral weight of excluding from the full application of our ethics, even as skin color or gender could not morally justify the exclusion of blacks and women" (Rollin). Although I believe he makes a compelling point, it lacks depth and standing. Written under the discipline of philosophy, there are limited methods for providing evidence; it would be difficult to support an ethical idea using statistics. The author can only provide new ways of analyzing situations through instances in history, and thoughts from him and other philosophers.

To further support his idea, he includes the thoughts of Darwin, that animals "can feel not only pain, but also the full range of emotions that figure in our moral deliberations about humans: fear, loneliness, boredom, frustration, anxiety" (Rollin). Rollin hopes these examples will force readers to ask themselves questions about the matter, such as, if animals have all of the same emotions that people do, shouldn't society look out for their best interests since they lack a voice? His evidence is not based on factual evidence or numbers, but it does allow the audience to contemplate his ideas, reflecting the discipline of philosophy. The purpose is not to prove facts, but to introduce the audience to new ideas and ethical ways of thinking.

To summarize, Tannenbaum's article informs the reader about animal rights laws, while Rollin wants the reader to consider the ethical standing of decisions in animal experimentation. Both pieces concern animal rights, but one takes an ethical approach while the other takes a legal approach to animals in experimentation and everyday life. The evidence the authors use is composed differently, and your interpretation determines how effective you find the piece. If you already agree with the author's ideas, the support the author provides for his or her arguments are not as valuable, though if you disagreed with the ideas presented, it would take strong supporting evidence to change your mind. Personally, I do not agree with vivisection, so I agreed with arguments made against vivisection, regardless of the supporting evidence. If more people became aware of the processes involved in vivisection, maybe they would be willing to stop using products tested on animals. "Monkeys are addicted to drugs and have holes drilled into their skulls, sheep and pigs have their skin burned off and rats have their spinal cords crushed. Tiny mice grow tumors as large as their own bodies, kittens are purposely blinded, and rats are made to suffer seizures" (PETA). According to the largest animal rights group, PETA, these are the common processes involved in animal experimentation; do you find them ethical? Consider the products you use regularly; do you know how many of them were tested on animals? Many of us might make this realization, though do not know we have the power to stop it. If the majority of people stop purchasing these products, companies will be forced to utilize other solutions to remain profitable. These ethical approaches will not rely on the strikingly different anatomy of animals, and it will provide data that is more realistic. Consider how the human body is not capable of properly digesting a majority of the items animals eat. How can we expect tests performed on these animals to produce results comparable to the human body?

WORKS CITED

"Animal Testing 101." *People for the Ethical Treatment of Animals*. N.p., n.d. Web. 06 Dec 2012.

Rollin, Bernard. "Ethics and Animal Research." Trans. Array *The Ethics of Animal Research*. Jeremy R. Garrett. Massachusetts: The MIT Press, 2012. Print.

Tannenbaum, Jerrold. "Animals and the Law: Cruelty, Property, Rights…Or How the Law Makes up in Common Sense What It May Lack in Metaphysics." *Social Research: An International Quarterly of the Social Sciences* 62.3 (1995): n. pag. Print.

AUTHOR PROFILE

I am a first year actuarial science major. I am nineteen years old and grew up in Madera, California. I have a love for animals and advocate for their ethical treatment, which inspired my piece.

—*Megan Talbert*

HOOKAH EFFECTS

Christine Sahyouni

Instructor: Vincent Rone

> **"**The second-hand smoke and cancer risks do not concern smokers who prefer the social and relaxing factors of hookah sessions.**"**

White clouds dissipate in the room, unleashing a sweet scent that lures smokers back to the nicotine packed hookah. This ancient ritual of nargile smoking has recently become a popular sensation in American society, despite the association of smoking with negative health effects, thanks to published scientific discoveries. The second-hand smoke and cancer risks do not concern smokers who prefer the social and relaxing factors of hookah sessions. These entertaining elements factor in the decision process which is discussed in "Time to Smell the Sweet Smoke" by Jim Bowman, who approaches hookah smoking from a popular culture/sociological perspective. This author conveys his point through the article: emphasizing an inflated tone, citing popular opinion, and creating a clear organization. Unlike Steven Fiala's article, "Measuring Indoor Air Quality of Hookah Lounges" that emphasizes a formal tone, cites scientific evidence, and divides the article chronologically to reach a conclusion. Although Fiala's article was more convincing, these two different academic disciplines approach the same topic using similar genre conventions to support contrasting ideologies. The author's tone influences the reader's understanding of a topic and should echo the appropriate guidelines of each genre.

An author's tone determines how a topic will be represented and how their message will be conveyed to the reader. Bowman focuses on the appealing and seductive qualities of hookah smoke, which seem to lure customers in who are well aware of the negative side effects of tobacco. The connotation of the word choices contribute to the tone as he describes hookah smoking as a "catalyst for reflection, measured conversation, and relaxation," and illustrates how "parents are unfamiliar with its charms" (Bowman 450). Although the author could be concise by using fewer adjectives to describe the hookah's social qualities, Bowman specifically inflates his tone. The diction of his words implies the author's personal stance in the essay, as well as how others may perceive smoking. Bowman's free tone mimics the hookah's seductive qualities, and the author's perspective is influential on the reader's opinion of hookah smoking. The tone leads readers to ponder how smoking with a hookah can be an intellectual and group-orientated experience. Bowman writes this article from a "fantasy theme [perspective] designed to 'provide insight into the shared worldview of a group of rhetors'" (444). Bowman set up his essay to examine the social effects of smoking instead of emphasizing the consequences.

The author's tone reflects this consistently throughout the article, even describing the negative health effects as "less killing, [but] tastes great" (Bowman 454). This ideology can relate to a reader who is personally content smoking a hookah. However, since the tone is inflated, it may hinder the readers to think rationally or statistically about the health risks involving hookah.

The article in the public health journal uses a formal tone with concise vocabulary to highlight the serious health risks of smoking. Fiala, Morris, and Pawlak define hookah tobacco smoke as a "potential health risk for patrons and employees" who inhale the second hand smoke (1). The article wants to avoid any bias in order to solely present research information; therefore, the connotation of words is important. Unlike Bowman's article, they use simple adjectives to reach the main idea without any lingering descriptions. The formal language of the article comes across when they describe "the concentration of particulate matter in the air [indicating] pollution from tobacco smoke" (Fialia, Morris, Pawlak 2). The authors choose to include details in order to achieve an in-depth analysis. If the authors decided to omit these details, then the paper might have lost the formal and educated tone that is consistent throughout the article. The tone reflects the intensity of research conducted in the experiment which increases the credibility of the article.

The type of evidence used reflects the quality, credibility, and research of each author's stance on hookah vs. cigarettes. Jim Bowman quickly introduces his article with quotations of ordinary people praising the smoking trend. For example, he quotes Catherine Rieder, an 18 year-old hookah smoker, who describes hookah smoking as "special [because] you can only do it once in a while" (Bowman 442). The author decides to use quotes by regular smokers in order to establish a familiarity with the reader. However, if the author had decided to use an official figure in society, then the author's article might have gained more credibility. Bowman includes a paragraph from an article by *The New York Times*, which characterizes cigarettes as being used by nervous people, in contrast to hookahs, which are used by balanced, patient people (449). These are analytical observations, but they have not been scientifically proven from a controlled experiment.

The author touches upon health risks, but considers them negligible as "many doctors seem to concur with the view that because the smoke goes through the water, many of the harmful substances are filtered out, and it is consequently less dangerous than cigarette smoking" (Bowman 545). This statement may hold some truth; however, there is no data to verify these conclusions, or maybe the author decided to leave out the details. Throughout the article, the author refers to popular sources like *Time* magazine, a Turkish journal of collectable art, and the *Washington Post*. These types of sources are acceptable considering that the author is writing from a Popular Culture perspective.

Since "Measuring Indoor Air Quality of Hookah Lounges" was written for a Public Health Journal, the authors use references to a large amount of data and experiments. The article introduces the main stance with scientific evidence of "air quality measurements ranging from 'unhealthy' to 'hazardous' according to Environmental Protection Agency standards" (Fiala, Morris, Pawlak 1). There are legitimate standards held by a widely recognized and respectable institution that works to see improvements in society. Scientific evidence is needed to support the claims and research in this article. They also refer to old studies performed about the effects of hookah smoke and repeat their conclusions to highlight the dangerous factors. This article compares hookah smoking to cigarettes containing "tar, carbon monoxide… inhaled more than 40 times the volume of smoke produced by a cigarette" (Fiala, Morris, Pawlak 1). This is a much different approach from Bowman's perspective on hookah vs. cigarettes. As an educated reader, I find the scientific evidence to be more convincing than opinions because it is considered solid evidence when it is valid and widely accepted. This is a much more direct and detailed description on the same specific subtopic on cigarettes vs. hookah smoking—proving why hookah smoking is unhealthy.

The division and organization of the article is crucial to the reader's understanding of the topic, and how they are influenced by the topic. Bowman's article opened with popular quotes and then traced the development of the hookah's historical ideology to its modern day uses. Since the author puts extra emphasis on examining the history of the hookah, it gives the reader time to understand why smoking is acceptable and embraced in certain cultures. Each subtopic in the essay is divided by a bolded title summarizing the main point of the following section such as, "A History of Toking in Turkey-From Ubiquiry to the Margins and Back Again" (Bowman 445).This is visually important for the reader to inform them when the author switches focus, and it helps divide the lengthy paragraphs, making it easy to look for specific information. The works cited is included at the end of the essay to keep the text simple and credible. There is also a chronological organization to the piece that builds the reader's knowledge of the history of the hookah in order to understand its modern day popularity.

"Measuring Indoor Air Quality of Hookah Lounges" presented evidence in a similarly structured manner that was concise, but was also aided by visual elements. The article opened with a general overview on the known health risks of hookah smoking, and then proceeded to describe each step of their experiment. The paragraphs were not as lengthy as Bowman's, but they were condensed with material requiring bolded subtitles in blue such as "Methods" or "Results" (Fialia, Morris, Pawlak 3). The article supplemented the data with graphs which helped the reader focus and understand the complicated terminology/statistics. Since the data was presented to the reader in alternative ways, the article can be read and understood by a wider audience. This is important in Public Health publications because they try to inform the public to take legal action after learning new conclusions from research. The works cited page is included at the end of the study, so that the reader can do further research; also it adds to the article's credibility. The organization of the paper is crucial to help an ordinary reader understand the data and analysis of an alarming public health concern.

Although, both of these articles are written in different disciplines, popular culture (sociology) and public health (research), they use similar genre conventions to achieve the author's specific purpose. The consistent tone of the articles, inflated or informative, is one of the most influential factors affecting the audience. The types of evidence such as popular sources or scientific evidence of the article, reflect the credibility and importance of

specific subtopics like cigarettes and hookah smoke. Finally, the organization of the papers is crucial to the reader's understanding of the topic. Bowman presents his article with an inflated tone, popular references, and multiple subtopics to examine the social aspects of nargile smoke. However, Fiala, Morris, and Pawlak's article was more convincing because it includes a formal tone, scientific evidence, and comprehensible organization appealing to a public reader. Ultimately, it is the reader's decision, depending on their personal perspective on hookah smoke, as to which article resonates more with them. Will you want to taste the sweet white smoke, or will you avoid the cancerous addiction?

WORKS CITED

Bowman, Jim. "Time to Smell the Sweet Smoke: Fantasy Themes and Rhetorical Vision in Nargile Café Cultures." *The Journal of Popular Culture* 42.3 (2009): 442–57. *Academic Search Complete*. Web. 29 Jan. 2013.

Fiala, Steven C., Daniel S. Morris, and Rebecca L. Pawlak. "Measuring Indoor Air Quality of Hookah Lounges." *Measuring Indoor Air Quality of Hookah Lounges* 102.11 (2012): 2043–045. *Academic Search Complete*. Web. 29 Jan. 2013.

AUTHOR PROFILE

I am a freshman biopsychology major. I am interested in economics and political science as well. I took writing 1 and 2, and as a result, my writing has drastically improved. The writing program polished my writing and helped me structure my essays. My other hobbies include dancing and playing the piano. I am also very involved in my Lebanese American culture and heritage.

—*Christine Sahyouni*

Photo by Marisol Jimenez

BOUNDARY
CROSSINGS

INSIDE THE WORLD OF SAM-I-AM

Sam-I-Am, American Icon, may be the most persistent creature in all of Whoville, but he is not without reason. A day in the life of Sam-I-Am.

Jared Payzant

Instructor: Silvia Ferreira

> **"'I can't remember the last time I had just a plate of regular eggs and regular ham...,' he says in deep thought with a concerned look upon his face."**

Sam-I-Am has many more secrets than the average Whoville civilian would imagine. The character Sam-I-Am, who played a significant role in the children's story *Green Eggs and Ham*, has a complex reality that most fans would find surprising. As he paces down the suburban path of his neighborhood, Sam-I-Am proceeds to enter a cartoonish-looking pink house of three stories. Although the house may look bizarre to an outsider, people enjoy and welcome its presence in the neighborhood, for it houses one of the most peculiar creatures indeed.

It has been 52 years since Sam-I-Am first starred in his major work, *Green Eggs and Ham*; though he has mellowed out quite a lot since then, his life is nothing short of bizarre. Sam sits in front of his large granite fireplace in his pink lounge chair with a crooked smirk across his face. This smirk may be disturbing, for the Whovillian boy from down his street is giving him a foot massage. As he casually sips on a vegetable-filled green power smoothie he remarks, "Nearly everything that I wish to ingest is the color green." He later admits that it has become a bit of a problem with his dietician. "It all started in preparation for the job. I began changing my whole diet around this character, and after *Green Eggs and Ham* was first introduced, I felt almost as if people were expecting me to eat only green foods." From there Sam proceeded to tell me that he ate that way to maintain a high stature in the media, and eventually it developed into a habit that engulfed his life. "I can't remember the last time I had just a plate of regular eggs and regular ham...," he says in deep thought with a concerned look upon his face. "That's not even the bad part; something in my mind won't let me eat it at a normal restaurant, it always has to be in some wacky situation, like on a boat, or on a train, or with a mouse in a house." Sam's persistence to remain in the light of fame was a driving force in the development of another guilty pleasure of his.

Most people who come in contact with Sam are aware of his power of persuasion. "I can persuade anyone to do anything," Sam boldly claims; "the key to persuasion is persistence." He tells me that he has gone to far greater lengths than those depicted in *Green Eggs and Ham* in order to persuade others to do things. "I once went on a two-week cruise to Alaska to persuade a man to sing the Happy Birthday song for me." Need I mention that it worked? Sam is so persuasive, in fact, he regularly talks to himself in attempt to persuade himself to do chores around the house. Sam is a peculiar creature in the way that he spends his time.

When Sam has time to spare he takes pleasure in going to garage sales and selecting treasures he can revamp and place throughout his strange home, always using persuasion to bring the price down, of course. In all of Sam's complexity he maintains a structured life and still continues to influence the citizens of Whoville. "Do you like green eggs and ham?" he asks to all those that he meets, never missing an opportunity to introduce someone to something he knows they will like. That is just the type of person he is, that Sam-I-Am.

REFLECTION

What could a translation from a children's story to a magazine article possibly look like? As I asked myself this question, I sought to find an answer through the method of creation. I made an attempt to translate Dr. Seuss's celebrated children's story, *Green Eggs and Ham*, into a magazine article, using the music and pop culture magazine *Rolling Stone* as a source of inspiration. Through this translation the audience changed tremendously, from children to educated American adults, to be brief. There were many factors to consider upon translating the story, such as context, audience, and what information to include and exclude. Through the translation, conventions of magazine articles were met and the audience, purpose, and context of the original source changed radically.

The reason I chose to translate *Green Eggs and Ham* into a magazine article was because I admire and appreciate a majority of the articles that I read in *Rolling Stone*. This magazine is a source of inspiration to me because it is entertaining, yet can be read intelligently, for it is also informative. Readers of this magazine are educated Americans who are interested in pop culture and currents events, both nationally and globally. I wanted my translation to speak to people in the same way, so I fitted it more to address this particular audience. I thought that this translation would be difficult, yet interesting to create, which is one of the reasons I chose to accept the task. The audience of the original source, children's books, is composed of young children, teachers, new readers, and parents with young children. The new audience that I intend to speak to is made up of informed and educated individuals who speak English; a large majority of these people are my peers, such as college students. These two sources also have different purposes; nearly every child's book teaches the children a valuable lesson to walk away with and helps them improve their reading skills, whereas the purpose of a magazine article is to entertain and inform the reader about a certain subject.

To integrate information from *Green Eggs and Ham* into a magazine article, I used one of the main characters, Sam-I-Am. The character Sam-I-Am was a very vital part of the translation because I chose to write the article as a profile of him. There were some complications with this because he is a fictitious character whom I knew nearly nothing about apart from the fact that he persistently tries to persuade another character to eat green eggs and ham. To achieve the translation between these two genres I had to include several fictitious details about the character that were not part of the original story. I presented the character as a celebrity who would normally appear in a *Rolling Stone* article after he finished a major work; in this case the major work was *Green Eggs and Ham*. By presenting my article in this manner, I was able to use an interview as part of the text and create quotes that I think Sam-I-Am would say if he had actually been interviewed. I excluded most of the storyline from the magazine article because people reading a magazine aren't interested in reading a short story, but instead want to learn about the person being interviewed and what their life is like behind the scenes. However, I did choose to incorporate many references to the story, such as Sam's desire to eat green things and ability to persuade others into doing things that he knows they will enjoy.

During the translation from children's story to magazine interview article, I found it much more difficult to create and add information than I had imagined it would be. I hadn't realized before how much of the translation I would have to create out of thin air. One of the reasons why it was so difficult was because I had to make the translation interesting when I added to the story, yet still hold relevance. I also found it difficult to structure the article and format it in a way that would be similar to a magazine article. To overcome the challenge of creating new material that wasn't in the story I tried to think of things that people would want to hear in an interview; there was really no other way around it. To get the structured layout of the translation, I used a *Rolling Stone* article as a reference. This article inspired me to use columns to further develop the structure of the article. To make the structure of the translation like that of a *Rolling Stone* article, I chose to include a large title and a heading. One of the most important components in my translation is the use of quotes because it helps clarify that it is indeed an interview. I really admire the flow of *Rolling Stone* articles, so that was an element of the translation I was striving for. To make it into a true *Rolling Stone* article I attempted to use their admirable incorporation of quotes into their articles in my own translation.

Through the process of this project, I learned a great deal about my sources that I hadn't previously been aware of. With the help of Kerry Dirk's article, "Navigating Genres", I learned that each genre has its own unique audience, purpose, and context. Taking these three things into consideration helped me in making my translation. Once I defined the audience, purpose, and context of both *Green Eggs and Ham* and *Rolling Stone* articles, the translation became much easier. Another source that helped me achieve the translation was Scott McClouds's *Making Comics*, because I learned about choice of

moment and image. Choice of moment and image are choices that the author makes to ensure clarity, organization, and flow. From my original source, I learned many of the conventions that the original author used to appeal to his intended audience, such as word choice, simple sentences, and a good theme. I also learned how carefully the author considered choice of moment and image. Dr. Seuss had to keep in mind that the story had to be drawn and rhyme to appeal to children, so choice of moment affected the words he used to rhyme in certain sections of the story and affected what he drew in certain moments. Through my translation, I also developed a greater appreciation for magazine articles because of their structure and the extent of detail that they include in their writing. They provide a lot of imagery and organize their articles with deep consideration, which is something to learn from. With the translation from *Green Eggs and Ham* to *Rolling Stone* article, the text served a completely different purpose for a completely different audience within a completely different context.

WORKS CITED

Dirk, Kerry. "Navigating Genres." *Writing Spaces: Readings on Writing.* Vol. 2. Ed. Charles Lowe and Pavel Zemliansky. Parlor Press, 2010. EBook.

McCarthy, Lucille P. "A Stanger in Strange Lands: A College Student Writing Across the Curriculum." *Research in the Teaching of English.* 21.3 (1987): 233–65.

Seuss, Dr. *Green Eggs and Ham.* New York: Beginner, 1960. Print.

AUTHOR PROFILE

My hometown is Costa Mesa, California, and I am an undeclared major here at UCSB. I plan on switching into the Film and Media major in spring. In my free time, I enjoy playing the drums and riding my unicycle.

—*Jared Payzant*

PORTS OF WRITING

Linda Phan

Instructor: Sasha Metcalf

AUTHOR PROFILE

I am a first-year economics and accounting major from San Jose, CA. Some things I enjoy include: Jason Mraz, yoga, and traveling. One day, I plan to travel the world. I also enjoy writing, and one day I plan to minor in it. One of my bucket-list items is writing a book.

—*Linda Phan*

"Ports of Writing is a popular destination where writers will find inspiration and learn about writing."

Ports of Writing

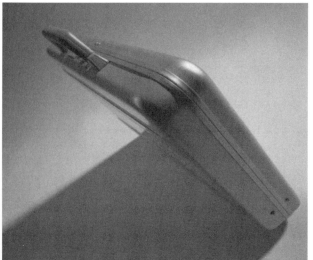

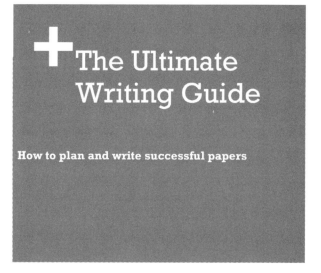

The Ultimate Writing Guide

How to plan and write successful papers

Overview:

Why Write?

Ports of Writing is a popular destination where writers will find inspiration and learn about writing. This guide will help writers to incorporate new elements of composition and sources into their writing practice to effectively communicate with their audiences.

Guide by Linda Phan
Metcalf
Writing 2

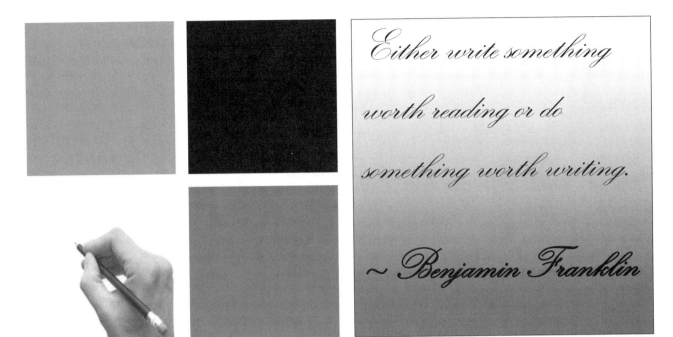

> *Either write something worth reading or do something worth writing.*
>
> *~ Benjamin Franklin*

+ See + Do
Attractions in Writing

Museum of Purpose

There is no better start to your trip than a visit to the Museum of purpose. This place is where tourists are able to admire exhibits and focus on what they want to establish. Tourists are able to examine their premises and assess the gallery of ideas.

Purpose is important because it establishes what the author hopes to achieve in the writing.

This museum leaves tourists with reflective thoughts about why they went on their trips and what they wanted to accomplish on their trips. Other highlights include a wall displaying genres and writing mediums located in the Hall of Writing.

Navigating Genres

Enjoy a ferry ride that takes tourists sightseeing around the various genre areas in the city. The three-hour tour encompasses geographic and notable locations. It is a great way for tourists to recognize the location's patterns and similar conventions. Kerry Dirk, the captain of the ship, tells tourists that genre is a way to categorize writing.

Writings that share a similar purpose, audience, tone, and style make them the same genre. The use of these conventions enhances the readability of a paper.

Likewise, the similar regions pointed out in the tour allow the audiences to discover the magnificence of the writing port.

+ Places in Writing

More diversity and experience in writing!

> **A writer never has a vacation. For a writer life consists of either writing or thinking about writing.**
>
> **~Eugene Ionesco (Playwright)**

Dictionland

Center of Performing Syntax

Tone Hall

This hugely popular theme park offers many different choices in rides for the thrill-seeking writer. In the "Land of Diction," park-goers will agree that the word choice ride is important.

Although there are similar types of rides, the attraction of each varies in their intensity.

Similarly, in writing, different word choices help the audience understand the sophistication of the argument and connections presented.

Many tourists like to stop by this attraction that looks into the culturally complex writing exhibited by writers. It is a venue for major concerts and events, with live bands singing songs about the relationship among sentences. The newest addition is the Syntax Monument, which has a unique architecture constructed from phrases and groups of words that have close bonds. The syntax exhibit is known for its cohesion and flow of sentences. The center helps audiences absorb more content in their future writings.

Many tourists like to stop by the Tone Hall of the town. It is significant because this is where the voice of the town gets heard. The founding authors of the town established Tone Hall in the very early writing periods. Inside the hall, conveyed by diction, point of view, and syntax, symbolic images of how the Ports of Writing was formed can be found. Tone is particularly important because it makes the writing distinct and gives it personality.

Restaurants

The Port's top writing dining spots will attract customers of all interests to great-value writings.

Writer's Bistro

After fun-filled visits to the many tourist locations, writers will find themselves looking for a place to eat to fuel up their brains for more writing. Hidden behind rows of hotels is a retro bistro serving a wide range of writers.

The restaurant menu has a variety of food to cater to all sorts of writerly taste buds. For example, the restaurant offers Asian fusion cuisine to cater to American tastes. There are many bistros within the area; however, not any are the same. Customers come into the Writer's Bistro for the uniqueness of the food, and they leave the Bistro satisfied.

Similar to how there are many different types of food for different types of people, a writer should keep in mind the variety of audiences reading their writing. The author should be able to tailor their writing to each audience.

There can be many of the same writings out there, but the approach and experience/perspective of the author keeps the writing new and refreshing to the audience.

Both writing and restaurants can make their product more appealing by considering the consumers, and by keeping aware of the content of their product.

+ Nightlife

The Peter Elbow Live Show!

The popular, sell-out writing show, *Teaching Two Kinds of Thinking by Teaching Writing*, narrated by Peter Elbow, examines first and second order-thinking. The show discusses how first-order thinking (unconscious, free writing) differs from second-order thinking (thoughtful rewriting). Elbow teaches us that through creative and expository writing, then engagement in critical assessment and revision, our writing will be more purposeful and controlled.

The viewers will enjoy the examples of how these two types of writing will work in a mutually reinforcing way in their writing.

MUST SEE SHOWS!

Late Night with Kyle Stedman

This late night show features comedy sketches and parodies about the annoying way people use sources. Stedman, who is also a writer himself, is the host. He informs the audience that although the use of sources is important, using them incorrectly makes writing ineffective. The show features sketches of annoying ways of using quotes, with a lineup of examples including: "Dating Spiderman" and "Armadillo Road Kill." Stedman follows up by dispensing advice to a live studio audience, telling them that whenever they use a source, they must support it with details in the sentences that follow the quote. Stedman then reenacts a scenario as a live example to the audience, reemphasizing that sources make their writing more credible.

"DEAR DANIELLE"

Danielle Butler

Instructor: Michael Joiner

> **"**I learned about the process of writing and that sometimes ideas change and develop; I just need to find the right genre to express those ideas.**"**

REFLECTION

In Writing 2 this quarter, students explored and studied many writing concepts, from comma placement to research of classroom literacy practices. All of these concepts seem to showcase the idea of genres and their importance in writing. Each genre consists of its own conventions that differentiate one from another, such as the intended audience and the purpose. From both Writing Project 1 and Writing Project 2, I have experienced the importance of taking the time to think about what I am writing and which genre will work best to successfully complete an assignment. I built on these experiences while working on this open genre project.

In my first Writing Project, I used a technological genre, Tweets, so I thought that using a different technological genre for this project would be a fun idea. Memes are a funny way to express ideas and opinions to share with others, so I created a series of Internet memes for the first peer edit. I created about ten memes, ranging from comma placement to commentary on some of the readings. However, I did not think that they showcased well what I had learned this quarter. I found that I was making memes about the class in general, and that it was difficult to create them based solely on what we had learned. This problem was highlighted in some of the comments I received on the peer edit because although some were funny, which is the purpose of memes, they were not useful to this project. Instead, I changed my genre to a newspaper advice column. Advice columns offer a more expressive form of communication from the writer to the reader, which allows me to use my own words and ideas, whereas a meme requires its own terminology and humor to get a point across. I chose this genre because it is a creative way to "flat out" explain what Writing 2 is and what we learned. It was easier for me to address both Writing Projects, articles that we were assigned, and other elements of the class, such as Grammar Day. I entitled the column "Dear Danielle" in *The Freshmen Bulletin*, which is a fictional newsletter that would be sent out to incoming UCSB freshmen during the summer. The purpose of the column is to address all questions and comments that the incoming freshmen may have. In this issue, I focus on Writing 2, and instead of answering individual questions, I respond to all of them in one reflective article.

All newsletters have a catchy title, so for mine I chose *The Freshmen Bulletin* because it is for incoming freshmen, by current freshmen. Advice columns also have a title that usually involves the use of a greeting from the writer. The greeting typically goes along with the name, either rhyming with it or starting with the same letter. Fortunately, I was able to use "Dear Danielle," as this creates a personal tone between the reader (those who ask) and the writer (the person who answers reader's questions). Additionally, the columns can also include a catchy signature, so I chose to include "Delightfully, Danielle" as a happy send-off that shows that I am interested in the questions. Some columns may use fictional names in order to protect the true identity of the writer, while others use real names. However, I chose to use my real name as this piece of writing is a personal account of my experiences that I am sharing with incoming students.

Aside from the titles and catchy phrases, the structure of an advice column is critical. Some advice columns answer individual questions, while others write articles about a topic that addresses many questions. I chose to go with the second option because I approach the article as if I received many questions about the Writing 2 course specifically. This method allowed me to express what is important to me, as well as include additional details that may not have been addressed in the questions. It also allowed me to insert my own opinions about other topics that incoming freshmen may not think to ask about. The actual structure of the page is also crucial to the newsletter/advice column genre. I used a template to create this newsletter, and so I had to work within the conventions set by the template; I found this helpful as I was able to change the format and add pictures and make it my own creation. The template also allowed a large title with eye-catching designs and fonts that draw the reader's attention. For the writing, advice columns consist of multiple columns rather than one large body of writing that reads left to right. In order to fit the parameters of this convention, I had to alter the font a few times in order to keep the column structure within one page.

To help prepare myself to write in this genre, I read some old *Daily Nexus* newspapers I found. While there are no advice columns, I read some opinion articles and some informative articles. I tried to combine what I found in both of these, as an advice column consists of informing the reader, while also having some type of opinion with a personal tone. In my column, I included small phrases that would be seen in an opinion article such as "Cool, huh?," which engages the reader and lets them see that I am writing this article directly to them. This form is inviting, which is crucial since I am welcoming these freshmen to the university.

Additionally, I have moments within the article which are strictly informative, but I also try to create an upbeat and personal tone of voice in order to keep the reader interested. When I explain genre conventions in the WP1 paragraph, I am informing the reader about how genres differ, but I use an example with which the incoming freshmen can relate: social media. Using such well-known websites allows them to better understand my point and easily see connections because they are familiar with them. I contrast these sites with a research paper and ask the reader short questions in order to keep their attention.

Another convention that is found in newspaper articles is paraphrasing or quoting a source. I used this convention in my article when discussing the articles that we were assigned in class. I mentioned the articles within my explanation of what we learned from each Writing Project to back up my comments and to further emphasize what was learned. For Writing Project 1, I chose the article "Navigating Genres" by Kerry Dirk because that article was one of the most helpful to me. It really explained to me what a genre is and set me up for the rest of the quarter. I mentioned certain highlights from the article, such as Dirk's explanation of location, in order to showcase to the freshmen some examples of differing conventions without trying to be too confusing. For Writing Project 2, I used two articles that we read: "The Concept of Discourse Community" by John Swales and "Annoying Ways People Use Sources" by Kyle Stedman. I chose to use Swales' article because it was a huge part of the second WP; however, this article had a lot of information, so I tried to keep my explanation concise and relevant. I chose Stedman's article to showcase how we learned to cite our sources in MLA style. I mentioned the "Dating Spiderman" from the article because it stood out when I read it, and it added some humor, which is typical of a newsletter column. I chose to paraphrase all of these because the article is my own narrative and explanation of the course. Paraphrasing allows me to state the point I am making within my own ideas, while quoting would cause a minor setback in the sentence and flow of ideas due to the necessity of an introduction to the quote, followed by analysis.

Prior to this project, I had a general knowledge of advice columns, but not enough to create my own newsletter. In order to complete this project, I used what Dirk said about studying other genres to familiarize oneself with them, and I feel like it worked well in developing the final product. I learned about writing articles from real newspapers and then used my imagination, with the help of a template, to bring all of my ideas together. I feel as though this Writing Project caused me to think harder about my writing as I had to address my concerns about my first genre not working, only to find another genre that contained the conventions that work best for the direction I wanted to take with the project. I learned about the process of writing and that sometimes ideas change and develop; I just need to find the right genre to express those ideas.

WORKS CITED

Dirk, Kerry. "Navigating Genres". *Writing Spaces: Reading on Writing*. Ed Charles Lowe and Panel Zemliansky. Vol. 1. West Lafayette: Parlor, 2010. 248–262. Print.

Stedman, Kyle. "Annoying Ways People Use Sources". *Writing Spaces: Reading on Writing*. Ed Charles Lowe and Panel Zemliansky. Vol. 2. West Lafayette: Parlor, 2011. 241–256. Print.

Swales, John. "Concept of Discourse Communities". *Writing About Writing: A College Reader*. Doug Downs and Elizabeth Wardle. Boston: Bedford/ St. Martins, 2010. 464–480. Print.

AUTHOR PROFILE

I am a first year biology major from Los Angeles, California. I have lived in California for most of my life, and I enjoy hiking and going to the beach. On campus, I served as a senator in my Residence Hall's Hall Council and have participated in HPH and EAB. After UCSB, I plan to attend medical school to become a cardiologist or pediatrician.

—Danielle Butler

SUMMER 2012

the FRESHMEN bulletin

THE WEEKLY NEWSLETTER JUST FOR UCSB FRESHMEN!

Dear Danielle,

The column that is here to answer all of your questions!

Dear Danielle,

The only advice column approved by the University for incoming freshmen, by current freshmen!

Please send questions/comments to deardanielle@thefreshmenbulletin.ucsb.edu.

HELLO UCSB CLASS OF 2016!

Congratulations on being accepted to the University of California, Santa Barbara! You have all made a great decision on choosing to attend this school.

My name is Danielle, and I am a first year Biology major in the College of Letters and Science. Here at *the Freshmen Bulletin*, we know how nerve-wracking the summer before college is, so the "Dear Danielle" column was created to help prepare all of you future Gauchos!

Here I will address your questions and give tips about campus, classes, residence halls, and just life at UCSB in general. I receive many questions, so I will pick the most popular and address them in my articles.

Many of you have sent questions regarding when and how to pick classes and which classes I recommend taking.

Fairly soon, you all will attend Orientation, where you will create your first-ever college schedule! This is an exciting time in which you have the freedom (kind of) to steer away from the high school curriculum and venture into the land of fun G.E.s and can pick the classes YOU want to take.

This can be scary, so in the next few issues I will focus on picking classes and giving tips on the best courses at UCSB.

Continued on page 2, see "Dear Danielle"

the FRESHMEN *bulletin*

DEAR DANIELLE, *CONTINUED FROM PAGE 1*

In this week's issue, I will focus on Writing 2, which is a required class that all of you will need to take (unless you achieved a 4 or better on an AP exam). CAUTION: Be sure you NEED this class before taking it. Writing 2 is an academic writing course, and it helps us to refine our academic writing at the college level. This class fulfills the College of Letters and Science and College of Engineering Area A1 Writing requirement. Despite all of these facts, I want to talk about this class because it really helped me with my writing, and I want to share some experiences and tips with you.

Upon entering the classroom, I thought the class would consist of essays upon essays. However, the class is designed to have three Writing Projects (WP) that take three weeks each. In these three weeks, we turn in Project Builders (PB) to build on our ideas, and we also have assigned readings that we sometimes have to answer questions about on GauchoSpace; GauchoSpace is an online resource for all students in which students can view grades, email professors, post in forums, or even chat with professors. Each WP focuses on different aspects of writing, and we study these in order to develop a 4-6 page essay.

In the first Writing Project, we studied and discussed genres. According to dictionary.com, a genre is "a class or category of artistic endeavor having a particular form, technique, or the like." In one class, we developed a list of different genres, and I was surprised to see just how many genres there were; in today's technological world, Facebook updates and Tweets even count as their own genres. In order to understand genres better, we learned about conventions, which are general rules or practices that are accepted by society. Each genre has its own conventions, which differ based on the intended audience (who will read your writing), purpose (why are you writing this) and context/location (when was it written, how was it published). For example, in a Facebook status you can use abbreviations, short sentences, and punctuation is not important. But would you do the same on a term paper? No. Because each genre calls for its own set of conventions. It is not appropriate to use abbreviations on a term paper, and people on Facebook will not want to read a well-structured, properly punctuated, long status update. Without even knowing it, we write in different genres every day and are aware of these differing conventions. I remember in the first few weeks of class reading an article by Kerry Dirk called "Navigating Genres." This article was my introduction to genres, and it addresses that we learn to write in different genres by referring to other genres to see what works and what doesn't. Dirk also tells us that location affects genre, and this was how I was finally able to grasp the concept of genres: genres differ depending on who you are addressing, where you are addressing an issue, and why and how. Cool, huh? I thought so.

Building off of what we learned in WP1, in WP2 we researched one of our classes to identify the literacy practices of that class. In a way, it was like finding the different conventions of each classroom, like each class was a genre. In order to understand this concept, we read "The Concept of Discourse Community" by John Swales in which he defines a discourse community (a community that has its own system of communicating and terminology within a field) using six characteristics. We used this information to observe our class and interview our instructors to come up with the literacy practices of the class, which include pieces of writing, how an instructor presents information, test questions, and how students should communicate in the class.

Another important part of this WP was citing sources. Pretty much, this is a repeat of high school with the MLA formatting of the Works Cited and citing within your writing. We read a pretty cool article called "Annoying Ways People Use Sources" by Kyle Stedman in which he relates those who drop a quote without a proper analysis to a date with Spiderman. Seems unusual, but it's actually very helpful.

On top of WPs, we learned about sentence structure and peer editing, and best of all, Grammar Day! (Okay, it wasn't the best day, but it isn't as bad as it sounds.) Each WP ended with a peer review and peer edit, spanning over 2 classes. These are a time for students to pair up and provide feedback before turning in our Submission Drafts. On certain days during WPs, we discussed sentence structure and how to structure our essays based on the academic essay genre. On Grammar Day, we observed how comma placement can completely change a piece of writing, making a love letter become a spiteful "anti-love" letter. We also made sentences that were up to 100 words! This seems difficult, but it is amazing how much detail one can add to make a four word sentence into a 100-word sentence. We used a baseball example involving a member of our class, and it was fun to see how everyone used their imagination to turn hitting a ball into a heavily detailed account. This class "requires" a "Hacker Manual" (a small, yet expensive, book about writing) and we use this on Grammar Day to pinpoint our most common mistakes and to work with partners to address how we can work on them.

Overall, I highly recommend you take Writing 2 within your first year, as it will set you up on the right path for academic writing in other classes--especially in WP2, where you can pretty much ask your instructor how to write and succeed in the class.

Don't forget to keep emailing me questions and comments!

Delightfully,
Danielle

PANCREATIC CANCER

Connie Chen

Instructor: Jessica Elliott

Dear WP3 Reader,

One day, I read an article about epidemics that surprisingly sweep across un-suspecting regions in urban areas and in third-world countries. It got me thinking, *are we really all that different?* I wondered if disease affects only a certain group of people or if there were other contributing factors. So, I looked into this notion further. I gathered information about the problem from professionals: economists studying gross domestic product input and production of agriculture in certain countries, sociologists analyzing and observing living conditions in third-world countries, and geneticists and doctors studying epidemiology and human disease susceptibility. After gathering information on these subjects, I became inspired to create a moving story of two people from two different regions suffering from the same disease—pancreatic cancer.

The following series of three compositions present the stories of two young girls diagnosed with pancreatic cancer—one contracted from malnutrition and third-world living conditions, another that contracted the gene at birth and enhanced her risk with an unhealthy diet. I chose to portray the stories of these two girls through an exchange of personal letters, one-on-one interviews, and an autopsy report of one that fell victim to the disease far too soon. The three texts will allow any interested reader to not only absorb information about their lifestyles and experience, but to understand how different texts can work together.

I enjoyed composing this assortment of texts based on the diverse writing conventions that each genre employs. First, the letter exchange between the two new friends is meant to depict their social standing, as well as their innocence and personalities, while also presenting clues that foreshadow an unfortunate death. My research included social and psychological factors that prompt poor food choices. In Meredith McDougall's case, her choices are prompted by naivety and innocence, but are also prompted by a sense of privilege. Being pampered with a "pink room with a castle bed" gives her the sense that she can do and get what she wants, such as lollipops and sodas. However, this privilege becomes a disadvantage in terms of her health. In another case, Ava Renana, who lives in a third-world country, has no choice but to consume whatever she can find in her village, even if it is dirty rainwater. These types of clues in each text will allow you to make connections

> **"After gathering information on these subjects, I became inspired to create a moving story of two people from two different regions suffering from the same disease—pancreatic cancer."**

within the story. I chose to foreshadow events through the letter exchange due to its ability to portray personal thoughts and actions. Meredith hid her malnutrition from her mother, which contributed to her quick death; her disease could have been treated sooner had her mother or a doctor known about her poor food choices. However, the information was only limited to the letter exchanges with Ava, who could not have told anybody who might be able to directly help Meredith.

Interviews have always served as a direct and simple way to convey information—they are, simply put, questions and answers; it doesn't require the reader to have prior knowledge on the subject. What I enjoy about interviews is that the responses are not simply answering the question; they convey emotion, opinion, and, further, form trickling thoughts on the subject. This text reflects an interview with a doctor who had seen both sides of the world—the privileged and the underprivileged—and has worldly experience with several diseases that exist in both regions. The interview with Ava depicts her limited experience in the world, which, in essence, saves her from the fears that one may face with this disease, and, instead, her limited experience provides hope that a better life does exist—even if it is too late for her to live it. Ava, in her own words, shows some understanding of this problem when she says in an interview, "Before, I thought my life was like everyone else's in the world. But, I hear people's stories, about a better life in America… I suppose if I had the chance to live in this cleaner world, then I would be able to live a longer life."

The interviews, made separately, also depict the other speaker's knowledge that contributes to the story. For example, Dr. Derek Montgomery tells the interviewer that Ava's pen pal, Meredith, has died from a disease that they both share, but chooses not to inform Ava. Although this action leads to Ava's curiosity towards her un-responded letters to Meredith, it presents Derek's good intentions and compassion for his patients, as well as wisdom that he has acquired through his years as a medical practitioner. An interview is an excellent source for information, and it allows the reader to understand the characteristics of a speaker.

The content of the interviews not only contributes to the emotional aspects of the story, but also presents information that I have acquired through the research that has inspired my composition, such as the nutritional and environmental causes of pancreatic cancer. I emphasized this research through one of the most difficult yet simple genres to compose: an autopsy report. Although it provides straightforward and detailed descriptions of a person's physical composition, it also provides a deeper analysis and explanation of a person's death. This autopsy report includes a pathological analysis that confirms reasons for Meredith McDougall's death, foreshadowed in the letter exchanges. It explains how her malnutrition has affected her internal organs and expedited her deterioration. The medical analysis also suggests what could have been done to prevent a sudden death. Although it does not provide a happy ending, I feel that the autopsy report provides a satisfying yet moving conclusion to the story.

In a multigenre project, making connections between different genres—from an autopsy report, to personal letters, to one-on-one interviews—requires a great amount of attention to details within texts. By unifying elements of each text, you will be able to understand the emergence of diseases from more than one academic point of view, but also grasp a new perspective of lives in different parts of the world. Although the outcomes of the story presented through these three texts is meant to serve a surprising end, I presume that without an awareness of the details I present, the outcome may not be comprehended the same way as I intend for readers. I hope this compilation of texts touches readers and raises an awareness of the various existence of disease in different regions.

Enjoy!

Sincerely,

Connie Chen

Dear Pen Pal,

Hi! My name is Meredith, but every body calls me "Merry Mere" becuz I'm always so happy no matter what! Hehe. I am 8 3/4 years old and I live in Beverly Hills, California. My faverite place in the werld is my room. My mommy decorated it when I was in her belly—she painted it everything pink and my bed is shaped like a cassle. What's your room like? Where's your faverite place in the world?

Your new frend,

Merry Mere ☺

Letter #2 September 20, 2011

Dear Meredith,

My name is Ava. I live in Ethiopia, Africa with my 3 brothers and 2 sisters. I am 14 years old and am the oldest of all my family, since my mother passed away 3 years ago. I only wish for room like yours. I share space with my brothers and sisters in my hut. My favorite place in my village is the spinning room. I work here and make clothes for work. It is a calm and quiet task and reminds me of my mom. She taught me to weave and sew. What is your mom like?

Ava

Letter #3 September 25, 2011

Ava,

I <3 my mom. She does evrything for me and scares my monsterz away. But, she looks sad when I get sick, even sadder when I get tummy aches and since my grammy Ann went to heaven, she cries when im sick. She takes me to the same doctor as grammy Ann's all the time now. His name is dr Derek. I like him because his office has lollipops and I get to take whatever I want! Plus. last week, I went thru this machine that felt like I was in a spaceship, and he looked at my insides and told me I am A-okay but my mom said we are gonna go every week! Yay, more lollipops! Plus, to grow my bones, they told me to eat lotsa vitamins but to stop drinking soda. But its so yummy, I trade my pudding for a soda everyday at school (shh, don't tell my mom!) I never get sick of it. I can drink that everyday until I die! What do you like to eat?

Your buddy,

Merry Mere!

Letter #4 March 15, 2012

Hello Meredith,

I sorry, it has been a while. Much has happened in the past few months. My village had another sandstorm and we have clean water no more. Doctors came to my village and helped us rebuild our home and gave us medicine. Also, they helped me celebrate my 15th birthday and gave me sweet bread. I am feeling thankful for these people. Doctors say the medicine will clean my body and make me strong for a while. Has your doctor made you strong?

Ava

P.S. I like to make flat bread made from handpicked grains with aged butter.

THE LIFE OF THE LIVING: AN URBAN AND RURAL VIEW
By Connie Chen *March 10, 2012*

15-year-old African native, Ava Renana, and American, Dr. Derek Montgomery, from Johns Hopkins Medical Center, separately speak about the everyday life in famine and poverty-stricken Ethiopia.

CC: *People know this region for its social conditions but don't know what it's like. What is your everyday routine like?*

AR: Every day is the same. Most nights, it's barely comfortable to sleep in the heat and the humid air. Every day, I go to work making clothes, then find water and food for my family. Most days, I can only collect the water from the muddy puddles outside of the huts, or, if I'm lucky I get rainwater from a leaky roof.

When the MEDLIFE clinic came, Dr. Derek told me that the water and food I collect is what has made me sick after all these years, but I have no choice; there is not much around here, and it is just something our village has to do on a regular basis.

CC: *How long have you known about your pancreatic cancer? Does anyone treat you or educate you about your disease?*

AR: Before the clinic came, I would get stomach pains and feel weak; I thought it was from long workdays or cholera, which many people have here, and I thought it had passed when the pain stopped. Then, one day, my airway closed, and I couldn't breathe, and I've felt weak since then. Luckily, the clinic came when it did. If it weren't for Dr. Derek and his

team, I would have never known that I had cancer. They have treated me, but I learned that there is no cure, and I have little time left. But I accept what I cannot change. So, I wait in the long lines in the sun, and I wait for the medicine that gets me some more time to watch my brothers and sisters grow.

CC: *Do you think if you lived somewhere else, you would have gotten this disease?*

AR: Before, I thought my life was like everyone else's in the world. But, I hear people's stories about a better life in America where there are good jobs, shelter, water fountains, and plastered walls that shield people from the dirty air. I suppose if I had the chance to live in that cleaner world, then I would be able to live a longer life.

In a separate interview with Dr. Derek Montgomery:

CC: *You started MEDLIFE mobile clinics seven years ago. In those years, what have you learned about the people and cities you visited?*

DM: There are a lot of inspiring people here. In the weeks we are there, hundreds visit the clinic waiting to be helped. You begin to realize the extremity of the horrible conditions these people experience, compared to the other developing cities my clinic has visited in the past. Yet, they're still humble and patient and continue with their everyday lives, taking care of their families, building a home, staying alive! You feel joy and thankfulness that you have the ability to help these people and make a difference in their lives.

CC: What kinds of diseases do you find most common in the villages you visit?

DM: Due to the malnutrition in these countries, cholera has been one of the most common diseases. But malnutrition also leads to more severe diseases, such as pancreatic cancer, which is difficult to treat. Unfortunately, we usually don't catch it until it's too late; we may be able to buy our patients an extra two weeks to the 3–6 months they have left. There are just so many factors in this type of environment—limited food sources, malnutrition, toxic air, and contaminated water—that contribute to the contraction of these diseases.

CC: Are diseases you see in these cities extant in the states?

DM: Diseases such as cholera are not as evident in the states, but pancreatic cancer definitely is. In my medical training, pancreatic cancer has risk factors such as an unhealthy diet, and it is hard to diagnose. It could also be genetic as well—the cancer could be present in their bodies from birth and escalate as they grow, accompanied by an unhealthy diet.

It is unfortunate that people become stuck living with consequences that they can't avoid. Some people have a just as small chance of survival living in Beverly Hills as others would in places like Ethiopia.

CC: Do you keep in touch with any of your patients?

DM: I do. I get updates from them, and I also try to get the patients to interact with each other from across the globe through pen pal letters. It allows each side to learn a little more about the different kinds of lives that exist in the world. One of my patients here in Ethiopia is actually a pen pal with one of my patients in America. There was a 10-year-old girl named Meredith, who was diagnosed in late September and got increasingly worse within the last five months, from mid-October until last month when we lost her. I… haven't had the heart to tell Ava because once you lose someone who is going through the same thing as you are, you lose hope. But keeping in touch with the patients in the countries we visit is also rewarding. By simply coming to them, giving them medicine, examinations, clean water, and food, we give them the chance to survive and to *live*.

AUTOPSY OF MEREDITH MCDOUGALL
Office of Connie Chen, Medical Examiner
Santa Barbara County Medical Examiner's District
Santa Barbara, CA
(818) 808-8586 Fax: (805) 555-1234

Autopsy Report

NAME:	Meredith McDougall
CASE NO.:	987111B
AGE:	approx. 10 years
HEIGHT:	4'7"
WEIGHT:	42.3 pounds
SEX:	Female

We certify that on the 25th day of February, 2012, at 9:30 in the morning, an autopsy on the body of Meredith McDougall was performed at the Santa Barbara County Medical Examiner's Office. We suggest that the cause of death was as follows:

ANATOMIC FINDINGS

A blood culture indicated *pernicious anemia* with only 25% hemocrit indicating malnutrition. Existence of *helicobacter pylori* bacteria in the stomach indicates the leading cause to the swelling of the stomach walls. Swollen and eroded stomach and esophageal tissue indicate long-term presence of *h.pylori* bacteria and acidic stomach fluid content with high concentration of carbonation and sugar. The deteriorated pancreas decreased patient's ability to excrete the bacteria properly.

CAUSE OF DEATH

Malignant neoplasm pancreatic cancer

EXTERNAL EXAMINATION

The subject has no lacerations on the outside of the body. The patient is evidently underweight, suggesting low absorption and digestion of nutrients (fats, carbohydrates, etc.).

INTERNAL EXAMINATION

CARDIOVASCULAR SYSTEM: The heart is measured a standard 200 grams and measured $5.5 \times 4 \times 3$ inches. There is little evidence of atherosclerosis—no blood clots in the descending aorta or major arteries connecting to the heart.

RESPIRATORY SYSTEM: The right and left lungs are measured at 230 and 218 grams, respectively. There are signs of intermittent respiratory distress; the patient's airway and lungs are swollen but unobstructed.

ENDOCRINE SYSTEM: Excretory organs withhold a harmful mass of bodily fluids—about 12 ccs of urine; slow excretion rate. The kidneys measure 95 grams (left) and 86 grams (right). Blood count to spleen and pancreas measure low white blood cells.

DIGESTIVE/ GASTROINTESTINAL SYSTEM: The abdomen is rigid and tender. The internal organ and its surroundings are ridden with cancerous cells and laboratory data confirms massive traces of *helicobacter pylori* bacteria in the intestines and bile. The pH of the stomach fluids are recorded as highly acidic, eroding stomach wall and esophageal tissues. Eroded esophageal tissue also suggests frequent regurgitation caused by mass chemical radiation; the patient's prescribed cancer treatment.

***SPECIMENS FOR TOXICOLOGY:** Alarming amounts of sugar and carbonation harming the kidney, stomach, and esophageal tissue.

CIRCUMSTANTIAL SUMMARY

The patient had regular checkups every week for 5 months, as symptoms grew worse. Prior to examinations, some cancerous cells were evident due to hereditary cancer genes. Malignant evidence was not evident at the times before regular examination. The patient began to experience sudden severe abdominal pain, blocked airways, then dramatic weight loss, and rapidly dropping vitals. Her young age and projected symptoms indicate that the cancerous cells were contracted genetically and immunity degenerated due to malnutrition. The spleen's lack of proper tumor-fighting cells and antibodies to properly respond to bacteria is predicted to be an innate physiological and genetic defect. Levels of antibodies are difficult to be measured or diagnosed in standard hospital check-ups.

Letter #5: June 1, 2012

Merry Mere,

I have not heard back from you in a year almost. I am finally well here. We now have clean water, and get donated clothes and food to our village. It is a miracle that your Dr. Derek came here to help us. He told me the medicine will help me live a bit longer. It has been 3 month and my body feel weak now but my mind strong, and I am watching my brothers and sisters grow. I hope you are well and grow too.

With my best wishes,

Ava

P.S. Late happy 10th birthday!

WORKS CITED

Fotso, Jean-Christophe. "Child Health Inequities in Developing Countries: Differences Across Urban and Rural Areas." *International Journal for Equity in Health* 5.9 (2006). BioMed Central. Web. 5 May 2013.

Gressler, Sabine, and Alexander Haslberger (Eds.) *Epigenetics and Human Health.* KGaA, Weinheim: Wile-VCH Verlag GmbH & CO., 2010. Print

Polednak, Anthony P. *Racial and Ethnic Differences in Disease.* New York: Oxford University Press, 1989. Print.

Sigerist, Henry E. *Civilization and Disease.* Ithaca, NY: Cornell University Press, 1970. Print.

AUTHOR PROFILE

I am a first-year biopsychology major from Northridge, California. Aspiring to become a physician, I look for avenues to broaden my knowledge of public health while incorporating my love of creative stories. I am very humbled and appreciative of this opportunity to do so.

—*Connie Chen*

LEVEL-UP SCRIPT

Lawrence Deang

Instructor: Christopher Dean

[Intro Music: Mario 8-Bit Theme Song]

Host: Hello UC Santa Barbara! This is Larry, and you're listening to UCSB's only gaming podcast where we talk about everything video game—retro to newest releases. Listen up, parents, because today we'll be breaking down a bad misconception about video games and the effects they have on your kids who play them. Now most people think that video games do nothing more than rot your brain and attention span. And, being a gamer, I will admit that this can be true for *some* of the games out there. *SOME*. But definitely not all! Games like "Legend of Zelda," "Tetris," and "Portal" are all perfect examples of games that will not rot your brain, just to name a few. But for time's sake, we will just be focusing on one game. And if you've been listening to the background music, you know that it must be Mario.

[Insert Sound Effect: Its-a-Me Mario! & Coin sounds]

[Another Theme]

Host: Now for all you old timers, if you don't know who Mario is, then prepare to be schooled. Mario has been on the gaming scene since 1981, first appearing in the arcade game called "Donkey Kong" (McLaughin). Since then, he has appeared on over 200 Nintendo video games, granting him more fame than Mickey Mouse (McLaughin). His most popular games are platformers, and those are the type of Mario games we will be using in our discussion. More specifically we're going to look at "Super Mario Bros" and the more recent game "Super Mario Galaxy 2."

Now back to the subject at hand. Playing video games has been said to do nothing but waste your child's time and rot their brains. But good games offer more than mindless fun. According to author James Gee, "games operate at the outer and growing edge of a player's competence, remaining challenging, but do-able, while schools often operate at the lowest common denominator" (Gee 2). That means that the player has to use problem-solving skills learned throughout the earlier levels to combat the challenges in the later levels. In a game like Mario—**Insert: Its-a-Me Mario!**—one does not simply just save Princess Peach, one must learn how to use power ups and how to defeat enemies. Now in the earlier 2-D scrolling "Super Mario Bros." game, it was a lot easier to save the princess due to its simple yet challenging gameplay. But Mario

> **"**Video games hold more than just entertainment. They can teach kids in ways most parents would never think of.**"**

has come a long way since then, and so has the difficulty and learning curve needed to play games in today's generation. An example is "Super Mario Galaxy 2."

[Insert Music: Super Mario Galaxy 2]

Host: "Super Mario Galaxy 2" takes place in—well the Galaxy! The game's physics simulate actually being in space; you run around small planets, fly in space, and use a variety of different power ups in your quest to yet again save the princess. In this game, and like many other games played today, players are pushed to solve problems in order to advance. This can help children apply these problem-solving skills in real-life situations. Motivation is another thing children gain from playing video games. In "Super Mario Galaxy 2," the learning curve is definitely much steeper than its previous games, but that learning curve is manageable due to power ups and tips from other characters in the game. Motivation is the willingness to make an extended commitment to engage in a new area of learning. It is a driving force; if motivation dies, learning dies and playing stops. And since good games like "Super Mario Galaxy 2" are highly motivating, players learn how motivation is created and sustained (Gee 2).

Host: It's time to get—**Insert: Dramatic Sound Affect DUN DUN DUUUUNNNNNNN—**

SERIOUS (Deepen pitch and dramatize)

[Insert: Mario Boss Battle Music]

Host: Let's try and take a step back from Mario and look at gaming as a whole. Playing is considered fundamental to the stabilizing processes that are essential for the development of cognitive structures. Through playing video games, children rehearse basic cognitive operations such as conservation, classification, and reversibility (Rosas 72). In video games, players also engage in "action at a distance," where they control the actions of the character on screen. Cognitive research suggests that this fine-grained action at a distance actually causes humans to feel as if their bodies and minds have stretched into a new space (Gee 3). And with today's games, multiplayer mode adds a whole new dimension in the ways kids interact and learn. When gamers play in multiplayer games, they often collaborate in teams, each using a different set of skills and sharing

knowledge. In this way, video games may be a better site for preparing players for modern workplaces than traditional schools (Gee 1). They offer a place where gamers can congregate and team up to accomplish a similar objective—and that's to win!

[Insert: Mario Underwater Theme]

Host: So are all games beneficial like Mario? No, but the point is that not all games are bad games that rot your kids' brains. Video games hold more than just entertainment. They can teach kids in ways most parents would never think of. Now if you're concerned about which games are like Mario, I would recommend you buy your child games like "Skyrim," "Pikman," "Rise of Nations," "Portal," "Legend of Zelda," "Tetris," and many more. Let your kids play video games with an open mind and remember, the most important reason they play them is to have fun. And on that note, I'll be talking to you gamers on the next podcast about "Halo 4" vs. "Call of Duty: Black Ops 2." Until next time, gamers! This is Larry, signing out!

[Insert Sound Affect: GAME OVER]

WORKS CITED

Gee, James Paul. *What Video Games Have to Teach Us about Learning and Literacy.* New York: Palgrave Macmillan, 2003. ACM Digital Library. Web. 24 Nov. 2012.

McLaughlin, Rus. "IGN Presents: The History of Super Mario Bros." *It's-a Mario! A Look Back at the Greatest Franchise in Gaming.* (2010): 1–5. *IGN.* Web. 24 Nov. 2012.

Rosas, Ricardo. "Beyond Nintendo." *Design and Assessment of Educational Videogames for First and Second Grade Students* 40.1 (2003): 71–94. *Science Direct.* Web. 25 Nov. 2012.

METACOGNITIVE ESSAY

In writing class, our third big assignment was to write a script for a podcast which we would then record after. I will admit, when I first heard about this assignment I was completely put off by it. First of all, I had never done or heard a podcast beforehand. Second, it was vastly different from the past two big assignments and from any other assignment I have ever done for writing. Lastly, I hate the sound of my voice. So when the podcast was first assigned to us, I had a very negative view on the entire thing.

When starting to write my script, I didn't know what I wanted to talk about. Since you can talk about anything in a podcast, I didn't know which direction I wanted to take it. Some initial ideas I had was having an educational podcast for kids, an informational podcast about what types of tennis gear people should buy, or having a podcast about the 1990s. After some thought, I decided on writing about the 90s since I would have more content to talk about. But there was another problem; the 90s holds too much content, and it would be too broad. In order to get some help on what I should write about, I decided to go to office hours and ask Professor Dean about how I should narrow it down. He asked me what the first thing is that comes to mind when I think about the 90s, and I told him "video games." After a good discussion, I was able to restrict my topic to writing about how video games can be beneficial to gamers and using Super Mario as an example to support my claim.

Writing the script was surprisingly very fun. Professor Dean helped me find sources by suggesting the author James Gee. I found his work was perfect for my topic and was very informative. While I was writing the script, I kept in mind that this is not like the last two papers in which I had a sense of professionalism. Here, it was different. I still had to have concrete details and arguments, but I also had to make sure it was entertaining enough for people to actually want to listen. In order to keep it entertaining, I came up with the idea of making my podcast like a video game. In video games, there would always be background music playing that fit the types of stages presented. If it was a beginning stage, the music would be simple. If it was a stage far into the game, it would be more powerful. If it was the end boss stage, then the music must be very dramatic. If it were the end of the game, the music would be peaceful credit music to fit the end of the adventure. And finally to end off the podcast, it must be with the sound effect used for a "Game Over." While writing, I thought about the background music that would go well with my podcast. The podcast soon became less of an assignment and more of a fun project.

When recording the podcast, I had more fun than I ever thought I would. Some challenges I had while making the podcast was learning how to use Garage Band and how to record my voice and insert music. Another challenge was that I was sick while recording the podcast, so talking for long periods of time became exhausting. Regardless, I was having so much fun learning how to use Garage Band and recording that it didn't really hinder me. I knew I wouldn't like the sound of my voice so instead of taking it really seriously, I decided to be more silly and record it how I think most radio people talk. I had fun with it, and I think the end result was that the way I projected my voice fit my topic well.

In the end, this podcast assignment became my favorite and the most fun I had out of the three papers we had. It was less serious than the rest, yet still challenged me in ways I have never been challenged before. The end result was an informative podcast about the benefits of playing video games with Mario as the main mascot of the whole discussion. I had a lot of fun, and hopefully that joy is reflected in my podcast.

AUTHOR PROFILE

My name is Lawrence Deang, and I am currently a freshman at UCSB. My hometown is South San Francisco, and I am 19 years old. I'm a biology major, but literature and writing have always been passions of mine. I hope to write a novel of my own one day.

—Lawrence Deang

SETTING THE BAR

Emily Zhou

Instructor: Randi Browning

> **"**By aiming for a distant goal, you raise your standards and allow yourself to pursue a path of success.**"**

Imagine if you could do something impossible. Les Brown once said, "Shoot for the moon. Even if you miss, you'll land among the stars." Although what Brown says seems physically impossible, he metaphorically implies that you must aim high if you wish to do your very best. By aiming for a distant goal, you raise your standards and allow yourself to pursue a path of success. Moreover, even if you don't achieve that goal, you can still take pride in the accomplishments that you make along the way. Brown's rule is one to live by and enables us to go beyond our capabilities. Although it initially seems impractical, setting the bar high when making goals allows us to succeed as these goals exceed our original expectations.

Personally, I find myself surpassing my own expectations when proposing influential goals because setting a high standard increases my motivation to succeed. For example, in high school I led my dragon boat team to first place by influencing my teammates to set goals that we collectively felt were unattainable. As the team captain, it was my duty to inspire my teammates to paddle to the best of their ability. Every practice, we set a new goal and hoped to achieve that goal by the end of the day. Initially, the team faced difficulties following through with the goals due to a lack of cooperation. Despite the odds, my teammates realized that the goals were actually achievable. As we inched closer and closer to race day, we began to aspire to improve our race times, and we felt overjoyed every time we succeeded. When it finally came down to race day, my teammates and I unleashed all our months' worth of hard work into a race that lasted less than two minutes. In the end, we felt more than satisfied with the results as we placed first. During the first practice, I made sure my teammates knew what they were up for, and I told them that although we started as a group of inexperienced paddlers, we could achieve the impossible if we set our minds to it. As a result, my teammates went beyond what they each thought they were capable of, and they knew I was in the background working just as hard as they were. After this experience, I realized that nothing is simply handed to you; you have to set the bar high in order to believe that you can actually achieve your own standards.

Success through high ambition also applies to society as a whole. For example, high expectations set in the education system ensure that the world has people who are at the highest standards of their profession. Establishing high standards allows everyone in the education system to know what to aim for. Students, parents, and teachers can share common expectations of what students should know and be able to accomplish. If society expects more out of students, students become inclined to learn beyond their levels of understanding, and this in turn raises the highest possible standards of education. Setting goals to improve educational standards creates the competition necessary to ensure that we get the best of the best. As time passes, these objectives, which used to seem unattainable, are finally achieved, and eventually, the new standards set for education become the norm. Consequently, people begin to plan more advanced standards for education, further developing new innovations to maximize our knowledge in every field. The cycle continues, as our quest for knowledge is never-ending. In order to establish a high-end society with people who are the best in their professions, society must set high standards for education to continue the cycle of development.

Les Brown's concept of aiming high also applies to significant historical events. The worldwide civil rights movement would not be possible without the emergence of influential leaders with high hopes in mind. For example, in the 1960s, Dr. Martin Luther King Jr. contributed to the African-American Civil Rights Movement through the promotion of civil rights using nonviolent tactics. As an orator and a leader, Dr. King aimed at ending segregation by race in the United States. Dr. King's "I Have a Dream" speech made his message well-known around the United States, giving recognition and voice to the civil rights issues. Consequently, Dr. King's speech made such a powerful impact that it eventually helped lead up to the Civil Rights Act of 1964. Because Dr. King set the bar high for what he wanted to advocate, he successfully had his voice heard by the people of America.

Whether the goals are on a personal level or a standard set by society, aiming high allows people to prosper as they learn to discover advances that potentially make the world a better place. Those who set the bar high enough when creating goals ultimately end up achieving goals well above their original intentions. In today's society, making reforms and advocating change are common and achieved due to the great intentions of the people leading them. Events such as the Civil Rights movement were all made possible by the powerful leaders who spoke with high goals. Issues in society continue to increase, but setting the bar reveals the solutions for these problems.

AUTHOR PROFILE

I am currently a freshman with plans to major in economics and accounting and Chinese. I have intentions of becoming a CPA and working in foreign countries so that I can travel while I work. My goal is to work a job I enjoy while seeing all the fascinating things in the world.

—*Emily Zhou*

FIRST AND SECOND ORDER THINKING

Maria Ericka (Mick) Castro

Instructor: Vincent Rone

> **"I was able to learn how to apply the skills I learned, like recognizing genre conventions and using first-order and second-order thinking, to create my genres rather than analyze them."**

REFLECTION

Humans are an organized kind of species. They like to take the things around them and try to fit them into categories. Humans need to create this organization. In writing we call this genre. Genres give readers direction to help them analyze a piece of writing, or help them create something to tackle a given or needed purpose. In this writing project, I, as a writer, had to utilize my knowledge of different genres to convey ideas I have learned throughout this class.

The power to choose the genres in which I could convey myself gave me a lot of room and flexibility for creative expression, which made this project a very enjoyable one. Before starting to write, I had to decide what genre I would write in. I wanted to take advantage of how much creative expression I was given, so I did not want to go with a traditional piece of paper with a bunch of words slapped together into sentences that made paragraphs. Naturally, I wanted to avoid genres like letters, academic essays, or narratives. There needed to be an element of challenge and fun to this project. This project was where I could challenge myself and show off my skill sets. I chose genres that had visual elements and challenged my ability to show the material I learned in this class. These genres were character concepts and nutrition facts.

For the first genre, I chose to create character concepts because it is a very familiar genre for me. In my free time I join role-playing communities online. There are several different types of communities that a role-player can join, such as blogs, forums, and chat rooms. These varying communities have two styles of role-play: literate and illiterate. Literate role-play is like writing a story, and it is usually used in forum and blog-based websites like Xanga, Livejournal, Gaiaonline, and Deviantart. Each role-player writes at least a paragraph of material that responds to another role-player and furthers whatever story develops in the interaction. Illiterate role-play is usually used in chatrooms like Skype, Omeagle, AIM, and IScribble. These role-plays, unlike literate ones, disregard grammar and tend to take the form of scriptwriting. However different these communities may be, the need for character concepts is universal.

As a role-player, I use character concepts as a way of introducing myself to other role-players. I want people to know the basic premise of who my character is before we initiate a role-play. This way, we can adjust to each other's creations without falling out of character. I also use character concepts to provide people with a visual of who they are interacting with, so they can better bring the role-play to life in their heads. By using past experience from the role-playing communities I've joined, I created two character concepts for this assignment.

The article by Peter Elbow, "Teaching Two Kinds of Thinking by Teaching Writing," served as inspiration for my character concepts. I took what I felt were the most important points of the article, which were first-order thinking and second-order thinking, and personified them. I created two "spirits" that embodied these two ideas. For first-order thinking I tried to portray a disheveled, scatterbrained girl who is an impulsive and creative free spirit. I added small details such as naming her Ichi Junzya, which literally means "first order" in Japanese, because when I think of Japanese culture I think of their fashion industry and "anime," which I find to be bright, colorful, and bursting with creativity and originality. I also drew her eating a piece of toast with a caption saying that she is, "Always flitting from one idea to another, so her diet consists of anything easy to make," to further reinforce the fleeting nature of first-order thinking. On the opposite end of the scale, Due Ordine, the spirit of second-order thinking, I portrayed as a stiff, neat, controlled perfectionist. Due's name literally means "second order," but for him I used Italian, which makes me think of a refined culture. I tried to make him look serious, analytical, neat, and controlled in his body language and fashion choices. In his hand I added a book with the word "order" on it to reinforce his need for control and order. For both characters I added short excerpts that portray how they would interact with the world. I changed the tone and the font of my writing to convey their personalities.

For the second genre I created a nutritional facts chart. This was an impulsive decision because I was at a loss for inspiration. I wanted an unconventional genre in which I could challenge my creativity like I did with the character concepts. It was not until I was staring at an empty carton of almond milk that I was struck by inspiration. When I turned the carton over to look at the nutrition facts, I thought it would be interesting and fun to challenge myself and create one of my own.

Admittedly, the first draft was not a stellar piece of work. I found myself frustrated with trying to figure out where to put my actual information. I was too boxed in with the structure of a nutrition chart. It was difficult to find a balance between the useless information and the actual content. The result of that draft gave me one place where I could incorporate information from the class. I was able to mention how to identify genres and their conventions in the ingredients. Unfortunately, as mentioned before, this information was only mentioned somewhat haphazardly. I drew from the "How to Read Like a Writer" reading by Mike Bunn that when looking for genre conventions, one must think about the audience of a genre, the purpose a writer gives to a piece of writing, and the content within the genre. I presented this in an unclear manner for my first draft by writing "GENRE CONVENTIONS" in the ingredients, then adding in parentheses "ANALYSIS OF PRESENTATION, CONTENT, WRITERLY PURPOSES, AND DEVELOPMENT." I provided no explanation or hints of the reasoning behind the decision to put these words in the ingredients section, and I expected my readers to figure out my meanings and reasoning on their own.

These flaws in my second open-writing genre did not go overlooked in my peer review session. My classmates, Sylvia and Eric, picked up on the imbalance between my content and superfluous information. They critiqued me for it, telling me that I obviously had trouble with finding a place to incorporate information from the class. In addition to the critiques, the two gave me suggestions to counter my imbalance. For example, Eric and Sylvia suggested that I could add my information in a "warning label" as well as a "recommendations label." I found these suggestions to be brilliant and immediately put them into my nutrition facts chart. In both labels I was able to take the two authors that I took information from and make them into doctors. This way, I could use quotes from the readings and stay true to my chart structure.

This writing project, as enjoyable as it was to make, put me through a learning process. Instead of analyzing someone else's work, I had to apply the concepts that I analyzed to the genres that I created. I became aware of the different audiences I targeted. Depending on my audience, I changed how

I wrote, which I feel can be seen in my character concepts through the excerpts I added at the end of each concept. Even within a genre like my character concepts I wanted to target different audiences or different types of role-players. I also learned how to think out of the box when presenting my information. I stretched my imagination to figure out where I could convey the things I learned, such as the keys to writing, and what to look for in genre conventions. I avoided using quotations or MLA format to cite my sources throughout my open genre pieces because they would seem out of place. Through this, I discovered that there were different ways to cite sources that were less formal. Instead of writing parenthetical citations, one can cite by saying from whom or where they got information.

Even though this writing project was an extensive project, I found that it was a very fun one nonetheless. To be given the reins to create two genres gave me the power and flexibility to guide my learning experience. The genres I chose allowed me to have a good balance between visuals and writing. This in itself let me have fun experimenting with what works best for this assignment. I was able to learn how to apply the skills I learned, like recognizing genre conventions and using first-order and second-order thinking, to create my genres rather than analyze them. I also learned how to present evidence in different ways without plagiarizing or using the standard MLA format. I found that an understanding of genre is not only good for analytical purposes, but it is good for applied purposes as well.

INTRODUCTION: CHARACTER CONCEPT

The genre of character concepts helps a reader, writer, or artist to understand a specific person, creature, or animate being in a story before jumping into it. For its audiences, this genre creates a connection between its reader and a character before a story even starts. As a concept writer and artist, I target role-players. I want people to meet and gauge who my characters are before they decide to delve into my world or I delve into theirs, and we have our personas interact. However, audience-wise this genre is very flexible. It can reach out to all kinds of people, from movie-lovers who want to have a more in-depth and comprehensive idea of their favorite character, or readers who want a neat, organized place to learn about characters before or during a story. When I write in this genre, I assume that readers know nothing about the personality I am describing. I expect that they want to learn some of the basic information of a character. For example, I expect that they would want to learn about the age, appearance, occupation, sex, and of course, personality. I want to give my audience a general idea of my creation without revealing too much of who it is. When I use these characters, I want people to figure out who they are as we interact. Sometimes I give a little bit of back-story for readers to better understand the workings of my characters. I also take into consideration how my audience would want me to present my information. I assume my audience would want an easy-to-read synopsis of a character, so I usually give them information in list or outline form with visuals.

NUTRITION FACTS

Nutrition facts are found at the back of a cereal box, milk carton, or any article of food to give a reader, and in this case, a hungry reader, information about the food they're eating. The audience, whether hungry or not, is anyone who would like to know what is in their food. For my nutrition facts, I wanted to reach to an audience who can relate to making writing projects, maybe specifically for this class. I have to assume that my readers understand elements in nutrition facts like serving sizes, ingredients, and expiration dates because such things are not explained by my genre. I have to expect my readers to know where to find the information they want to have. For example, regular nutrition fact charts have information like the calories, the amount of fat, and the amount of sodium in a product. There were some elements that I did add that are not traditionally on nutrition fact charts. For example, I added elements. However, in my chart, I replaced this information with elements like brain power, stress and knowledge. Then I also had to take into consideration the presentation of my information. I wanted to make a nutritional fact chart as close to a real one as I could, because the information I presented was not the same as a real nutrition fact chart, but a parody of one.

Ichi Junzya

Sex: Female

Species: Spirit

Age: N/A

Occupation: First-order thinker

Personality: Ichi is a quiet and shy spirit that needs some coaxing and time warming up to you. Once you establish a relationship with her though, she is a fun-loving and spontaneous spirit. She can be talkative once inspired, but she tends to speak without thinking. She can be insightful and full of creative energy, but she is a scatterbrain jumping from idea to idea. She is easily influenced by biases, opinions, and things of that sort, but that is just because she is a free-floating creative spirit.

"I'm gonna challenge you. Let's take ten minutes to write whatever comes to mind. I want you to create a stream of consiousness with no restrictions. I know it's going to be hard at first. Just let go and trust me. I'll give you ideas, and before you know it you'll be writing up a storm. Don't worry about whether what you're making sense or not, we'll get Due to look at this peice later."

Never brushes this.

Always flitting from one idea to another, so diet consists of anything easy to make.

Get back onto the topic Ichi.

I can see my nose!

Due Ordine

Combed, slicked back hair, cause he can't stand an unruly mess covering his eyes.

Order for Dummies Due's go-to book for advice.

Sex: Male
Species: Spirit
Age: N/A
Occupation: Second-Order Thinker

Personality: Due is a rational minded being. He is guided by logic and control. To many, he can come off as a perfectionist or overly picky, but his intentions are mostly good. His lot in life is to keep his first-order thinking counter-part, Ichi, in check. He keeps her from sounding too crazy or nonsenscial. Due is meticulous by nature, and he can spend a great amount of time over-thinking things, but that is only because he strives to refine and more clearly communicate ideas.

"Okay, let's see what you and Ichi wrote. Think of me as your editor. You've written this wonderful piece of work, but it's your first draft. Chances are, you haven't put much thought into it. That is a bad thing, but Ichi tends to write before thinking. You have a lot of material here, but let's separate the diamonds from the coal. Let's take out the repetitive and superfluous material, and organize your thoughts so that they make sense to your readers."

This paper... Ichi has been here...

WRITING PROJECT

Nutrition Facts

Serving size 4–5 pages

Servings per container 1

Amount per Serving

Work Load: 3–5 Hours	With Distraction: 1–2 days

		% Daily Value*
Total Brain Mass and Power	5g	**35%**
First-Order Thinking	4g	**80%**
Second-Order Thinking	1g	**20%**
Knowledge	100g	**25%**
Genre Conventions	30g	**30%**
Audience	40g	**40%**
Evidence	10g	**10%**
Analysis	20g	**20%**
Stress		
On Schedule		**Medium**
With Procrastination		**Dangerously High**

Ingredients: PAPER, INK, AWARENESS OF THE ASSIGNMENT, GENRE CONVENTIONS (ANALYSIS OF PRESENTATION, CONTENT, WRITERLY PURPOSES, AND DEVELOPMENT), ANALYSIS OF AUDIENCES, ANALYSIS OF PURPOSE, TOPIC, WORD CHOICE, GRAMMAR, PUNCTUATION, BLOOD, SWEAT, TEARS

CONTAINS WORK

DISTRIBUTED BY VINCENT RONE, WRITING 2 TEACHER

TAKE A DEEP BREATH AND RELAX BEFORE OPENING

FINISH WITHIN 5–7 DAYS

Recommendations: According to Dr. Lennie Irvine, to the get most out of your writing project:

- Understand what you are writing and how you approach the task.

- Write at least two drafts.

- Use your best judgment or "writer's sense" to best convey your ideas.

WARNING: Dr. Kerry Dirk warns that depending on the location and context of each genre, the nutrition facts may vary. Genres, after all, are classifications that are responses to different situations or contexts.

WORKS CITED

Dirk, Kerry. "Navigating Genres." *Writing Spaces: Readings on Writing.* Parlor Press, 2010. Print.

Elbow, Peter. "Teaching Two Kinds of Thinking by Teaching Writing." *Embracing Contraries: Explorations in Learning and Teaching.* New York: Oxford University, 1986. Print.

Irvin, Lennie. "What is "Academic Writing?" *Readings on Writing.* Parlor Press, 2012. Print.

AUTHOR PROFILE

My name is Maria Ericka Castro, but I go by Mick for short. I am a first year working on sociology and economics double majors. I absolutely love drawing, meeting people, and enjoying the little things in life.

—*Maria Ericka (Mick) Castro*

Photos by Shannon Mirshokri

PHOTOGRAPHER
PROFILES

PHOTOGRAPHER PROFILES

SAMANTHA BROWN
I usually joke around with people about my sense of direction by saying, "I let the wind guide me" or "I follow the wind." Honestly, that is sort of the truth. My being here at UCSB is a windfall to me.

LORIEL DAVILA
I am a first-year student with a double major in pre-biology and Spanish. UCSB is the best choice I ever made!

MARISOL JIMENEZ
My name is Marisol Jimenez, and I'm from San Jose, California. I'm currently a pre-biology major, but I plan to switch into anthropology or sociology. If there is one thing I love to do, that is to take lots of pictures—I enjoy capturing the moment and later looking back at photos to reminisce about the past.

SHANNON MIRSHOKRI
Shannon Mirshokri is a first-year pre-psychology major at UCSB. She loves to do community service, and she started the school organization Swipes for the Houseless, which helps feed homeless individuals in Santa Barbara.

LEO VARGAS
As a kid, Leonardo (Leo) Vargas was exposed to the world of visual arts and culture. Now Leo is studying communications and art at UCSB, and he wants to work in the advertising field after graduation.

YUQING (AUGUSTINA) WANG
I'm an international student from China. I love writing short poems and taking pictures.